Architecture and Revolu

In 1989 Europe witnessed some of the most dramatic events of the twentieth century, with the fall of the Iron Curtain and the collapse of the Soviet Bloc. But what are the repercussions of these changes for architects and planners? What problems are there to be solved? What role does architecture play in the new Europe? *Architecture and Revolution* explores the consequences of the recent 'revolutions' in Central and Eastern Europe from an architectural perspective.

A fundamental part of the problem for Central and Eastern Europe as it struggles to adapt to the West, has been the issue of the built environment. The buildings that have been inherited from the communist era bring with them a range of problems. Some are environmentally inadequate or structurally unsound, others have been designed to serve a now redundant social programme, and others carry with them the stigma of association with the previous regime. The question, however, as to what needs to be done extends beyond straightforward practical concerns. For while the physical rehabilitation of towns and cities remains a pressing problem, no less than remedying the environmental pollution inherited from Soviet bloc industry, there are underlying theoretical issues to be addressed first of all.

Architecture and Revolution is the first volume to address these issues. It contains a series of essays which offer a novel and incisive take on some of the pressing questions that now face architects, planners and politicians alike in Central and Eastern Europe, as they consider how best to formulate the new architecture for a new Europe. The essays have been written by a range of renowned architects, philosophers and cultural theorists from both the East and West. The views expressed represent a snapshot of informed opinion soon after the opening up of Central and Eastern Europe. As such this volume constitutes an important document in the shifting sands of European history.

Neil Leach is Reader in Architecture and Critical Theory at the University of Nottingham.

Architecture and Revolution

Contemporary perspectives on Central and Eastern Europe

Edited by Neil Leach

London and New York

First published 1999
by Routledge
11 New Fetter Lane, London EC4P 4EE

Simultaneously published in the USA and Canada
by Routledge
29 West 35th Street, New York, NY 10001

Typeset in Galliard by Routledge
Printed and bound in Great Britain by Biddles Ltd,
Guildford and Kings Lynn

British Library Cataloguing in Publication Data
A catalogue record for this book is available from the British Library

Library of Congress Cataloging in Publication Data
Architecture & revolution: contemporary perspectives on Central and
Eastern Europe / edited by Neil Leach.
p. cm.
Includes bibliographical references and index.
1. Architecture, Modern–20th century–Europe, Central.
2. Architecture, Modern – 20th century–Europe, Eastern.
3. Architecture–Europe, Central Public opinion.
4. Architecture–Europe, Eastern–Public opinion. I. Leach, Neil.
NA958.A745 1999
720'.1'03–dc21 98-26183
CIPCIP

ISBN 0-415-13914-7 (hbk)
ISBN 0-415-13915-5 (pbk)

Contents

Illustrations

Figures

Photo Credits

Associated Press, 19.4; Natasha Chibireva, 10.1; Catherine Cooke, 1.1, 2.1, 2.2, 2.3; Chris Duisburg/Studio Libeskind, 9.1; Government Archives, 19.3; Wolfgang Köhler/Action Press, cover; Landesbildstelle Berlin, 19.2, 19.5, 19.6, 19.7; Neil Leach, 4.1, 7.1, 7.2, 7.3, 15.1; Mark Lewis, 20.1, 20.2, 20.3; Dod Miller/Network, Figure 2, Figure 3; Constantin Petcu, 15.2; Bill Robinson/ Sigma, Figure 1; Ullstein Bilderdienst, 19.1.

Contributors

Evgeny Asse is an architect and educator. He is Associate Professor at the Moscow Architectural Institute. He has published many articles on architectural design, and his own architectural work has been published and exhibited internationally.

Andrew Benjamin is Professor of Philosophy at the University of Warwick. He has held visiting professorships at various schools of architecture. He is the author of numerous books including *Art, Mimesis and the Avant-Garde, The Plural Event* and *Present Hope*.

Andrei Bokov is the chief architect of the Design Institute 'Mniipokoz' in Moscow. He has published many articles in Russian. His design work has been published and exhibited internationally.

Jonathan Charley is Lecturer at the Department of Architecture and Building Science, University of Stratclyde. He is the author of *Architectures of Resistance: Histories and the Production of the Built Environment* (forthcoming).

Hélène Cixous is a writer and academic. She is Professor of Literature at the Université de Paris VIII. She is the author of several works, many of them translated into English. Her books in English include, *Angst, The Newly Born Woman, Coming to Writing and Other Essays, Readings: The Poetics of Blanchot, Joyce, Kleist, Lispector and Tsvetayeva* and *Rootprints*.

Catherine Cooke is Lecturer in Design at the Department of Design and Innovation at the Open University. She is the author of *Russian Avant-Garde* and *Chernikov: Fantasy and Construction*, and the editor of several volumes on Russian Constructivism and Deconstruction.

Augustin Ioan is Lecturer at the Institute of Architecture in Bucharest, and fellow of the New Europe College. He is the author of several books in Romanian. His books in English include *Symbols and Language in Sacred Christian Architecture*. He is also co-author of the award-winning documentary film, *Architecture and Power*.

Vyacheslav Glazychev is Professor of History and Theory at the Moscow

Architectural Institute and President of the Academy of the Urban Environment. He is the author of several books in Russian on the history and theory of architecture.

Bart Goldhoorn is an architect, writer and critic. He has published many articles in Russian, and is the editor of the architecture journal, *Project Russia*.

Selim Khan-Magomedov is an eminent architectural historian. He is a member of the Russian Academy of Architecture and Building Science and the International Academy of Architecture. He is the author of numerous books in Russian. Those which have been translated into English include, *Alexander Vesnin and Russian Constructivism, Pioneers of Soviet Architecture: The Search for New Solutions in the 1920s and 1930s* and *Rodchenko: The Complete Work.*

Fredric Jameson is Distinguished Professor of Comparative Literature at Duke University. He is the author of numerous works, including *The Prison-House of Language, The Political Unconscious, The Ideologies of Theory* (2 volumes), *Marxism and Form, The Seeds of Time*, and *Postmodernism: or, The Cultural Logic of Late Capitalism.*

Neil Leach is Reader in Architecture and Critical Theory at the School of the Built Environment, University of Nottingham. He is the editor of *Rethinking Architecture*, author of *The Anaesthetics of Architecture* and co-translator of Leon Battista Alberti, *On the Art of Building in Ten Books.*

Daniel Libeskind is an architect and educator. He has held a number of distinguished academic posts and visiting professorships, and his work has been published and exhibited internationally. He is the subject of a number of monographs in various languages, and is himself the author of several books including *Chamber Works, Theatrum Mundi* and *Fishing from the Pavement.*

Laura Mulvey is an academic and film maker. She is Postgraduate Programme Tutor at the British Film Institute, and the author of several books, including *Visual Pleasure and Narrative Cinema, Citizen Kane (BFI Classic)* and *Fetishism and Curiosity.*

Constantin Petcu is an architect and researcher. He teaches at the Université de Paris and the Institute of Architecture in Bucharest.

Doina Petrescu is an architect and researcher. She teaches at the Université de Paris and the Institute of Architecture in Bucharest.

Renata Salecl is a philosopher and sociologist who works as a researcher at the Institute for Criminology, University of Ljubljana. She is the editor of several volumes on psychoanalysis, and author of *The Spoils of Freedom: Psychoanalysis and Feminism after the Fall of Socialism.*

Ioana Sandi is an architect, trained in Romania and England. Her articles and design work have been published in several international journals.

Dorin Stefan is an architect and Lecturer at the Institute of Architecture in Bucharest. His work has been published and exhibited in several different countries.

Bernard Tschumi is an architect and Dean of the Graduate School of Architecture, Planning and Preservation at Columbia University, New York. His architectural work has been published and exhibited widely, and he is the author of several books, including *Manhattan Transcripts*, *Architecture and Disjunction* and *Event Cities*.

Dalibor Vesely is Lecturer at the Department of Architecture at the University of Cambridge. He has held visiting professorships at a number of universities, and was a founding member of the Central European University in Prague. He is the author of *Architecture and the Conflict of Representation* (forthcoming).

Acknowledgements

Much of the material for this book emerged from a conference held in Romania in 1995. The conference took place against the extraordinary backdrop of Bucharest, a city violated by the architectural interventions of the former communist dictator, Nicolai Ceausescu, and a city whose architecture is itself scarred by bullet holes that bear witness to the bloody 'revolution' that took place in December 1989.

The conference bore the title, 'Beyond the Wall'. It was a conference which took place both geographically and temporally *beyond* the wall. Likewise it sought to transcend walls – or boundaries – between different cultures and different disciplines, by bringing together architects, philosophers and cultural theorists from both the East and the West. This was the first such conference to be held since the collapse of communism, and while the event itself was staged in Romania, it addressed pressing questions concerning architecture and the built environment that related to the whole of Central and Eastern Europe.

I am grateful to all those who took part in this conference, and to those who contributed to this volume. I am particulary grateful to all those who helped in the organisation of the conference. Most especially I must thank my conference co-organiser, Mariana Celac, for her tireless work in managing the logistics of the event in often very difficult circumstances. Likewise I should like to thank the support team in Bucharest, notably Augustin Ioan and Alexandru Beldiman, the president of the Union of Romanian Architects.

I must also thank our sponsors, the Soros Foundation for a Free Society, the British Council and the NEC Group. It was only through their generous sponsorship that such an event was possible.

Finally, I must thank my editors at Routledge, especially Tristan Palmer for his vision in setting up this publication, and Sarah Lloyd for seeing it through to completion.

Introduction

Neil Leach

Figure 1 A West Berliner takes a hammer to the wall by the Brandenburg Gate, dawn, 10 November 1989

In 1989 Europe witnessed some of the most dramatic events of the twentieth century. The fall of the Iron Curtain and the collapse of the Soviet Bloc were as unexpected as they were sudden. These were events that might have been anticipated with time, but which could hardly have been expected at that precise moment. Although there had been tell-tale signs, the very speed of change took the world by surprise. While many Western observers had been following the steady rise of the Solidarity movement in Poland, few would have predicted that by May 1989 Hungary would have started to dismantle portions of the Iron Curtain along its border with Austria, and that by 9 November the Berlin Wall itself would have been breached. By 25 December 1989, Nicolai Ceausescu the last surviving communist leader, had been tried and summarily executed, and Central and Eastern Europe was largely free of communism.

Figure 2 Tanks take to the street to support the people of Romania, 22 December 1989

Equally, few would have predicted the problems that were to emerge following the initial euphoria. Social and economic difficulties, internal conflicts, racial tensions and even civil war: these are just some of the ills that have afflicted Central and Eastern Europe, as it struggles to adapt to the agenda of capitalism. Without the economic and political infrastructure that exists in the West, the East has little framework against which to work through its rehabilitation. Indeed, many are actually worse off under the present conditions. Without the social safety net of communism, those in the East have less security under capitalism. Entrepreneurs have often seized the initiative, whilst much of the rest of the population has been trapped in a spiral of poverty. Capitalism has not proved the paradise that it once might have seemed.

A fundamental part of the problem in Central and Eastern Europe has been the issue of the built environment. Architecture has been inextricably linked with social developments. Clear parallels may be drawn between the utopian social projects of the first half of the twentieth century and the utopian architectural ones. Both represented dreams, noble enough in their intentions; but they were dreams which, against the backdrop of late twentieth-century scepticism, have clearly failed. In many cities in Central and Eastern Europe these two dreams came together, not least in the concrete tower blocks that blight many of the cities. Indeed, if we are to believe Vaclav Havel, it was precisely these tower blocks that helped to precipitate 'revolution'. In his play, *Redevelopment, or Slum Clearance*, architecture serves as an allegory for the machinery of government.[1] The insensitive process of redevelopment comes to embody the lack of humanity in the political regime. The tower block becomes synonymous

Figure 3 The image of the executed Nicolai Ceausescu, televised to the world, 25 December 1989

with totalitarian rule, and the failure of the architecture comes to represent the failure of the regime.

Architecture has failed to change the world. Yet the key question remains as to what architecture might best suit a world that has itself changed. The buildings that have been inherited from the communist era bring with them a range of problems. Some are environmentally inadequate or structurally unsound, others have been designed to serve a now redundant social programme, and still others carry with them the stigma of association with the previous regime. The problem is compounded by the financial situation. While it is an economic imperative to re-use existing buildings, vast sums are required to refurbish and readapt them.

The question as to what needs to be done extends beyond straightforward practical concerns. For while the physical rehabilitation of towns and cities remains a pressing problem, no less than remedying the environmental pollution inherited from Soviet Bloc industry, there are underlying theoretical issues to be addressed first of all. These have a significant bearing on the framework within which these very practical problems are tackled. For unless the deeper theoretical issues are considered, redevelopment is likely to follow its own paths of self-interest, as dictated by the marketplace. Berlin provides ample evidence of the perils of such an approach, as big business takes over and redevelops many of the sites vacated by the Wall and its defences with little thought for the consequences of this action. As a result, important monuments to a traumatic past are being erased for the sake of purely financial interests.

The essays in this volume track some of the pressing theoretical concerns that face politicians, architects and urban planners alike, as they consider how best to formulate the new architecture for a new Europe. The volume is divided into thematic sections, ranging from background historical questions to more specific contemporary ones. The essays have been written by a range of architects, philosophers and cultural theorists from both the East and the West. They offer a variety of perspectives. No attempt has been made to package them into a coherent position. Instead the volume serves as a platform for a debate between a range of often contradictory views, from the somewhat restrained to the uncompromisingly avant-garde, and from the abstractly theoretical to the resolutely practical. Already we might begin to question some of the conclusions. Change happens fast in the East, and the parameters are constantly being revised. Yet this does not detract from the value of the volume. The views expressed represent a snapshot of informed opinion soon after the opening up of Central and Eastern Europe. This volume constitutes an important document in the shifting sands of European history.

Historical perspectives

The whole problem of devising a new architecture for a new society is, of course, not a novel one within the twentieth century, and much might be learnt from the earlier precedents. Catherine Cooke sketches out the dilemmas that faced the constructivists and other avant-garde movements following the communist revolution in Russia. She reveals the fragmentary impulses that lie behind these movements, contrasting the ideological idealism of the aesthetic theorist and anarchist, Alexei Gan, with the strategic pragmatism of architects such as the Vesnin brothers. Through her anecdotal details of the very real problems that faced these individuals, Cooke brings to life the struggles of an architectural moment that has been all too often idealised in contemporary Western culture. She dispels too one of the common myths about this period, that architecture was dominated by a coherent movement in league with political changes. She describes instead an essentially disparate, bourgeois profession slowly coming to terms with the new ideological situation. Throughout her account we find resonances with the current conditions in Eastern Europe, with architects struggling to find a new architecture for a new age, amid the chaos and shortages of a society in turmoil.

Jonathan Charley questions whether the recent 'revolutions' can really be considered revolutionary in comparison with political changes in the early part of this century. In a world where the term 'revolution' has been appropriated to refer to little more than ephemeral changes in fashion, Charley attempts to define what a true 'revolution' might mean. 'Revolution', for Charley, is not a mere aesthetic term. It is fundamentally a political term that must be grounded in concrete economic and social relations. In the context of the built environment, this refers to questions such as property ownership and labour relations within the building industry. Western culture, for Charley, far from coming to terms with capitalism, has become increasingly stifled by capitalism. He therefore offers a manifesto for the built environment, calling for various strategies of resistance to counter this development.

Augustin Ioan, meanwhile, sets debates about architecture and popular politics within an historical context and makes comparisons between Postmodernism, as it is commonly understood within architectural culture as a style often characterised by largely superficial historicist motifs, and Socialist Realism. For Ioan, Socialist Realism represents a 'democratisation' of architecture – 'let the people have columns' – while Postmodern architecture plays upon an eclectic medley of codes in an attempt to popularise architecture.

Architecture and memory

Turning to the contemporary Central and Eastern Europe, Fredric Jameson pursues the problem of architecture's role in commemorating the past. His piece has a particular relevance in the context of Bucharest, a city whose historic fabric was so violated by Ceausescu. Architecture, as Jameson observes, is a problematic category in the context of all this. Not only must we distinguish between the function of a work of art to subvert aesthetic ideology, as opposed to general ideology – and for Jameson one is allegorical of the other – but such questions inevitably depend on what Jameson terms the 'transaesthetic'. For Jameson political content is dependent on a sense of historical memory: 'the building can only serve as a history lesson if its public and its viewers still have a sense of memory.' If political content is merely allegorical, once the existential and social context has been forgotten, the associations will be lost. All this begins to expose a problem for reconstruction in our present age in which 'the appeal to the past becomes a matter of sheer images.' Within such a context, architectural projects which aim to resurrect the past must be treated with caution. In an age when authenticity is prone to collapse into its opposite – the 'inauthenticity' of Disneyland – how is one to reconstruct the fabric of the city without resorting to a Disneyland architecture?

Working from within an overtly philosophical trajectory, Andrew Benjamin reflects upon the question of how to think the housing of change in 'post-revolutionary' Central and Eastern Europe. Benjamin approaches the question through Descartes's call for a renewal of philosophy. Drawing upon Descartes's famous analogy between architecture and philosophy, Benjamin asks what implications this might hold for an architecture of change. Yet the shortcomings of Descartes's own project, a project that excludes consideration of the body soon become clear. With Descartes, architecture is not thought as such, and the body and memory need to be policed. Rather, Benjamin argues, we should look to an alternative model which perceives architecture as being both 'the locus and agent of change', a model which could allow for the body and the memories associated with that body. Benjamin thereby sets the scene for a discussion of architecture, memory and change, pursued by Renata Salecl.

Like Jameson, Renata Salecl also considers the question of how to deal with the problem of the remains of visible monuments to a previous regime. She focuses on the need for identity and therefore for a symbolic order by which to define that identity. Nostalgic memory may itself provide that stable identity, offering a myth of a happy past as a means of escaping the actual trauma of the past. The problem now is whether to erase or accommodate the monuments to previous regimes. Ceausescu himself had attempted to erase the past and to create a new symbolic order by the demolition of existing townscape and the construction of his palace. By reappropriating the palace for democratic government, and renaming it the 'People's House', the people of Bucharest had paradoxically carried out Ceausescu's vision for the palace as the symbol for an ideal, total society. It is against the fabric of this building recoded as an emblem for a new Romania that a new sense of Romanian national identity might be forged.

In my own piece, 'Architecture or revolution?', I attempt to offer an overview of the problematic relationship between architecture and political revolution, tracing a number of theoretical views from the twentieth century on the relationship between politics and aesthetics. In distinguishing between the aesthetic and the political, I argue that architecture can only be politicised by association, thereby challenging the commonly held belief that architectural form is in and of itself political. I question the capacity for architectural form to influence political behaviour, which is often assumed within standard architectural discourse, and claim that architecture in itself can have no direct political agency. Yet architecture may still play an important indirect role in the formation of new national identities.

Strategies for a new Europe

Few could be more qualified to comment on the current architectural dilemmas in Central and Eastern Europe than Daniel Libeskind, who was himself born in Poland and, after moving to Israel and then the United States, now practises in Berlin. Throughout his recent work, Libeskind has displayed a consistent approach neither to erase the past, nor to be locked into a nihilistic reconstruction of the past. He is concerned to respond to history and to open up the future in a responsive manner. As such he is keen to avoid the closure implicit in abiding steadfastly to conventional notions of *genius loci*, and is vehemently opposed to the totalitarian mechanism of the master plan. Instead he calls for strategies of transformation and metamorphosis of existing realities, as he attempts to open up a domain for the creation of unpredictable, flexible and hybrid architectures.

Libeskind's concern to commemorate the past is reflected in his architectural designs for Berlin which serve as a concrete articulation of the need to retain a sense of historical memory. Memorials to the tragedies of the past, for Libeskind, should not be erased. Europe needs to live with its history and to retain monuments to its traumatic past. Libeskind's commendable stand against the commercial redevelopment of the sites once made vacant by the wall, such as Alexanderplatz and Potsdamerplatz, echoes a consistent theme to be found throughout his work. In his entry for a competition to design a housing estate on the site of the former Sachsenhausen concentration camp, for example, Libeskind deliberately ignores the brief and proposes instead a memorial to the victims of that camp. Likewise his Jewish extension to the Berlin Museum attempts to evoke the memory of a culture that has been eradicated. The central void that runs through the zig-zag layout of the museum – a void which visitors are forced to cross and recross as they make their way through the musem – is empty of artifacts. The principle exhibit to a culture that has been all but eradicated is an absence of any exhibit. The void becomes a death mask of a culture, the invisible made visible by its conspicuous absence in a physical location that seems to demand its presence.

In his concern for a sense of history, Libeskind appears to echo the views of Jameson. But the differences between Libeskind as architect and Jameson as literary critic begin to emerge in Anne Wagner's interview. Libeskind sees the role of architecture as fundamentally different to that of literature. Architecture, for Libeskind, is not a language, and does not conform to the rules of language. Indeed, its connection to language remains highly problematic. Literary descriptions of architecture may vary, but the work itself will always endure. As such he sees architecture in terms of real space, as the space of lived experience, and as the space of memory which is itself prompted by encounter with the physical. Libeskind therefore speaks in terms of icons, but not icons as in language or culture at large; indeed architecture, for Libeskind, moves in a very different direction to culture itself.

Dalibor Vesely, Libeskind's former teacher and himself a refugee from Czechoslovakia during the era of communism, looks to the discourse of anthropology as a means of understanding how human beings are corporeal and situated in the world. Contemporary interest in simulated architecture and architecture of the image are merely illusory, caught up in the trap of hallucination. Unless we can begin to grasp the fundamental situatedness of human beings we will continue to produce an architecture out of touch with the human condition. 'What makes meaningful representation possible', Vesely observes, 'is the communicative context of culture in which we are always situated.'

This contrasts somewhat with the more radically avant-garde approach of Bernard Tschumi, who calls for a new architecture for the new cultural conditions.

Architecture, for Tschumi, should always question the limits and refuse to be constrained by tradition. What is required is an architecture of disruption and disjuncture, which through strategies of repetition, distortion and superposition opens up new possibilities that reflect the complexities of our contemporary moment. Tschumi's seemingly anarchic approach echoes that of the early Russian anarchists, outlined by Cooke.

Meanwhile in my own contribution, 'The dark side of the *domus*', I attempt to expose some of the problems within phenomenology which has begun to dominate much recent architectural thinking, especially within Central and Eastern Europe, and I question whether such a potentially nostalgic and limiting approach has much relevance any more. What the new Europe needs, I maintain, is a new approach to architectural theory more responsive to the fluidity and flux of today's society, one that is more in tune with the technological conditions of our contemporary existence. Echoing Libeskind, I call for a more flexible approach towards architecture in the New Europe.

The section is concluded with a roundtable discussion led by Bart Goldhoorn with the Russian architects and critics, Selim Khan-Magomedov, Vyacheslav Glazychev, Andrei Bokov and Evgeny Asse. They address the role of architecture in a post-totalitarian society, its professional standing, institutional status and methods of expression. Their discussion brings into sharp focus many of the questions that now face architects elsewhere in Central and Eastern Europe. Under the new economic conditions, should architects try to maintain total authority, or should they accept that this authority must necessarily wane, and explore instead new kinds of relationships with both client and builder? Should a new centralised system of regulation be introduced, such as exists in the West, or should there be a more *laissez-faire* approach to reflect the newfound political freedom? Should architectural education reorientate itself to address, on the one hand, the very practical questions that face architects today, and, on the other, a more reflexive concern for ethical and cultural issues? And should new schools of architecture be established to cater for the highly varied needs of a new society? What emerges is an image of a society in flux, uncertain of its direction, and always threatening to descend into a market-led chaos. In this respect the East remains the 'wild West' of Europe.

Romanian questions

Various Romanian architects then focus on the more concrete realities of the Romanian condition. As such they offer a telling account of the struggle to find a framework for architectural theory. Constantin Petcu adopts a structuralist line in painting a picture of Bucharest prior to 1989 as a city within a generalized semiotic rupture. This rupture represented a rift between the 'perfect reality' as conveyed in official state pronouncements and 'social reality' itself. Architecturally this rift was reflected in the disjunction between the 'official architecture' of the regime and the existing architecture of the city. At an individual level, the pressure for citizens to act as state automatons prompted an 'architecture of urban camouflage', where the conformity of the architecture embodies the principles of the huge stadium performances in which the people themselves became the spectacles. Yet these images served only to mask the resistance that this oppression spawned. The dictatorship of Ceausescu could therefore be seen in semiological terms as a 'dictatorship of false signs'.

Doina Petrescu interrogates the paradox of the palace of the former Romanian dictator, Nicolai Ceausescu, as both 'wonder' and 'monster'. This building, now known as 'the People's House', is reputed to be the second largest building in the world behind the Pentagon.[2] It stands at the end of a 4 km long avenue of grand buildings which was driven through the centre of old Bucharest, causing the destruction of much of the historic fabric of the city. Although still unfinished at the time of Ceausescu's overthrow and execution in 1989, the building has been partially completed, and is now redeployed as the House of the Parliament and as a conference centre. The palace is presented as a Medusa-like monster which serves to petrify the people through the wonder at its sheer scale. For Petrescu, Ceausescu was caught up in a psychotic delirium for architecture, an 'architecturomania'. This psychosis allowed him to attempt to replace reality by the product of his own monstrous architectural hallucination. Yet the monster is etymologically linked to the wonder. Monsters both terrify and awaken the spirit with their sphinx-like provocation. And in this awakening, they offer a glimpse of hope. Understood dialectically, the People's House anticipates its own reversal, and in so doing 'it marks the crisis and the imminence of change'.

Dorin Stefan's article is one drawn straight from the melting pot of contemporary Central and Eastern Europe, a desperate search for a new architectural identity. In his enigmatic, poetic writing Dorin Stefan reflects upon the very practical crisis within the architectural profession. 'Pre-revolutionary' Romania at least allowed for the possibility of a 'de Chirico-esque' dream of a better world, even though Stefan – like many others – found himself 'locked out of the citadel' as the empty eclectic emblems of official state architecture were preferred to the modernist vision of the architectural elite. Beyond the 'revolution', this utopian dream has degraded into a dystopian nightmare. The promise of a better future has evaporated in the chaotic aporia of the 1990s. A shortage of skilled labour through economic emigration and the absence of any legislative framework for the building industry have forced architects like Stefan to adopt guerilla tactics – 'the art of architectural compromise' – and to supervise building construction on a more *ad hoc* basis, as strict specification gives way to 'design guidelines', and detailing becomes a question of improvised 'stitching'.

Ioana Sandi presents an image of Eastern Europe awakening from fifty years of sleep, 'with the mind of a child and the old-fashioned values of its grandparents'. This sleep has left it ill-prepared to deal with the demands of capitalism. Unlike its western counterpart, now 'saturated with infrastructures and communications networks', Eastern Europe has become 'a vast expanse of wilderness'. How, then, is the East to adapt to the ways of the West? Sandi describes the passion with which Romania, with its obsession with fast cars, television and

McDonald's, is rediscovering a sense of the political, ethical and economic. And architecture, she notes, still has an important role, although a new sense of architectural identity needs to emerge.

Tombs and monuments

In 'Berlin 1961–1989: The Bridal Chamber' I attempt to theorise the Berlin Wall from an architectural perspective, comparing its social role with that of walls throughout history. Illustrating my argument with images of the early construction of the Berlin Wall, and of the bricking up and demolition of buildings in its immediate vicinity, I claim that the wall can be understood as a form of 'anti-architecture', a grotesque denial of the social art of building. 'All that architecture has stood for over the ages', I conclude, 'was now being subverted, challenged and denied by the logic and the violence of the Wall'.

Laura Mulvey outlines the intentions behind her documentary film, 'Disgraced Monuments', compiled with Mark Lewis, which considered the fate of the communist statues of Central and Eastern Europe. In many ways her concerns echo Fredric Jameson's interest in 'disgraced' buildings. The statues act as indexical markers, emblems of the 'disgraced' regime. Mulvey reads the treatment of these statues within an historical perspective, as part of a tradition of iconoclasm that marks all moments of political change.

Finally, Hélène Cixous offers a highly reflexive and lyrical account of her first visit to Prague to view the tomb of Kafka. For many the opening up of Europe has provided access to the treasures that had remained for so long inaccessible. Yet her piece circles enigmatically over themes of access and denial. Even when she eventually visits Prague, she questions whether she really understands the city. Prague, for Cixous, can never be fully captured by the onto-hermeneutical process. It is not Prague, but Pragues, promised Pragues to which she perhaps would never gain entry. 'Promised Pragues. You dream of going. You cannot go. What would happen if you went?'

Cixous's visit to Prague is somehow emblematic of the experiences that many from the West have had in visiting the once inaccessible territory of Eastern Europe. None can fail to be moved by the grim, concrete reality of the built environment in the East, but how much can those from the West really understand of the problems that face the people there?

Notes

1 Václav Havel, *Redevelopment, or Slum Clearance*, trans. James Saunders and Marie Winn, London: Faber, 1990.
2 This statistic is based on its gross floor area. In terms of interior volume, the 'People's House' is in fact the third largest building in the world behind the Pentagon and the Nasa assembly building in Florida.

I
Historical perspectives

1 Sources of a radical mission in the early Soviet profession

Alexei Gan and the Moscow Anarchists

Catherine Cooke

Ten years after the 1917 revolution, there were several clearly identifiable theories of a consciously 'revolutionary' and 'socialist' architecture being practised, taught and debated in the Soviet Union. Some were purely modernist; others sought some synthesis of modernity with classicism. As soon as these various approaches start to be formulated with any rigour and launched into the public domain, we can evaluate them as more or less subtle professional responses to certain dimensions of Bolshevik ideology.[1] However, preceding that stage and underpinning it was a process of personal adjustment and collective refocussing whereby a relatively conservative capitalist profession faced up to a new context and started mentally defining its tasks or writing a new narrative for its practice.

This earlier part of the process, during the Civil War, is infinitely less accessible than what happened once building activity revived in 1923–4. The earliest stages of the process were also being conducted in a political environment which was very different from that of the mid-1920s, an environment that was more fluid and more plural than mainstream accounts from either East or West have suggested. In the phrase of Paul Avrich, who is one of the few (besides survivors) to insist on documenting the minority radical groups of the revolution, both Eastern and Western orthodoxies have to differing degrees been written 'from the viewpoint of the victors', that is privileging the Bolsheviks.[2] In reality, important voices were also coming from other directions. Such was the Bolshevik terrorisation of dissent that for decades the safety of individuals and their historical reputations demanded that these censoring filters be applied. In the new situation, however, it becomes possible to start opening up the early biographies of some key individuals to show a much richer picture.

In the context of architecture, the first person whom we find rethinking the city as an active political agent in Marxist terms is Alexei Gan in his typographically dramatic little book *Constructivism*, published in 1922.[3] Gan is well known for playing various roles as theorist, publicist and typographical designer at the heart of Moscow avant-garde art and architecture from 1920 onwards. His *Constructivism* opens with a lengthy quotation from the Communist Manifesto of 1848 and his reference point throughout is 'the proletariat with its sound Marxist materialism'. However, he is merciless in his critique of the Bolshevik Party's cultural leadership.

Figure 1.1 Alexei Gan at work on a magazine cover, 1924, photographed by Alexander Rodchenko

Commentary on Gan's book has conventionally focussed on his venom against 'old art'. This is traditionally and reasonably attributed to the productivist artists' natural vehemence in 1922 in face of a revival of easel painting after the Party's economic retreat into a quasi-capitalist New Economic Policy (NEP) in the previous year. By encouraging private enterprise and free markets, this was reviving the concept that creative work in its conventional media legitimately existed to provide accoutrements or entertainments as objects of consumption. Certainly the aesthetic consequence of this economic retreat is one of Gan's most direct targets, but he extends that critique into merciless attacks on the Party's new cultural hierarchy in the Commissariat of Popular Education, Narkompros:

The Communists of Narkompros who are in charge of art affairs are hardly distinguishable from non-Communists outside Narkompros. They are as much captivated by the idea of beauty as the latter are by notions of the divine....Their words promise the future whilst they reverently transmit and popularise the past. Whether in painting, sculpture or architecture, this is impelling them in the direction of the most reactionary déclassé maniacs.... As if guided by a prayer book they venerate the art of those very cultures about which they are so scathing when they discuss the theory of historical materialism.[4]

The origins of the voice we hear here have always been obscure. Its political explicitness, and even more its political edge, are very different in their confidence and sharpness from anything we hear in the statements of other creative people in Russia at that time. What we can now see is that this voice which mocks 'our responsible and so very authoritiative *leaders* [his emphasis]...who paint themselves up to look like Marx',[5] and which challenges them to face the implications of their own ideology, has its origins not in Bolshevism but in anarchism.

In the materialist view which Gan brought to Soviet architecture, he conceptualised the built environment as one dimension of 'the intellectual-material culture of Communism.' He explicitly propounded this view of its socially-formative role in an effort to overcome 'the lack of even minimal Marxist understanding' amongst all practitioners 'whether in painting, sculpture or architecture'.[6] The aggressiveness of his voice, in both discussions and writing, made it effective propaganda. If his Marxism seems at times suspiciously *plus royalist que le roi*, however, this is perhaps because his own political allegiance had once been very publicly displayed as lying with a rival ideological group: a group by which the Bolsheviks had felt sufficiently threatened since the Revolution to make it an early target of their increasingly dreaded new secret police, the Cheka.

The vacuum of ideology in the post-revolutionary profession

Those who emerged as leaders of the radical archiectural avant-garde of the 1920s had not been conspicuous as social or aesthetic dissidents before the revolution in the way that the bohemian, iconoclastic artists had been. There was very little in Russian architecture before the war that was socially innovative by the standards that would be applied thereafter. As progressive structural and servicing technologies arrived from Europe at the turn of the century, a form of art nouveau developed that was declared by sympathetic commentators to be inherently 'democratic', but such a term was very relative.[7] A building boom among the new middle classes gave a dramatically new shape and scale to city centres, but it was the architectural expression of a reformist political option that was increasingly doomed after 1905.[8] It left a material matrix that can be physically and ideologically reinhabited with Russia's return to a capitalist culture today.

But in 1917, it bequeathed the new regime a building stock whose very robustness made it ill-adopted to change.

When building ceased in 1913–14 the modernising, westernising decade of the 1900s had created a Russian architectural profession which, though relatively small, was not significantly different in its profile from those of the West. Above all, it was similar in the extent of its political engagement, which was generally minimal. Very few architects fled when their world collapsed in October 1917. One senses that they stayed with their buildings as doctors stay with their patients, more engaged by the professional act of ministration than by high politics. Where, then, and amongst whom do we first see signs of personal engagement with the new ideology?

Conspicuously, it was not in the old capital. Between signing and ratifying a peace treaty with Germany at Brest-Litovsk but with German advances still underway, Lenin transfered his new government to Russia's historic centre of Moscow on 10–11 March 1918. From that date, the city resounded with political voices as the new leaders moved conspicuously around it and the new 'people's commissariats' embarked on their social and economic reorganisation of the country, mainly from requisitioned hotels. Petrograd, formerly St Petersburg, was now a relative backwater.

A conceptual context for rethinking the built environment had been created by some of the new government's earliest legislation, which nationalised all real estate and redistributed housing space.[9] For the middle and upper classes, the ensuing process of 'quartering, eviction and concentration' were the most exquisite torture and violation. For the former have-nots, this effected a vast improvement but also gave them shelter of a manifestly ill-adapted kind. Architects suffered with the rest, but for them the new legislation was also the first draft of a new scenario.

The first task through which professionals in both cities engaged with the new Soviet government was that of effecting emergency repairs and protection to architectural monuments damaged by fighting or vandalism. This was taken very seriously by Commissar of Popular Education, Anatoly Lunacharsky, as part of his Marxist ideological obligation to preserve the cultural heritage and artefacts made by the working populace.[10] This obsession with preventing pillage and vandalism created caretaking jobs for a large number of young architects in the immediate aftermath of the Revolution, and the new legal reality became daily more tangible as they moved freely around buildings that were hitherto 'private'. Having passed from multiple to single ownership, this space was manifestly accessible to reshaping as one whole.

Once the Bolshevik party had asserted its authority with such brutality during the Civil War, useful debate in any field had to accept the Party's values as their premise. Even interpretation of their constantly evolving policy was a complex task that imposed rapid learning curves on all concerned. In a profession such as architecture, those who led the way were inevitably those who combined a suitable predisposition with useful prior experience; the vast majority of its members were essentially ignorant of the minority ideology which now ruled them. At all three levels of the built-environmental task, at the levels of urbanism, architecture and theory, the early work of professionals reveals a complete ideological vacuum.

An Architectural Studio for the Replanning of Moscow was set up by the city council, Mossoviet, in August 1918, just five months after the Party leaders moved into the Kremlin. The announcement in *Izvestiia* made clear that it was motivated by the historic urge of all post-revolutionary regimes to make their new citadel 'beautiful'.[11] As if the logic was obvious, it declared that 'the overall political perspectives of the urban economy cannot be developed without such a plan.'[12] The notion that the plan should depend upon the politics (not vice versa) would be precisely Gan's message in 1922.

The Studio was headed by the fifty-year old academician Ivan Zholtovsky, famed for his adulation of Palladio, who had wide pre-revolutionary experience in and around Moscow. Zholtovsky was known to the cultured Lunacharsky and made himself personable to the new government.[13] Zholtovsky later recalled his personal briefing meeting with Lenin. The leader was plainly still living out the parallel with the French Revolution that had sustained him, as colleagues remarked, through the first days of their own takeover. This was the element of heritage to which their own plans must refer. In Zholtovsky's words, 'Vladimir Ilich talked about how Moscow must be rebuilt in such a way that it became something with an overall aesthetic conception to it, whilst also being convenient for the individual citizen.'[14] Lenin stressed to him three times, 'Remember, just don't make it in bourgeois taste!', which in Russia at that time meant either the overdecorated eclecticism of late nineteenth-century commercial architecture or the art nouveau which followed it. Zholtovsky loathed them both as much as his new client did, but their shared preference for classicism derived from personal tastes rather than Marxist theory.

The plan which resulted at the end of 1918 proposed a traditionally imposing administrative centre of classical building around the Kremlin, a ring of fully-serviced suburbs of the kind obligatory in model city plans worldwide during the 1910s.[15] The most apposite criticism of it came from less glamorous planning people in the new economic administration, VSNKh. These men from highway engineering and the pre-war Garden Cities movement could see that this was 'an architectural plan without any basis in traffic flows *et cetera*', and failed to 'take into account the new socio-economic structure of our life'.[16] But Zholtovsky's office continued and was joined by another academician with strong Moscow experience, Alexei Shchusev.

Dividing the city into eleven design studies, they provided almost the only employment available for architects and allied professionals of all ages during the next three years. They surveyed, planned and designed while the city decayed around them. Its spaces were gaily decorated for every revolutionary festival, but building interiors were systematically stripped by the freezing and starving population. As Berthold Lubetkin described it: 'Since the floorboards had been used for firewood we slept, wrapped in old newspapers, across the bare joists.'[17]

Shchusev took Zholtovsky's strategy into greater detail as a Plan for the New

Moscow, which was presented on 2 January 1923 and 'approved' by Mossoviet. A mass of documentation and project work remains, and what is evident today became increasingly clear to those who could muster another perspective on the task at the time: namely, that all this was meaningless.[18]

At the scale of architecture, the context of the revival after the end of the Civil War in 1921 was defined by the nature of the New Economic Policy as the chosen engine of the recovery. When it was launched in March 1921, the NEP completely reversed the approach hitherto applied under the name of War Communism. Instead of attempting to eliminate private ownership, wage differentials and even money itself, these now became the officially approved motors of economic revival. Lenin himself admitted that it was 'a retreat'.[19] The extent of private enrichment by the devious and energetic 'NEP-men' was equivalent to that of the 'New Russians' under Yeltsin's regime today. In August 1922 a decree 'On the Right to Build' launched one of the government's main vehicles for absorbing these private monies. A raft of privileges enabled individuals and cooperatives to build and operate housing which they could pass on as an inheritance.[20]

Hungry and unemployed architects saw in this the hope of some work. An experimental Trade Union of Architects, formed after the February revolution of 1917, had collapsed and the old established Moscow Architectural Society, MAO, had re-established itself earlier in the year and retrieved its old headquarters. In June Fedor Shekhtel, doyen of art nouveau, resigned after fifteen years as its President and was replaced by Shchusev.[21] In the vacuum of architectural publishing MAO achieved two issues of a new journal, *Arkhitektura* (Architecture) which give us a unique close-up on the core of the profession at this date.[22]

On 1 July 1917 the Society's new Board declared to its members: 'Before us stands a ruined Moscow, a new social environment and entirely new legal norms, under which the work of architects must proceed in quite new directions.' They were gratified that 'in virtually all organisational activity related to the revival of construction…the Society has links into their practical work.' On principle, however, the message they took into that work was devoid of political content. As MAO's Board proudly reported:

> our representatives…are, by the very essence of it, expressing views which are free of any one-sided bias and provide the possibility for problems to be solved in the interests of the generality, which is so necessary at the present time amongst the endless arguments between different interest-groups.[23]

This was professionalism in its old mould, entirely benign but on principle non-partisan. It was appropriate to the humanitarian urgency of the moment, and MAO's busy lecture programmes had the same tone. But there was no attempt here to discover what Marxism said or should mean for the field.

The only attempt at such theoretical investigation was being made by their nearest equivalent in the fine arts, the new Russian Academy for Artistic Sciences, RAKhN.[24] RAKhN's diligent researcher in the Marx–Engels Institute did not find much, but as part of Lunacharsky's sprawling Narkompros empire, art historians were forced to address such issues, however lamely. So too was RAKhN's rowdier subsection, the Institute of Artistic Culture (InKhuK), where small groups of young abstractionists hung out.[25] MAO, by contrast, was an independent professional society of the old kind. In February 1922 RAKhN had created its own research section on 'the science of architecture', but the boundaries of 'theory' here were predetermined by the appointment of Zholtovsky as chairman. The researchers established a studio 'to work on the problems of current architecture', but it was 'closed for lack of resources' by the end of the year.[26] In this torpid environment it is no wonder that somewhere outside the old professional establishment a voice protested that the Revolution seemed to have been 'forgotten' and that 'theory' should perhaps be addressing the new ideology.

Alexei Gan: the city as political agent

Gan's constantly repeated challenge to one creative field after another was precisely this: 'where is the new ideology?' We see him raising the question first among the painters, then the film-makers and finally the architects.

Gan was at that time a close colleague of Alexander Rodchenko, of whom the abstract, so-called 'leftist', art community were increasingly in awe, but Rodchenko's wife Varvara Stepanova noted in her diary for 7 January 1920: 'Gan says our art is not proletarian, that it carries no ideology but only develops on the level of professional achievements.'[27] A month later Gan made a similar critique of Narkompros's Theatre Section, TEO, who were planning the political festivals. They must, he said, stop 'borrowing every alien myth from classical Greece to the French Revolution' and 'protect the class essence of real history'. The revolutionary festival must be reconceptualised as 'a Mass Action'. It was 'not something to be borrowed, but a form to be created'. For the forthcoming May Day he proposed that 'entire proletarian masses of Moscow' should enact their own vision of 'the Communist city of the future' in real space, filling 'not only the entire city of Moscow but even its outskirts'.[28]

A year later, in the spring of 1921 when Rodchenko, Stepanova and the other InKhuK artists with whom Gan was forming the First Working Group of Constructivists had moved on from painting to making three-dimensional assemblages, Gan's message to them was unchanged: they were 'operating upon material haphazardly'. Their work was still 'conceptualised in a narrowly-professional way and artificially cut off from life'. They should be 'tackling the tasks posed by the Communist culture which is arising in front of us' and which was above all 'dynamic'.[29]

When he became editor of a new film journal *Kino-Fot* in summer 1922, Gan addressed his message to the film-makers. Film was one of the 'material-technical "organs" of society.'[30] Here too, he warned, 'unless the soldiers of the "left front" [stop their] endless series of formal experiments [and] carry it into real life, the cause will be lost.' He quoted the founding theorist of Marxist aesthetics at them:

Plekhanov wrote that 'In order to understand the way in which art reflects life one must understand the mechanism of life.' But our self-styled 'left front' has no such understanding of the mechanism of life…which is why voices of protest are so often raised against their work among Communists who are literate in Marxism.[31]

In his book *Constructivism*, put together that summer and published in December, he reiterated these various dimensions of his message and addressed them to architecture.

With its most aggressively political assertions highlighted by its boldest typography, the book's aim was to force people to recognise:

> what Marx wrote in *The Poverty of Philosophy*, that 'theoreticians of the proletariat must set themselves the cognitive task of giving themselves an account of what is really going on in front of their eyes, and of becoming the interpreters and explainers of that reality.'[32]

The problem, he said, was 'a lack of Marxist literacy': 'The lack of even minimal numbers of Marxist-educated people has a notable effect even in the circles of politically reliable party comrades.' But the situation was worsened because:

> even our supposedly qualified Communists are sometimes intellectually extremely lightweight and take a slighting attitude to subjects they know little about. All this reflects itself disastrously on our practice, on our thinking, on the approach to multi-facetted and diverse phenomena of life, on the solution of a whole series of questions that are currently arising in connection with the building of communism and its way of life.[33]

With construction work about to restart Gan could see that no one had begun to analyse the political significance of buildings:

> As material-technical 'organs' of society, the capitalist towns that we inherited are staunch allies of counter-revolution. Soviet communism has already discovered that the capitalist town not only does not accommodate even the most timid measures of Revolutionary reorganisation, but more than that! *It stubbornly obstructs the path of that reorganisation.* Its small and awkward buildings have been totally unable to accommodate the operational requirements of the various new Soviet organisations. They are too cramped, just as the streets and squares which we inherited have not afforded the spatial conditions that we need for mass parades and vast assemblies.[34]

The varied heights of capitalism's buildings and 'the eclecticism of their architectural forms' were 'obscuring the logical structure bequeathed to us by this fragmentation of economic activity', which NEP was about to revive. In the spirit of Marx's injunction, therefore:

We must get human consciousness organised. We must force the revolutionary activists and the working masses to see this disformity, this misfit, to see it just as clearly as they see a misfit when some reorganisation [of their lives] brings disorder into their space at home.[35]

If 'misfitting' buildings could obstruct social change, then buildings that 'fitted' would clearly assist it. But the design problem this posed was not so simple, because 'Communism by its essence is dynamic.' 'It requires dialectically-thinking and theoretically-literate masters who can give material shape to fluidity and its specific content', but 'our actuality and reality do not contain such people.' This is not 'an aestheticising task' but a 'constructive' one, says Gan. It is not a matter 'of building something which abstractly gives a visual illusion of the dynamic.' It is a matter that:

> if communism today requires a building *for today*, that building must be provided in a way which takes into account that tomorrow society will be needing forms for its next stage and that this next form must be provided in a way that does not reject yesterday's, but is supplemented and supplements it with the next successive requirement in its turn.
>
> Thus [the architect] cannot build today if he is does not know the essence of what communism is and what it may require tomorrow.
>
> How then ought this work to be approached?...
>
> Only through an absolute knowledge of the principles of the communist economy and mastery of the economics of the transition period from capitalism to communism, through intense attention to the political and economic strategies of revolutionary action.

In this context, 'usefulness has to be judged from the point of view of the current moment in the proletarian revolution.' Society's forms of external expression under communism will emerge, says Gan, from a synthesis of the sociopolitical and the technical, not a conflictual battle between them. Henceforth 'usefulness must be understood as achieved through the organic properties and requirements of communism on one hand and the conscious approach to industrial material on the other.'[36]

It sounded theoretical, but Gan was also typically practical. No amount of 'communicating one's fantasies about the communist city' would serve 'to create a clear understanding in the citizen's own mind about the meaning of public ownership' in this sphere. 'Planning activities must be brought out of the studio and onto the streets to attract all citizens of the proletarian republic into this great and collective work.' But:

> the first stage towards solving the city as 'the communist expression of material structures' is to get orientated.
>
> First of all we must study the experience of the last five years, in the course of which the proletarian revolution, as the first stage towards the

communist transformation, has visibly altered the bourgeois capitalist city. Then we must observe how NEP is restoring it all again.

So the first stage must be:

> A plan of fact-finding: (1) what needs to be done at the present moment. (2) Who can take part in the work. (3) What professional resources and groups exist right now? (4) What has the revolution given us? (5) What attempts have been made so far? (6) Information on towns past and present. (7) Building materials, and (8) the approach to restructuring the city in a manner sympathetic to Communist ideals.[37]

Whatever form this urban restructuring might take, it would not involve 'monumentality.' ' "Monumentality"...cannot be the defining concept of new communist buildings', Gan declared, because it 'is saturated by judgements of taste and sanctified by aesthetics.'[38]

So much for Zholtovsky and Shchusev as architects of communism. Indeed, their planning approach was headed for sharp criticism by even the Party's own newspaper *Izvestiia* as 'creating a museum of a city' and 'representing a purely aesthetic approach to planning';[39] but their careers were established. It was the much younger architects who took up Gan's challenge, most importantly those around the three brothers Vesnin and around Moisei Ginzburg, who later formed the Constructivist architecture group with which Gan was intimately involved. Unfortunately, the informal debates through which that group coalesced and argued out its position are not documented in verbatim records like those kept by the artists around Gan in InKhuK. From 1924, it was principally Ginzburg who carried the baton of theory forward, as scribe if not the sole thinker, and the period of fuller professional documentation began.[40]

The political illiteracy of which Gan accused his creative colleagues was characteristic of the entire Soviet population, and the Bolshevik Party used every opportunity and medium to rectify it. On 1 November 1922, just as Gan's book would have been coming off the presses, a government decree obliged every higher education institution to augment their professional curricula with compulsory courses in subjects such as 'historical materialism.'[41] Such moves helped to spread a superficial awareness of the new catechisms, but the process by which each profession would analyse its tasks and reconceptualise its practice was infinitely slower. Even before Gan's architect colleagues started to develop the implications of his theories (indeed, so far as we know, before he actually had any architect colleagues except perhaps Alexander Vesnin), statements from the Party leaders in 1920–1 were becoming ominously indicative that myth would be prefered to systems analysis.[42] However, that outcome could not be prejudged, and Gan's theory promised potent tools.

The primary theoretical concept which he articulated was that of seeing the built form (like other 'material-technical "organs" of society') as an active agent influencing social change in 'revolutionary' or 'counter-revolutionary' directions at any given moment or stage of political development, and doing this through the structure into which it organised space and material. (This concept was later developed into the Constructivist architects' notion of the building's spatio-material organisation as a 'social condenser'.)

Gan's second key contribution was his insistence that the mechanisms by which these 'material-technical "organs"' operated in any real context, and the processes by which they could be 'constructed' to have those effects, were permeated throughout by politics and required serious research. He echoes here the classic *ABC of Communism* in which the Bolsheviks gave a popular explanation of their 1919 Party Programme. 'Marx's chief instruction to all his followers', it said, 'was that they should study life as it actually is...precisely after the manner in which we might study a machine, or, let us say, a clock.'[43] Thus Gan's geologically inspired science of Tectonika would be the 'new discipline' which described how materials and ideology had interacted in different historical cultures. Equipped with this, designers could move on predictively, 'to create a system of forming objects...whose service to society was not just utilitarian but conformed to social aims.'[44] (The Constructivist architects later devised their 'functional method' to be such a system.)

The special drive of Gan's theory came from his constant insistence that the forming of these active 'material-technical "organs"' depended, in every field, upon the synthesis of profound ideological understanding with an equally profound mastery of domain-specific knowledge, what the *ABC* called knowledge 'taken from life'. Repeatedly he stressed this to his colleagues in film-making: 'You must know the mechanisms of film.' 'Revolutionary ideology' in cinematography, he said, demands a mastery of what its 'real material' is and of how this impacts on 'real, concrete, consumers', not just as 'agitation' but at the profound level of their self-understanding.[45] In the *ABC*'s words, they must know 'how the wheels of our clock are actually fitted.' In *Constructivism*, Gan praised Rodchenko for similarly 'concrete' work on in developing 'the system which must be studied in the field of producing [three-dimensional] form.' In every field, 'creating such systems means proceeding by lengthy practical sequences of live experiments built on the foundations of social relevance.'[46]

Gan's political allegiances

If we stand back from the specific messages about the arts and architecture in Gan's writing at this time, three general themes are conspicuous. The first is a familiarity with Marxist texts that is beyond anything we find amongst the artists around him. The second, built on that foundation, is an extraordinary boldness in his criticism of the Bolshevik Party and its cultural leaders. The third is his constant concern with the need not just to teach people ideological facts but to engage them in the subtler business of understanding what ideology means for the 'mechanisms' of their lives. With new biographical information on his activities in the years preceding InKhuK and the ideas of his book, we can begin to identify the origins of Gan's particular slant and concerns.

His own trade skill seems to have been typesetting, I suspect without the artistic pretensions now implied by the word 'typographer'. Unlike Rodchenko, who came to the use of letter forms from art and is better described in today's terms as a graphic designer, Gan's work and his discussion of it indicate an intimate familiarity with the craft disciplines of metal type. Certainly he was not an architect, as Stites has described him,[47] nor is there any hint of the art school background which Lodder has rather assumed.[48] On the contrary, in the remarkable diary which Stepanova kept from January 1919 and through the debates of 1921 in InKhuK, we see Gan constantly trying to get inside the artist's mind to get a feel for what drives it.

There were many conversations in which Gan plainly irritated people, as a non-painter and relative outsider, by trying to label and classify their work. On 14 January 1919 Stepanova reported her husband Rodchenko declaring 'I am sick to death of Gan. He understands nothing about art.'[49] A year earlier the balance had been the other way, with the artists indebted to Gan. In March 1920, Gan's different motivations are clear. She registers the gulf between them with the disdainful remark that 'Gan considers agitation is just as important as making works [of art].' As a result, 'he sees Malevich' who was still then, with Tatlin, the towering artistic figure of avant-garde circles in Moscow, 'as a propagandist for something new, not as an artist.'[50] Back in January she had been pleased to sell Gan Igor Grabar's classic five-volume pre-Revolutionary *History of Russian Art* for five thousand rubles to teach him some art history.[51] In her most cutting judgment on 11 March 1920:

> Certainly Gan still has a lot to learn and see, but he is impeded in this by his desire to be some kind of 'new person' – and how! But I think there is a bit of decadence nested in there somewhere, and not enough rigorousness and seriousness in order to be a new person.[52]

By this time it is clear that Gan needs the artists as some kind of *raison d'être* and is becoming ever more closely integrated in their professional activity. A year earlier, the balance was still the other way. At a meeting on 14 January 1919, Gan became exasperated at their factiousness over who to include in a forthcoming exhibition:

> I just don't understand. This is your family business, but now you have got a split. Here am I, for example, working with the anarchists, the maximalists and the bolsheviks. They are all calling each other names the whole time, but they don't tear themselves apart over it.[53]

At a moment when the Bolsheviks were doing their best finally to eliminate the anarchists, this remark of Gan's is a telling indicator of his personal situation and the problem of allegiances he was later forced to navigate.

From Gan's role in the Moscow anarchists' newspaper a year previously and from his other activities at that time, we can now see more clearly where his origins lay, the cause of his dilemma and the sources of these features in his polemical writing. Of the various strands of Russian anarchism which originated with Kropotkin, Bakunin and others in the late nineteenth century, the anarcho-syndicalist movement which grew amongst industrial workers after 1905 was particularly strong in Moscow by the autumn of 1917. On principle, the anarcho-syndicalists were less organised than the Marxist-inspired Bolsheviks and were therefore less effective (as well as lacking membership records), but common estimates suggest they were about three times as numerous as the Bolsheviks in their own capital. Throughout Russia the two movements had made common cause in the revolutions of February and October 1917. After Kerensky's Provisional Government was driven out, however, no common hatred of the Tsarist Whites could persuade the anarchists to accept the centralising, bureaucratic policies being imposed by the Bolsheviks. Through the first shaky months after Lenin and his colleagues seized power, the balance of forces in many of Free Russia's town and city soviets and among the general population was relatively even.[54]

In the spring of 1917, when many vulnerable state figures fled after the February revolution and the Tsar's abdication, both anarchists and Bolsheviks expropriated their homes as headquarters, as indeed the Provisional Government expropriated several palaces of the Imperial family. With freeing of the press, a flood of new newspapers emerged from proliferating groups which combined their own views with general news. Anarchist groups in Petrograd produced several newspapers, and September 1917 saw the launch in Moscow of 'a weekly public-affairs and literary newspaper of the anarchist persuasion' called *Anarkhiia* (Anarchy).[55]

Amid the general disruption of the October takeover, *Anarkhiia* ceased publication. In early March 1918, however, it reappeared as a daily, not least as a mouthpiece for anarchists' increasing fury at the concessions with which the Bolsheviks were buying peace from a still belligerent Germany at Brest.[56] The second issue in March, its twelfth in total, contained its first piece signed by Alexei Gan on 'The revolution and popular theatre.'[57] The next, on 5 March, had one of anarchism's main ideologists Lev Chernyi, personal acquaintance of Kamenev and other leading Bolsheviks, declaring that for anarchists the socialist state was as much their enemy as its bourgeois predecessor and promising 'by all means to paralyse the governmental mechanism.' On the 7th, *Anarkhiia* greeted the signing at Brest-Litovsk with the proclamation 'Peace concluded. Long live the war!' (their own war with Bolshevism).[58]

Amidst ever more detailed proposals from Chernyi and others for entirely decentralised production and 'complete absence of internal power structures',[59] the fifteenth issue launched a regular back-page section on 'Culture' (*Tvorchestvo*, literally 'creative work') covering literature, theatre and art, whose editor was Alexei Gan. With a daily print run of twenty thousand, this was a worthwhile platform to which he was soon bringing not just the usual fare of events and reviews but polemic pieces from rival groups of avant-gardist painters in Moscow and Petrograd. These included Tatlin, Rodchenko, Altman,

Punin and the regular voice of Malevich, who was always the most fluent of them in print.[60]

The issue of 6 April carried Malevich's article 'Architecture as a slap in the face to reinforced concrete', which is well known through its republication in December that year in Narkompros's Petrograd paper *Iskusstvo kommuny* (Art of the Commune).[61] Malevich's plea for a 'reincarnation' of Moscow architecture that would 'allow the young body to flex its muscles' was effectively *Anarkhiia*'s architectural manifesto. In typically colourful language, it denounced current architecture as 'the only art with the warts of the past still growing endlessly on its face.' It was a brutal attack on the 'sick, naive imaginations...absolute lack of talent and poverty of creative powers' of 'Messieurs the individualist architects.' His example of how 'iron, concrete and cement are insulted' was Moscow's historicist Kazan Railway Station and its architect Shchusev (though his name is not mentioned), who won the job in 1911 and was still completing it.

By the time Lenin and his new government arrived in Moscow on the 10–11 March, the anarchists had expropriated twenty-five mansions as their local headquarters across the city.[62] *Anarkhiia* ran articles describing the buildings and their contents. The central headquarters of the Moscow Federation of Anarchist Groups and editorial address of *Anarkhiia* was the former haunt of Moscow businessmen, the Merchants' Club, a superb piece of Jugendstil by Ivanov-Shits of 1908. With the spacious rooms of a gentlemen's club, its library and theatre, this 'House of Anarchy' ran a rich cultural programme which, as one participant recalled, included '[hobby] circles of proletarian art-printing, poetry and theatre', as well as their propaganda.[63] Its basement was the depot whence guns and bombs were issued to a somewhat uncontrolled range of dissidents which included (said the Bolsheviks) White Guard officers and criminal vandals as well as their own Black Guards.

Gan was superintendent of one of their grandest expropriations or 'exes'.[64] The former owner of the house, Alexei Vikulovich Morozov, was a member of Moscow's biggest multi-millionaire dynasty. Gothic interiors had been done by Shekhtel with vast Faustian murals commissioned from Moscow's leading symbolist painter, Vrubel. Special wings contained Morozov's nationally famed collections of Russian china, silver, icons and twelve thousand portrait engravings.[65] On 19 March, Gan described the collection in his *Anarkhiia* piece on 'The Morozov mansion.'[66] Ten days later the culture page announced plans for a museum in the house; Gan was to be its chief curator and had invited Grabar to address the project's 'initative group'.[67]

To what extent it was this shared concern of Bolsheviks and anarchists for protecting the heritage that brought artists like Tatlin and Malevich into contact with anarchism and Gan, and to what exent they were already involved in the movement, is not so far clear. (Was Malevich's canonical 'Black Square' of 1915 perhaps also an anarchist black flag?[68]) Rodchenko's memoirs illuminate the situation at the mansion, but they do not clarify this issue. Indeed, whether through his own caution or later family editing, they are carefully silent on

Gan's central role there and suggest little engagement by Rodchenko with the anarchists' cause:

> Tatlin and Morgunov, having got mandates from Mossoviet, went to Gan in order to make arrangements about protecting private mansions from plundering and to watch over them. They took me along to the meeting. There I made the acquaintance of Alexei Gan.
>
> They assigned me to protecting the mansion of Morozov where there were engravings and china. A group of 'anarchist-communists' was lodged there. I walked over every day and my work consisted in moving everything of artistic value into one room, of which I kept the keys.
>
> The anarchists were quite a few, of whom several were women. What they did in the evenings I never knew, as I went home at five or six. Not that they did a stroke during the day, in my opinion. They would go out somewhere, come back and sleep. I don't know where they ate. They seemed quite ordinary people if somewhat sentimental. They played the mandolin and had arguments.
>
> Their attitude to me was rather hostile and watchful, as if I was some kind of observer from Mossoviet, from the communists.[69]

Much of these artists' writing in *Anarkhiia* and elsewhere at this time rings with a natural artistic anarchism that does not of itself indicate ideological conversion, though coincidences of vocabulary and common themes need analysing further. The only example that I have found so far of a direct identification between their work and anarchism is by Malevich, in one of his last *Anarkhiia* pieces published on 20 June 1918. A suprematist painting, he says, starts by establishing that 'single plane...from which each author can build entirely in his own way' which is the basis of 'true abstraction'. This, and the presence in the work of 'one inviolable axis on which everything is built...constitute the assertion "this is how I want it" from which follows the final affirmation "I am an anarchist in my very essence." '[70] The very date of this piece is interesting in relation to the larger events..

Through March and early April 1918 the paper's political pages increasingly reflected hostility not just to the Bolsheviks' actions, but to an onslaught of propaganda which blamed anarchists for every act of vandalism or civil disorder in the city. This climaxed in Trotsky giving a week of anti-anarchist pep talks to Red Guard troops in the Kremlin to stir their fury before being dispatched by the Cheka, in the early hours of 12 April, to flush the anarchists out of their twenty-five houses. The process was confused and vicious, leaving forty dead or wounded and over five hundred people under arrest in the Kremlin. As described by an editor of the other Moscow anarchist paper, *Golos truda* (Voice of Labour), who was one of them, they were 'kept in abominable conditions and treated in the most insulting manner.'[71] Whether Gan also went through this experience, we do not know.

The next day's *Anarkhiia* had not yet gone to press when the raid started, and it was a fortnight before it managed to resume.[72] When it did, both production and secretariat were at 'temporary addresses', the latter at 1 Nastasinsky Lane, just across the street from their routed headquarters in the Merchants' Club. 'Nastasinsky 1' was a building the anarchists had long frequented. Since the previous November its basement had housed the famous Poets' Café, where the futurist artists and writers who founded it, Kamensky, Mayakovsky and Burliuk, would paint their faces and declaim outrageous poems to earn themselves a nightly crust. Moscow had a dozen such places which regularly saw full-scale battles between gangs and the militia, but as the writer Lev Nikulin recalled, 'it is hard to say what particularly attracted the Anarchists to the Poets' Café.' The main attraction was probably its proximity to their base. In Nikulin's words,

> There were no alcoholic drinks here, no ladies of easy virtue, that is to say none of the ingredients which abounded in the Anarchists' den under the black flag. But they still came to the café as if it was their home, sat comfortably on the benches and played ostentatiously with their revolvers.[73]

Rodchenko and other artists also came here, and indeed had helped decorate it. This café may have been one of their initial points of contact with the anarchist movement. By the time *Anarkhiia* set up its office and resumed publishing from here, the basement café had closed. According to a neutral Moscow newspaper report of 15 April, 'the "official" reason was departure of the moguls of futurism for the provinces.'[74] The larger picture, however, suggests it may have been a response to the purges three nights previously. As Mayakovsky opened the 'gala programme' of the closing evening he spotted Lunacharsky, not for the first time, sitting at one of the tables. Challenged to speak, the Commissar 'captivated the audience' by talking 'with great gusto' but 'by no means felt obliged to flatter his hosts and relentlessly criticised the noisy and anti-aesthetic publicity tricks of the futurists, their contempt for the classics', and perhaps aptly identifying the source of this liaison, 'their tendency to pretend they were Anarchists at any price.'[75]

The Cheka's effectiveness in disrupting the movement's affairs was now reflected in a daily note on *Anarkhiia*'s front page: 'In view of the routing of the Moscow Federation and the disappearance of all materials and books from our dispatch section, the *Anarkhiia* office requests all subscribers to send us their addresses again as soon as possible.'[76] Similar raids on anarchists followed in Petrograd and provincial cities through the next six weeks, producing such a pressure of political news that Gan's culture section was driven out for a week in late May.[77] But none of this resulted in his diminished participation; on the contrary, other front-page notices announced his very public identification with leading ideologists of the Moscow Federation. Thus we read that:

> On Tuesday 14 May, at 5 pm, the initiative group in the Moscow Post

Office is organising a PUBLIC MEETING in the newspaper dispatch department of the Main Post Office on Miasnitskaia Street, which will be addressed by comrades Vl. Barmash [*Anarkhiia*'s editor], the Gordin brothers, Al. Gan, Kaz. Kovalevich, Yakovlev and others.[78]

Both Kovalevich and Barmash were known for terrorist activity. They had histories of imprisonment stretching back to the 1905 revolution, and records with the Tsarist Okhrana which preceded the Bolshevik Cheka.[79] Clearly Gan identified himself with these people on public platforms, not just in journalism.

On 30 May his culture section was back with the announcement that a volume would be published called *Anarchy: Creative Work* with articles by Gan, Malevich, Rodchenko and two regular pseudonymous authors, Sviatigor and Plamen. Its three sections would be titled 'Agitation', 'Dynamite and Form', and 'Information'. Its programme had that same anarchist ring:

> We shall fly up through the heads of bosses, retailers, critics, and the vegetarian and narrowly Party organisations now dominating the cultural section of the cooperatives and the Proletkult, and drop down into the very midst of the masses with the dynamite of destruction and the forms of our creative inventiveness.[80]

The book was never published, and the newspaper's regular section continued till its 99th and last issue on 2 July, which had statements on artgroup politics from Tatlin and Rodchenko.[81] By now Bolshevik power was increasingly dominant and anarchism was in severe retreat. In December, delegates who came to Moscow for their All-Russia Conference were arrested, and by then no anarchist journals remained. Over the next two years, 1919 and 1920, the mass movement was wiped out by the Cheka, and small factions with increasingly unworldly programmes grouped and regrouped amongst intellectual membership.[82]

Cultural education for the Bolsheviks

These episodes fully explain Gan's political awareness and his later critiques of Bolshevik cultural policy. Meanwhile, it was perhaps that 'unseriousness' which Stepanova had perceptively noted that now enabled him to work with them as well. As to what that work was, I recently discovered some indications in an unexpected source: in the *Prikazy* (Orders) of the Moscow District Commissariat for Military Affairs for the spring of 1919.[83]

The civil war was at its height, and these flimsy little bulletins were gazetting the movements of Red Army regiments and personnel from one activity and garrison to another on a daily basis. The whole military effort to save the new regime was threatened by the soldiers' ignorance of the Bolshevik programme and ideology for which they were fighting. In the Red Army as throughout the population, this problem began to be tackled urgently during early 1919, at three levels: directly, with political information and agitation; less directly, through 'cultural-educational' activity, and at the fundamental level, in teaching people to read and write. At the global level of its leaders and general policies, this vast programme is extensively documented.[84] Through references to the Administration for Political Education in these Orders, however, we get a close-up view onto personnel and activities in the Moscow District command.

Most of the Orders from this Administration were published over the names of two people, 'Military Commissar Yaroslavsky' and 'Head of the Political Education Administration Vukolov.' An Order of 2 May 1919, however, also bears the third name of a Departmental head under the latter: 'Head of the Cultural Education Department Alexei Gan.' Significantly, he is the only signatory I have found in two years of these Orders who is given a first name, clearly identifying him as a person with some individual, non-military identity. The Order in question announces 'that all water-sport societies, that is yacht-clubs, sailing and rowing societies, are hereby taken over by the [Moscow District] Commissariat [for Military Affairs]' and whether 'requisitioned or confiscated...their property must be registered with the Administration [for Political Education] within two weeks.'[85] There is clearly some continuity here with Gan's earlier work on expropriated buildings. Some indication of his job's content appears a year later in Orders which now formally define the tasks of such a Cultural Education department within its Military District:

> It conducts cultural education [*vospitanie*] and all-sided enlightenment [*prosveshchenie*] of troops in the spirit of the idea of communism. It organises and executes instruction in clubs, theatres, libraries, reading rooms, schools, lectures, excursions, orchestras, choirs and all kinds of cultural enlightenment establishments and within the military units themselves, in accordance with the programme of the Political Education Administration of the military district, helping with distribution of instructors in the area. It works in contact with the local organisations of the Russian Communist Party [RKP] and Narkompros.[86]

From this work we can see how Gan might have come to realise that capitalism's buildings did not fit communism's needs and so constrained them as to be themselves 'counter-revolutionary.' It is less indicative of the real depth of his Party commitment. This order states that the person at Vukolov's level will be chosen 'from amongst local members of the RKP' and must then select his own staff. Whether this means that Gan was a Party member in the spring of 1919 we do not know, but when the artists came round to his lodgings at 5 pm, as Stepanova describes,[87] he would be just back from a day organising 'cultural education of troops in the spirit of the idea of communism.' In this context, it is not surprising that he was impatient with their introspectiveness and indecision as well as their political naivety. From the artists' point of view, as their diaries and transcripts show, his questioning served as grit in the oyster. Their world was dramatically radical in its internal, professional aspirations and was psychologically desperate for change, but it was still, like the troops, politically illiterate.

The next two years were no time to advertise any anarchist sympathies in Moscow.[88] Every increased threat from the Entente powers who were blockading the country and every movement towards Moscow by White forces increased the propaganda pressure to support the government for national survival, and every sign of counter-revolution was deemed to be inspired by 'the anarchist underground.' For Kropotkin's funeral on 13 February 1921, a few leading members of the movement were let out of prison by Kamenev, Chairman of Mossoviet, in deference to the old man's special status. That was famously the last time that anarchism's black flag was paraded through Moscow's streets.[89] Those who had contributed to *Anarkhiia* knew that colleagues not imprisoned were in hiding, had emigrated or, like Chernyi in September 1921, simply been shot.

By December 1921, little was left beyond a brave group of Anarcho-Biocosmicists who sought a social revolution in interplanetary space, but not on Soviet territory.[90] According to one scholarly Soviet source, they had formed a year before around a declaration made on 16 December 1920 by A. Sviatigor, whom we know as a pseudonymous colleague (or alter ego?) of Gan's in the proposed of collection of *Anarkhiia* papers over two years earlier. According to this source, the Biocosmicists 'comprised two groups of anarchists: the group of poets and the group of artists.' On 17 April 1921 'twenty-six Sviatigor supporters in Moscow formed a Club of Creator-Biocosmicists' (*Kreatory-biokozmisty*).[91] Was Gan in this? One Western authority has said that Lunacharsky dismissed him from heading the mass festivals section of Narkompros's TEO at the end of 1920 'because of his extreme ideological position.'[92] During 1921–2 he seems to have been earning his living in the printing trade again, and in summer 1922 began *Kino-Fot*. With so many contacts among Moscow printers, it has always seemed curious that he produced *Constructivism* in the town of Tver a hundred miles away. However, even the NEP did not make such direct Party criticism as his acceptable. Tver had had a strong anarchist group; perhaps it also had a friendly printer?[93]

The potency of Gan's ideas for architecture was proven in their subsequent development by colleagues in that profession. His particular contribution lay in the tendency astutely observed in 1920 by two of Rodchenko's painting students, the Chichagova sisters. They visited Gan about a project and noted how 'in his characteristically energetic manner he started to theorise about our task.'[94] In as far as he was engaged with the anarchists he exemplifies Emma Goldman's observation, writing as a participant: 'The anarchists, the future unbiassed historian will admit, have played a very important role in the Russian Revolution – a role far more significant and fruitful than their comparatively small number would have led one to expect.'[95]

Notes

1 For general accounts see Anatole Kopp, *Town and Revolution*, London, 1970; S.O. Khan-Magomedov, *Pioneers of Soviet Architecture*, London, 1987; C. Cooke, *Russian Avant-Garde: Theories of Art, Architecture and the City*, London, 1995.

2 P. Avrich, *The Russian Anarchists*, Princeton, NJ, 1967, pp. 4–5.

3 A. Gan, *Konstruktivizm* (Constructivism), Tver, 1922.

4 Gan, *Konstruktivizm*, p. 14.

5 Gan, *Konstruktivizm*, p. 15.

6 Gan, *Konstruktivizm*, for example pp. 11, 14, 16, 49, 57.

7 For example, V. Apyshkov, *Rational'noe v noveishchei arkhitekture* (The Rational in the Latest Architecture), St Petersburg, 1905, pp. 55, 63.

8 W.C. Brumfield, *The Origins of Modernism in Russian Architecture*, Berkeley, CA, 1991; C. Cooke, 'Fedor Shekhtel: an architect and his clients in turn-of-the-century Moscow', *AA Files* 5, January 1984, pp. 3–31.

9 'O zemle' (On the Land), 26 October 1917; this draft by Lenin was affirmed on 19 February 1918. For the texts of these in English, see M. McCauley, ed., *The Russian Revolution and the Soviet State 1917–1921: Documents*, London, 1975, pp. 241–7 (though first date is Western style and second misprinted). The further decree of 20 August 1918 confirming 'Abolition of private ownership of urban real estate' appears in T. Sosnovy, *The Housing Problem in the Soviet Union*, New York, 1954, Appendix I, pp. 228–9. Lenin's own draft of 8 November 1917, 'On requisitioning the houses of the rich for alleviating the needs of the poor', was finally passed on 20 February 1918 as 'Fundamentals of the law on confiscation of apartment houses'. On these, see Sosnovy, *Housing Problem*, p. 12. On the specific measures taken to redistribute housing in Moscow, see N.M. Aleshchenko, *Moskovskii sovet v 1917–1945 gg* (Moscow City Soviet during 1917–1945), Moscow, 1976, pp. 193–4.

10 For well documented accounts, see later sections of V.P. Lapshin, *Khudozhestvennaia zhizn' Moskvy i Petrograda v 1917 godu* (Artistic Life in Moscow and Petrograd in 1917), Moscow, 1983. Trotsky also describes his colleague's earnest concerns in L. Trotsky, *My Life*, London, 1930, pp. 300–1.

11 *Izvestiia* report, 15 August 1918, reproduced as Document 18 in V.E. Khazanova, comp., *Iz istorii sovetskoi arkhitektury 1917–1925 gg: dokumenty i materialy* (From the History of Soviet Architecture 1917–25: Documents and Materials), Moscow, 1963, p. 32.

12 Programme for the organisation of Mossoviet's Planning Department, 5 September 1918, Document 19, in Khazanova, *Iz istorii 1917–25*, pp. 32–3.

13 For Lunacharsky's high estimation of Zholtovsky, see A.V. Lunacharsky, 'Ob otdele izobrazitel'nykh iskusstv' (On the Department of Fine Arts), ms, 1920, in I.A. Sats and A.F. Ermakova, *A.V. Lunacharsky: ob iskusstve* (A.V. Lunacharsky on Art), vol. 2, Moscow 1982, pp. 79–83.

14 G.D. Oshchepkova, *I.V. Zholtovsky: proekty i postroiki* (I.V. Zholtovsky: Projects and Buildings), Moscow, 1955, pp. 9–10.

15 The Plan is illustrated as Document 25 in Khazanova, *Iz istorii 1917–25*, p. 40, also in V. Quilici, *Città russa e città sovietica*, Milan, 1976, fig. 132, p. 142.

16 Account of meeting, 20 December 1918, from archives, is Document 22 in Khazanova, *Iz istorii 1917–25*, pp. 37–8.

17 On the festivals, see V. Tolstoy, I. Bibkova and C. Cooke, eds, *Street Art of the Revolution: Festivals and Celebrations in Russia 1918–33*, London, 1990. On the condition of buildings, see H. Carter, 'Rebuilding Soviet Russia: 2 – The condition of urban Russia', *The Architects' Journal*, 20 September 1922, pp. 373–7; B. Lubetkin, 'The Revolution, 1917', in M. Reading and P. Coe, *Lubetkin and Tecton*, London, 1992, pp. 128–33.

18 *Pravda* announcement, 21 December 1922, is Document 28 in Khazanova, *Iz istorii 1917–25*, p. 42. Examples of the urban design schemes are illustrated as Documents

23, 24, 26 and 31–33 in Khazanova, *Iz istorii 1917–25*; in G. Muratore, ed., *Architettura nel paese dei Soviet 1917–1933*, Milan, 1982, figs. 77–8, 84; and in Khan-Magomedov, *Pioneers*, figs 712–15, 731.

19 For example, Lenin's speech to Moscow Party workers October 1921, in Aleshchenko, *Moskovskii sovet*, p. 225.

20 Provisions of the act are discussed in: Sosnovy, *Housing Problem*, pp. 44–5.

21 I. Mashkov, 'Moskovskoe Arkhitekturnoe Obshchestvo, 1867–1927 gg' (Moscow Architectural Society 1867–1927), *Ezhegodnik MAO* (MAO Annual) 5, Moscow, 1928, pp. 9–14.

22 *Arkhitektura*(Architecture), 1923, nos 1–2; 3–4. Though described on its cover as *Ezhemesiachnik MAO*(MAO's Monthly), these were both double issues.

23 P. Antipov, 'Khronika' (Chronicle), *Arkhitektura*, 1923, 1–2, p. 47.

24 I.P. Denike, 'Marks ob iskusstve' (Marx on art), *Iskusstvo: zhurnal' RAKhN* (Art: the Journal of RAKhN) 1, Moscow, 1923, pp. 32–42; for a discussion, see Cooke, *Russian Avant-Garde*, pp. 122–3.

25 For general accounts of InKhuK, see Khan-Magomedov, *Pioneers*, and S.O. Khan-Magomedov, *Rodchenko: The Complete Work*, London, 1986.

26 'Arkhitekturnaia sektsiia' (The Architecture Section), *Iskusstvo: zhurnal' RAKhN* 1, pp. 431–3.

27 Varvara Stepanova, *Chelovek ne mozhet zhit' bez chuda* (A Person Cannot Live Without a Miracle), Moscow, 1994, p. 92.

28 A. Gan, 'Chto takoe konstruktivizm?' (What is constructivism?), *Sovremennaia arkhitektura* (Contemporary Architecture) 3, 1928, pp. 79–81; Proposals for the organisation of May Day festivities, from TEO Narkompros, February 1920, published as Document 38 in Tolstoy, Bibikova and Cooke, eds, *Street Art*, pp. 124–5.

29 A. Gan, 28 March 1921, paper 'O programme i plane rabot Gruppy konstruktivistov' (On the programme and work plan of the group of constructivists), in S.O. Khan-Magomedov, *InKhuK i rannyi konstruktivizm* (InKhuK and early constructivism), Moscow, 1993, pp. 98–9. Part of this is translated in Khan-Magomedov, *Rodchenko*, p. 92.

30 A. Gan, 'Kinematograf i kinematografiia' (The cinematograph and cinema), *Kino-Fot* (Cinema-Photo) 1, 25–31 August 1922, p. 1, translated in R. Taylor and I. Christie, eds, *The Film Factory: Russian and Soviet Cinema in Documents 1896–1939*, 1994, pp. 67–8.

31 A. Gan, ' "Levyi front" i kinematografiia' (The 'Left Front' and cinema), *Kino-Fot* 5, 10 December 1922, pp. 1–3, translated in Taylor and Christie, eds, *The Film Factory* pp. 75–7.

32 Gan, *Konstruktivizm*, p. 21.

33 Gan, *Konstruktivizm*, pp. 11–12.

34 Gan, *Konstruktivizm*, p. 63.

35 Gan, *Konstruktivizm*, p. 63.

36 Gan, *Konstruktivizm*, p. 60.

37 Gan, *Konstruktivizm*, pp. 63–4.

38 Gan, *Konstruktivizm*, p. 61.

39 Khazanova, *Iz istorii, 1917–25*, p. 9.

40 On this later development of theory, see Cooke, *Russian Avant-Garde*, ch. 5.

41 C. Lodder, *Russian Constructivism*, London, 1983, p. 286, n. 75.

42 For example, Lenin, 'Speech to the 3rd All-Russia Congress of the Komsomol', 2 October 1920, in V.I. Lenin, *Collected Works*, vol. 31, Moscow, 1965, pp. 283–99; Lunacharsky, 'Ob otdele izobrazitel'nykh iskusstv' (On the Department of Fine Arts), 1920, in A.V. Lunacharsky, *Ob iskusstve* (On Art), Moscow, 1982, vol. 2, pp. 79–83; and Lunacharsky, 'Iskusstva v Moskve' (Art in Moscow), speech to 3rd Congress of the Comintern, July 1921, in *ibid.*, pp. 94–100.

43 N. Bukharin and E. Preobrazhensky, *Azbukha kommunizma*, Moscow, 1919, translated as *The ABC of Communism*, London, 1969, pp. 66–7.

44 Gan, *Konstruktivizm*, pp. 63–4.

45 A. Gan, 'Kino v shestom oktiabre' (Cinema at the sixth anniversary of the Revolution), *Zrelishcha* (Spectacles) 61, 1923, pp. 20–2.

46 Gan, *Konstruktivizm*, p. 65.

47 R. Stites, *Revolutionary Dreams: Utopian Vision and Experimental Life in the Russian Revolution*, Oxford, 1989, p. 198, describes him as 'a major Constructivist architect'.

48 Lodder, *Russian Constructivism*, p. 243.

49 Stepanova, *Chelovek*, p. 66.

50 Stepanova, *Chelovek*, pp. 108–9.

51 Stepanova, *Chelovek*, p. 93.

52 Stepanova, *Chelovek*, p. 109.

53 Stepanova, *Chelovek*, p. 66. The Maximalists were the Soiuz S-R Maksimalistov (Union of Socialist-Revolutionary Maximialists), an ultra-radical offshoot of the Socialist Revolutionary Party (SR) lying roughly between the anarchists and the Bolsheviks. For sources on them, see Avrich, *Russian Anarchists*, p. 203.

54 There are inevitably several historical views on the anarchist movement in Russia. For Western scholarship, see Avrich, *The Russian Anarchists* and P. Avrich, ed., *The Anarchists in the Russian Revolution*, documents with introductory texts, London, 1973. For the accounts of leading members forced into emigration, see most notably G.P. Maximoff (Maksimov), *The Guillotine at Work: Twenty years of Terror in Russia (Data and Documents)*, Chicago, 1940; also A. Skirda, *Les anarchistes dans la révolution russe, Textes de: A. Skirda, A. Gorélik, A. Berkman, V. Serge, E. Goldman*, Paris, 1973. For the Bolshevik account, see S.N. Kanev, *Oktiabrskaia revoliutsiia i krakh anarkhizma: Borba partii bol'shevikov protiv anarkhisma 1917–1922 gg* (The October Revolution and the Break-up of Anarchism: The Battle of the Bolshevik Party against Anarchism, 1917–22), Moscow, 1974, and G. Kostomarov, ed., *Moskovskie bolsheviki na zashchite sovetskoi stolytsy v 1919 godu: sbornik dokumentov* (Moscow Bolsheviks Defend the Soviet Capital in 1919: Collection of Documents), Moscow, 1947.

55 *Anarkhiia* was the organ of the Moscow Federation of Anarchist Groups, itself formed in Moscow in March 1917. The first issue appeared on 13 September 1917; the editorial office was at 12 Moronovsky Lane, and the editor was Vladimir Barmash. The main Petrograd papers were *Burevestnik* (Stormy Petrel), *Kommuna* (The Commune), *Golos truda* (Voice of Labour) and by autumn 1917 also *Svobodnaia kommuna* (The Free Commune). Anarchist papers from other towns are listed in Avrich, *The Anarchists*, p. 68; Maximoff, *Guillotine*, pp. 344–5; Gorélik in Skirda, *Les anarchists*, p. 67. Until lately these have been unavailable in Soviet libraries ('never existed') and western library searches have so far failed to locate *Anarkhiia*. The chance to open up this topic was created by first republication of all Malevich's contributions to it in: D.V. Sarab'ianov *et al.*, eds, *Kazimir Malevich: Sobranie sochinenii v piati tomakh: tom 1* (Kazimir Malevich: Complete Collected Works in Five Volumes, vol. 1), Moscow, 1995, where footnotes on pp. 331–7 give new detail on Gan's anarchist connections.

56 The manifesto of the Moscow Federation published in *Anarkhiia*, 6 November 1917, i.e. four days after the end of violent fighting in which the Bolsheviks took Moscow, included a strong cry for peace to be negotiated without any accommodation to 'German imperialism'. (Kanev, *Oktiabrskaia revoliutsiia*, pp. 122–3, 287.) By February 1918 anarchists papers were pouring 'a stream of obloquy' at the terms being negotiated (Avrich, *Russian Anarchists*, pp. 182–3). Different secondary sources variously give references to the paper by date, number of issue, or both. It reappeared as a daily, but with some irregularity for correlation is often difficult. Offices were initially in their headquarters but in late March moved to 1 Nastasinsky Lane, where the famous futurist artists' haunt 'The Poets' Café' was located. Herman

Askaraov was editor at one stage. When the government moved to Moscow central figures of Petrograd anarchism followed and brought *Golos truda* with them, among whose editors was Grigorii Maksimov, author, as Maximoff, of *Guillotine*.

57 A. Gan, 'Revoliutsiia i narodnyi teatr', *Anarkhiia*, no. 12 (March) 1918, cited in Sarab'ianov, *Kazimir Malevich*, p. 331.

58 L. Chernyi, 'Gosudarstvo i anarkhizm' (The state and anarchism), *Anarkhiia*, 5 March 1918; 'Mir zakliuchen. Da zdravstvuet voina!', headline in *Anarkhiia*, 7 March 1918. Quoted in Kanev, *Oktiabrskaia revoliutsiia*, respectively on pp. 102, 307.

59 Chernyi's article in *Anarkhiia* for 12 March 1918 outlined a proposal for a federative system of national organisation with a 'great federation' or national assembly and city federations below it, and to individual persons free to produce their own food, goods and so on or enter into exchanges with any other unit, 'without dealing through middlemen'. Article quoted but not named in Kanev, *Oktiabrskaia revoliutsiia*, pp. 130, 262.

60 Launching, Gan's role and general contents of the 'Tvorchestvo' section, from Sarab'ianov, *Kazimir Malevich*, p. 331. Print run, from Kanev, *Oktiabrskaia revoliutsiia*, p. 56. Maximoff, *Guillotine*, p. 345, indicates this is typical for such papers in Moscow and Petrograd, where *Golos truda* and *Burevestnik* each sold about 25,000.

61 K. Malevich, 'Arkhitektura kak poshchechina betono-zhelezu' (Architecture as a slap in the face to reinforced concrete), *Anarkhiia*, 6 April 1918, p. 4; Russian text in Sarab'ianov, *Kazimir Malevich*, pp. 69–72. Later republished, with additional ending, in *Iskusstvo kommuny*, no. 1, 7 December 1918, pp. 2–3. For English translation of the latter see T. Andersen, ed., *K.S. Malevich: Essays on Art 1915–1933*, vol. 1, Copenhagen and London, 1968, pp. 60–4.

62 Sources vary between 25 and 26: maybe 25 plus their headquarters? Some sources describe them all as 'mansions' (*osobniaki*), others refer to 'buildings' (*doma*). Avrich, *Russian Anarchists*, p. 180, reports their principled preference before the Revolution for taking only private homes. After the Revolution their strength on Mossoviet enabled them to operate a 'special desk' in its requisitioning office handling their own expropriations (Maximoff, *Guillotine*, p. 407). Most were too large for their needs and contained ordinary residents too. Maximoff describes their management of property as exemplary and adding to their popularity among local populations.

63 Maximoff, *Guillotine*, pp. 405–6. For plans of the building at 6 Malaia Dmitrovka (later Chekhov) Street, see T.V. Moiseeva, ed., *Pamiatniki arkhitektury Moskvy: Zemlianoi gorod* (Architectural Monuments of Moscow: Zemlianoi Gorod Area), Moscow, 1989, pp. 197–9. For period photos and drawings of the interiors, see M. Raeburn, ed., *The Twilight of the Tsars,* Hayward Gallery, London, 1991, pp. 214–7.

64 This is clearly stated by Sarab'ianov in his *Kazimir Malevich*, p. 337, presumably from sources in *Anarkhiia* including Gan's own piece of 19 March (see note 66 below). His role is notably not mentioned by Rodchenko, see my following text and note 69. Maximoff's statement, *Guillotine*, p. 408, that 'registration of art treasures in the Morozov house' was under supervision of Piro refers to the house and post-impressionist art collection of another Morozov, Ivan. On the anarchist takeover of this, see B. Whiney Kean, *All the Empty Palaces*, London, 1983, p. 255.

65 For plans of the house and associated buildings at 21 Vvedensky (later Podsosensky) Lane, see Moiseeva, ed., *Pamiatniki: Zemlianoi gorod*, pp. 288–9. For period photos of the Shekhtel/Vrubel interiors, see E.I. Kirichenko, *Fedor Shekhtel'*, Moscow, 1973, pp. 34–5, and Raeburn, ed., *The Twilight*, pp. 50, 198–9. On owner, collections and their fate after 12 April 1918, see E.B. Sametskaia, 'A.V. Morozov i sozdanie gosu-darstvennogo myzeia keramiki' (A.V. Morozov and the creation of the State Museum of Ceramics), *Muzei–6*, Moscow, 1986, pp.159–64.

66 A. Gan, 'Osobniak Morozova' (The Morozov Mansion), *Anarkhiia*, 19 March 1918, cited in Sarab'ianov, *Kazimir Malevich*, p. 337, note 3.

67 *Anarkhiia*, 29 March 1918, cited in Sarab'ianov, *Kazimir Malevich*, p. 337, note 3.

68 His 'blasphemous' presentation of this picture in the exhibition 0.10 (Zero-Ten) in Petrograd, December 1915–January 1916, high in 'the icon corner', as well as its fundamental role in suprematism, has made it much discussed. See C. Douglas, '0.10 Exhibition', in S. Barron and M. Tuchman, eds, *The Avant-Garde in Russia 1910–1930: New Perspectives*, Los Angeles and Cambridge, MA, 1980, pp. 34–40; J.A. Sharp, 'The critical reception of the 0.10 exhibition: Malevich and Benua', in A. Calnek, ed., *The Great Utopia*, Guggenheim Museum, New York, 1992, pp. 38–52; and L.S. Boersma, *0.10: The Last Futurist Painting Exhibition*, Rotterdam, 1993. All these and criticism at the time discuss the works in relation to each artist's personal development and the politics of the art world. Where they broach broader political implications, for example by Sharp, the assumption is that the 'left radicalism' in these works of Malevich's and Tatlin's coincides with the political aspirations of the Bolsheviks.

69 V.A. Rodchenko, comp., *A.M. Rodchenko: Stat'i, vospominaniia, avtobiograficheskie zapiski, pis'ma* (A.M. Rodchenko: Articles, Reminiscences, Autobiographical Notes, Letters), Moscow, 1982, pp. 86–7. These reminiscences were written during 1941–2.

70 K. Malevich, 'Vystavka professional'nogo soiuza khudozhnikov-zhivopistsev. Levaia federatsiia – molodaia fractsiia' (The exhibition of the Trade Union of Artist-Painters. Left Federation – Young Fraction), *Anarkhiia*, 20 June 1918, p. 4; republished in Sarab'ianov, *Kazimir Malevich*, pp. 117–23, where annotations make no comment on these passages.

71 Maximoff, *Guillotine*, pp. 355–7 gives the most authoritative account as he was arrested near his workplace at *Golos truda*. He reproduces related government and newspaper documents in *ibid.*, pp. 383–9. See also Avrich, *Russian Anarchists*, pp. 184–5. The Bolshevik side is told in Kanev, *Oktiabrskaia revoliutsiia*, pp. 318–24. Official documents quoted in Sametskaia, 'A.V. Morozov i sozdanie', record supposed damage to contents found at the Morozov house, this being another virtuous pretext for the Cheka's purge.

72 Maximoff, *Guillotine*, p. 356. In *ibid.*, p. 410 he says *Anarkhiia* was closed for 'more than a month' but issue numbers/dates indicate it was about two weeks.

73 From Nikulin's unpublished reminiscences in W. Woroszylski, *The Life of Mayakovsky*, London, 1972, pp. 209–11.

74 Report in the Moscow literary and cultural newspaper *Figaro* of 15 April 1918, quoted in Woroszylski, *The Life of Mayakovsky*, pp. 212–14. Woroszylski describes *Figaro* as a daily, but standard Russian press listings of that date describe it as weekly.

75 *Figaro*, 15 April 1918.

76 *Anarkhiia*, nos 56 and 57, 11 and 12 May 1918, p. 1.

77 Sarab'ianov, *Kazimir Malevich*, p. 331. It was absent from nos. 63–69, in mid–late May.

78 *Anarkhiia*, nos. 56 and 57, 11 and 12 May 1918, p. 1.

79 Peter Goodman, 'The anarchist movement in Russia 1905–1917', Ph.D. thesis, University of Bristol, 1981, p. 230.

80 *Anarkhiia*, no. 72, 30 May 1918, quoted in: Sarab'ianov, *Kazimir Malevich*, p. 331.

81 Sarab'ianov, *Kazimir Malevich*, pp. 330, 347. The 'two further issues' he describes as appearing in September and October 1919 were a paper of the same name but no connection: Avrich, *Russian Anarchists*, p. 188.

82 The documents in Kostomarov, ed., *Moskovskie bolsheviki*, give a grim picture of the developing campaign in late 1919. For a general account, see Avrich, *Russian Anarchists*. On the fate of the last journals, see Maximoff, *Guillotine*, p. 357.

83 *Prikazy Moskovskogo Okruzhnogo Komissariata po voennym delam* (Orders of the Moscow District Commissariat for Military Affairs), Moscow. Issues surveyed are 2 May 1919–27 Dec 1920.

84 V.G. Kolychev, *Partiino-politicheskaia rabota v krasnom armii v gody grazhdanskoi voiny 1918–1920*(Party-Political Work in the Red Army During the Civil War 1918–1920), Moscow, 1979, has extensive bibliography.

85 *Prikazy*, 2 May 1919, no. 871, pp. 6–7.

86 *Prikazy*, 23 Feb 1920, no.168, 'Polozhenie o Politichesko-Prosvetitel'nom otdele Gubernskogo Komissariata po voennym delam utv. 22 ianv. 1920' (Regulations on the Political Education Departments of Gubernia Commissariats for Military Affairs, affirmed 22 January 1920), p. 7.

87 At this stage, and later as InKhuK, they generally met in each other's lodgings around central Moscow. Gan at this stage seem to have been in 'apartment 62, 29 Dolgorukovskaia Street' (Stepanova, *Chelovek*, p. 66). Domestic photographs convey the atmosphere, e.g. Khan-Magomedov, *Rodchenko*, p. 69, showing a group over teacups including Stepanova, Popova and Alexander Vesnin; and A. Lavrentiev, *Varvara Stepanova: A Constructivist Life*, London, 1988, p. 55, which includes Gan.

88 Maximoff, *Guillotine*, includes a photograph of the eighteen-member Kropotkin Funeral Committee, of which he was a member with Chernyi, Barmash, Askarov others who wrote in *Anarkhiia*. The caption includes notes on dates of murder or deportation of each person in and after 1921. Other leading figures expelled are listed by Anatole Gorélik, in Skirda, *Les anarchistes*, pp. 81–3. When Maximoff himself emerged from Moscow's infamous Butyrka Prison in January 1921, those still prominent in the Moscow movement told him 'Abandonnez l'idée d'oeuvrer à Moscou, capitale des bolchéviks – Moscou la rouge où il n'y a pas de place pour les anarchistes', *ibid.*, p. 77.

89 Avrich, *The Anarchists*, pp. 26–7, 153.

90 Avrich, *The Anarchists*, p. 27; Maximoff, *Guillotine*, p. 362; Kanev, *Oktiabrskaia revoliutsiia*, pp. 38–9.

91 Kanev, *Oktiabrskaia revoliutsiia*, p. 49. His source on the Club of Creator-Biocosmicists is the journal *Biokosmist*, 1922, no. 1, p. 3. On the *Anarchy* papers, see note 74 above.

92 J. Bowlt, *Russian Art of the Avant-Garde: Theory and Criticism 1902–34*, London, 1988, pp. 214–5.

93 Maximoff, *Guillotine*, p. 406, mentions Tver as one of several towns of central Russia where there was 'anarchist educational and propaganda activity of the same extensive character as in Moscow' during 1918.

94 Reminiscences of Galina Chichagova in Rodchenko, *A.M. Rodchenko*, p. 142.

95 E. Goldman, *My Disillusionment with Russia*, London, 1925, p. 251, quoted as Document 54 in Avrich, *The Anarchists*, p. 165.

2 The Vesnins' Palace of Labour

The role of practice in materialising the revolutionary architecture

Catherine Cooke

By the autumn of 1922, when the Moscow Architectural Society (MAO) began engaging with the prospect that Russian building activity would start again, circles outside the profession, as we have seen, were urgently prompting them to some theoretical engagement with the new Soviet ideology. Alexei Gan's *Constructivism* came out in December that year. But the professional issue of what a real Soviet building would be like, as a fully resolved work of architecture rather than a diagram, was not yet broached. Three-dimensional experiments being conducted among artists were to have enormous long-term importance as a source of new formal languages for architecture. By their very origins, however, they crucially lacked any input from that domain-specific knowledge which Gan had stressed as the essential partner of ideological understanding in creating the 'material-technical "organs" of the new society.' In his argument, it was only the practitioners in possession of such knowledge who could produce the catalyst to launch a new direction in each field.

By the time MAO started to publish its new journal *Architecture* in early 1923, even its stolid new fifty-year old President Alexei Shchusev was declaring: 'We must participate in the creation of life and not be passive contemplators of it.'[1] However, his strangely ecclesiastical vocabulary gave his words little conviction. The more committed voice of that generation came from the architect-planner Vladimir Semionov, whose engagement with radical politics had forced him to leave Russia in 1908 for four years of professional travel in Britain and Europe. Writing before the war, he had felt forced 'to eschew politics, though the centre of gravity of the whole question lies precisely in that.'[2] After losing a decade of professional life in the upheavals, he now urged his colleagues to embrace the fact that 'this new world…presents [us] with the task of an architecture which is genuinely public'; that 'the changed circumstances call for new methods and forms.' It was their task, he said, in a powerful agenda of 'priority tasks', 'to understand these new conditions…and to find forms which respond to the real situation.'[3]

Editorials in the journal's two issues by a practitioner who was twenty years younger, but who also knew Europe and had built, started to connect the task with contemporaneous debates in Europe. As 'technical editor', the young Moisei Ginzburg contributed two pieces which reflected the recent arrival in Moscow, following the end of the Entente's blockade, of some copies of *L'Esprit Nouveau*.[4] With Corbusian illustrations of Buffalo grain silos, he challenged the Moscovites to conceive a new aesthetic sensibility derived from 'the realities of our life'; to see 'engineering and industrial structures' as 'elements of our life not to be covered up but to be seen as a source of new aesthetic values.'[5] If the European phrases about 'the mechanisation of our lives' seemed inappropriate to Russia's present ruined state, they were familiar to those in the arts reared on the message of futurism. Indeed, a year earlier this had been the theme of an impassioned credo delivered to the artists in InKhuK by Alexander Vesnin, one of the profession's rising prewar stars of a middle generation between these two.[6] As one of three brothers known throughout Moscow practice as a highly capable team, Alexander designed the cover for MAO's new journal while his older, more academic brother Leonid was on its editorial board. Alexander's typography was as intentionally crude as Alexei Gan's in *Constructivism* a few months earlier. It provoked outrage from the connoisseurial brigade in the person of historian Igor Grabar.[7] Even here, the Vesnin brothers were already making their presence felt, and with architectural competitions now beginning again, they were soon an inescapable force.

As Gan had said to the painters, the worthy new aspirations expressed in *Architecture* by leading members of the profession was 'not proletarian, that is it carries no ideology.'[8] At the same time, quasi-architectural experiments in form going among the so-called rationalists and others, though given plausibly Soviet functional names, were entirely devoid of that real professional content which, as Gan insisted, really materialises the ideology.[9] The people who first brought together these two aspects of the architectural task into a palpably real proposal for an ideologically new building were the three brothers, Leonid, Victor and Alexander Vesnin, in the first competition for a public building in the Soviet capital.

For its combination of social innovation with technical boldness their third-prizewinning scheme for a Palace of Labour was described by Ginzburg four years later as the project which led his generation 'along the thorny path of independent, thoughtful and creative work.'[10] The Vesnins themselves were a nodal point of Soviet architecture for several decades, not least because so many areas of creative and professional life intersected in their buzzing studio in central Moscow's Denezhnyi Lane. (Even after modernism's demise, in 1933, Leonid's premature death caused Mossoviet to rename it Vesnin Street.) In the nature of Soviet history writing, however, their three richly different and complementary talents later became merged into one historical and professional personality. Likewise, the sources of their commitment to the Soviet social and political project were reduced to the usual formulaic assurances that 'they immediately embraced the October Revolution.' Some rich memoirs published in the late 1980s by one of their wives, and better access to project documentation on this scheme, now make it possible to build a much richer account of where their ideological commitment originated, of how their definitive professional manifesto emerged, and of how it was received at the time.

Figure 2.1 Victor and Natalya Vesnin at the time of their marriage in 1915

The first image of an ideological architecture

When 'The Right to Build' became law in August 1922, MAO sent a letter to all local and central government agencies urging them to use architectural competitions 'to obtain the best possible solutions to the rebuilding and replanning problems across the country...and to ensure the rational application of scarce building materials.'[11] That autumn Mossoviet responded by inviting MAO to collaborate immediately on running two competitions. The briefs were conventionally practical. The competition for workers' housing sought projects that would 'offer correctives' to 'the best models from the West and America' so that 'the working class can provide itself with a capacity for work that is rooted in being a healthy individual.'[12] The resulting schemes were socially fairly conventional, as was appropriate to the NEP, and Leonid Vesnin took one of two first prizes.[13]

The brief for a vast Palace of Labour just off Red Square was equally practical in tone. Mossoviet saw the building as prestige accommodation for their own administration and for meetings of their 2,500 city councillors. It would provide a headquarters for the Moscow Committee of the Party, a museum of social history, and a public eating facility seating 1,500. Dominating all this was a hall for national events to seat 8,000, including 'representatives of foreign governments' and the press. The final brief was written by Zholtovsky, Semionov, Shekhtel and three others of that generation. Its great stress on high daylighting levels, ease of circulation and different entrances to its various parts dictated a highly penetrable and, in that sense, 'democratic' building. The conception of an agitational and informational hub was embodied in the requirements that there should be balconies at street level 'for orators to speak from, on all four facades', and that towers, if desired, 'should accommodate things like an observatory and radio station.' Another option was 'a landing place for aeroplanes.' The only aesthetic specification was that inside and out, the Palace should have a 'rich look appropriate to its idea but expressed in simple contemporary forms not belonging to the specific style of any past epoch.' In urban terms, it would be an element in the 'New Moscow' city plan which Shchusev was then finalising. The brief therefore stressed that 'massing must be compatible with Theatre Square', the Bolshoi and the urban spaces around it.[14]

The competition was announced on 5 November 1922 to coincide with celebrations for the fifth anniversary of the Revolution. Submissions were due on 5 February 1923. This was not long for a big scheme, but the priorities were clear: 'Designers should allow themselves to be led mainly by the overall idea of the building's composition and not sacrifice this to secondary details of its planning.'[15] On 30 December, a further ideological charge was overlaid on the task when the tenth All-Russian Congress of Soviets approved the union of their Russian republic with the new Ukrainian, Belorussian and Transcaucasian republics to form the single USSR. Speakers dreamed of a World Socialist Union as the next stage, and one up-and-coming Party leader, Sergei Kirov, spoke with great passion of the need this created for a much larger assembly place, a 'magical palace' for 'these exceptional parliaments of ours' which 'must be an emblem of our developing power, of the triumph of communism not just here but also in the West.' Such a building might even 'give the final push to the European proletariat, the majority of which is still not convinced of the triumph of revolution and still doubts the rightness of the Communist Party's tactics.'[16] That was an excessive faith in architecture and Kirov made no reference to the Palace of Labour, but his widely reported words clearly raised the ideological temperature surrounding the competition.

Trained but inexperienced architects who were abstractly exploring 'form' in InKhuK (notably the future rationalists Ladovsky and Krinsky) refused to enter the competition in protest at the presence of Zholtovsky and Shekhtel among MAO's six worthy and traditional representatives on the jury.[17] (Grabar was another member. Their Chairman was Lev Kamenev, Chairman of Mossoviet and a member of the Party's Central Committee. For years he has been written out of the story as a non-person.) One suspects these dissenters also feared ridicule for their incapacity to make a 'real' building from such enormous volumes. In that, they were sensibly cautious. The task was almost impossible for the technologies available anywhere, but forty-seven design teams submitted attempts. These demonstrated above all one thing: that in the Russian profession at large, the umbilical cord to historical architectures had been stretched but not cut. The exception was one scheme under the pseudonym 'Antenna' which, as a later Soviet commentator put it, 'shocked and alarmed those of the jury who represented the Academy tradition', specifically Zholtovsky and Grabar, as something 'so unusual, that it blasted the foundations of traditional architecture.'[18]

On 2 March 1923, all the entries went on public display in MAO's building. *Pravda* published details and the public poured in for guided tours. Petrograd

Figure 2.2 Alexander, Leonid and Victor Vesnin, competition entry under the pseudonym 'Antenna' for the Palace of Labour, Moscow, 1923: perspective view from the Historical Museum (South)

architects demanded a later showing in their own city, or at least special train trips down to Moscow.[19] 'Antenna' became a sensation, particularly amongst the young architects and students. One can see why. It challenged the well-meaning romanticism of the others like a single revolutionary fist punching the Moscow air. Shchusev later recorded how it generated such violent disagreement in the jury that Zholtovsky insisted no prize should be awarded to this scheme.[20] Argument continued in and around the jury until their last meeting on 16 May, when the prize list was announced pseudonymously.[21] Everyone knew that 'Antenna' was by the Vesnin brothers, and sheer pressure of opinion in the professional community had meant they were given third prize. The first prize went to a vaulted mass, half-Byzantine half-Renaissance, by young Petrograd architect Noi Trotsky. The second went to a modernised Roman Coliseum with a landing strip on piloti above, from two Moscovites.[22] Five days later envelopes were formally opened, names were announced and fresh-faced photos of the prize winners appeared with perspectives of their schemes in popular magazines like *Pravda*'s fortnightly *Prozhektor* (The Searchlight).[23]

Even when reproduced in such an unwonted context, the energy of the Vesnins' totally unrhetorical proposal was palpable. By its immaculate attention to how the socially unprecedented activities inside would actually function, it asserted a total belief in the 'realness' of the new world the councillors represented. Human figures, in the most widely reproduced perspective, are so small that its scale is ambiguous without the historic city around it. But the worker was being shown something structurally lucid and totally convincing; suddenly the public domain would have seemed to be about 'his' world. In this image, his life in a factory or (as they all were) as self-builder of log huts, was now manifestly identified with the state, with the Soviets who represented him and with a governing Party that claimed to be effecting a 'dictatorship' of proletarians like him. The presence of several boldly framed structures among central Moscow's prewar commercial buildings gave the project a further realism. The most notable precedent was the vast multi-functional business complex nearby called *Delovyi dvor* (Business Court), completed by the architect Ivan Kuznetsov in 1913, which was now home to the central organisation of Soviet trade unions.[24] This closed the end of Old Square as dramatically as the Vesnins' Palace would close the spaces to east and west of it. In 1913, a few classical trimmings at the entrance had been deemed to give dignity but the workers' mind could readily imagine the building stripped of these, stretched and recast a little into the Vesnins' Palace.

The plausibility and lucid materiality of their scheme were entirely intended. Their notes declared its four guiding principles to have been: 'constructiveness [this was a well-established Russian word for an object which speaks of how it is 'constructed'], *utilitarnost'* [fulfilment of utilitarian function], rationalness and economicalness.'[25] Nothing here had the quality of being 'accidental', which Gan identified with capitalist building.[26] Where other projects evoked dark, defensive fortresses, the Vesnins' scheme had genuinely fulfilled the brief's requirement for high levels of daylighting and penetrability. Their images alone had already fulfilled the psychologically energising task which Alexander had defined a year earlier in his credo to InKhuK. In the new world, he said, 'every object' they created 'must enter into life as an active force, organising man's consciousness, influencing him psychologically, arousing in him an upsurge of energetic activity.'[27] Here too was 'usefulness' as Gan defined it when he wrote: 'usefulness must be understood as achieved through the organic properties and requirements of communism on one hand and the conscious approach to industrial material on the other.'[28] This was the first Soviet building which could be described in his phrase as 'the communist expression of material structure'. It both reflected a deep cultural change and would shape that change, by a material and spatial organism that was entirely free of what Alexander had called 'the superfluous ballast of representing anything'.

The roots of experience and commitment

The unique qualities of this design derived from the synergy between these three brothers whose complementary skills and temperaments made them a model of what management science today would see as the ideal team. This complementarity was commented upon by many colleagues. Since 1909, it had been observed at close quarters by Victor's wife Natalya who kept house for a studio where students were always coming and going and old friends from Petrograd-Leningrad would sleep on the floor when they rallied round to help on a big scheme:

> Alexander worked tormentedly at times and was often disappointed with himself. He had the greatest creative flights of invention, often exceeding any real possibilities of the time. Leonid stood with both feet on the ground. He was the most realistic of them. When the two younger ones soared off into some dizzy fantasy he would bring them back to reality half-jokingly, with a single sensible argument. With his immaculately trained eye and the breadth of fundamental architectural knowledge derived from an Academy training, he had an unquestioned authority among them. He was the connecting link between Alexander and Victor. Victor had an extraordinary engineering imagination. However audacious the concept proposed he would seek to embody it adequately in a concrete way that could be practically executed....Even when he had engineers on a job he would work through all the calculations himself to be thoroughly satisfied.[29]

As Natalya could see, marrying into the trio, 'this teamwork began in earliest childhood on drawing expeditions together.' Their encounter with life's difficulties also came early. After a comfortable provincial childhood in reasonable affluence, their mother died in 1901 at the birth of their sister Anna and soon after that their father's chronic rheumatism forced him into ten years of life as an immobile invalid. At the time of the 1905 revolution the boys were sharing a flat in St Petersburg and collectively profiting from the resources of both the great Russian architecture schools, as Leonid was in the Academy of Arts school and the other two in the Institute of Civil Engineers. They were energetic in student political activism of the kind which caused the Tsarist government to close all higher education establishments after that year's uprisings. When their schools reopened, the Vesnins did not return. They now had two sisters and an invalid father to support and stayed with them in Moscow, only later returning to complete their qualifications. They took on all the architectural work they could get in any decent office and built a high reputation for their energy and the quality of their output, particularly in technical preparation of schemes.[30]

This work with different practices and their numerous competition successes meant the brothers were already very popular and well respected throughout the Moscow profession when Natalya first met them in 1909. As she records, however, they were far from being aspirants to the establishment. Like many in their student generation they were acutely aware of Russia's dire reality, and their own early plunge to the threat of poverty had given them a personal understanding of it. When Natalya first knew them they would 'go for long country walks [with friends from the arts and theatre] talking about how they wanted to achieve something big enough in their lives that would contribute to all this...and ended up talking of political themes.'[31] Their links with the artistic community came partly through friends in the theatre and partly through maintaining their childhood habits of serious art practice. In St Petersburg they all took classes at the studio of the painter Tsionglinsky. Back in Moscow in 1905 they went to Yuon, and a few years later to Tatlin, who took people into his studio to make some money. Through joining that bohemian cooperative on Ostozhenka Street, the Vesnins became exposed to the political and social iconoclasm of Russian futurism, of Tatlin's friends like Mayakovsky, and of his first abstract experiments with 'real materials'.

Having known Natalya for some years, Victor was the first to marry. She brought to the trio both political awareness and experience. Her father was a 'sharply anti-autocratic' lawyer fighting the cases of workers and peasants. He was a profound admirer of Russia's first revolutionaries, the Decembrists, and 'constantly talked of the need for decisive changes'. Several of their family friends were involved in revolutionary activities. As war approached in the summer of 1914, Natalya was staying in the country with an aunt and letters to Victor recorded her own depression at the horrors of rural poverty among peasants driven suicidal with despair.[32]

When the couple married in April 1915, Tatlin was their best man. By then Leonid had been called up on the home front, while Alexander's astigmatism meant his call-up was delayed. Victor was now in a firm working in factory-building, and found himself exempt from call-up as this was 'war priority employment'. Natalya moved with him up to the 'factory belt' where he was happily building vast chemical plants. Among her letters she kept one that Alexander wrote to them on 4 March 1917, which conveys clearly where they stood politically at this first stage of the revolution. One of Alexander's friends at the base where he was now serving 'rushed in to read us Nicholas's declaration that they are all abdicating' (the Tsar abdicated for himself, for the young Tsarevich and for Grand Duke Mikhail, who was potentially the boy's regent):

> All my soldier friends cheered so loudly it did not go quiet for ages. A new life is beginning in our workshops just as all it is across Russia. Everyone is in terrifically high spirits and has a great desire to work to be useful to the nation. I am now impatiently waiting to see when the riots will begin in Germany and whether the Hohenzollens will be overthrown too. I'm sure they will. I think the freedom movement really is beginning in all countries and it's the only thing that can ultimately justify this ghastly brutal war....All the police and home guards here have been disarmed and until a popular militia is organised in this area it is only we soldiers who are ensuring order. I already told you how we had a meeting and decided to elect one person from each section of the workshops onto our soldiers's soviet.[33]

The brothers went through the October revolution in their different locations and were then demobbed. Back in Moscow by early 1918, Victor found himself in the company of Tatlin, Rodchenko and Shchusev on Mossoviet's special committee to decorate the battered city for the first Soviet May Day. He received the most prestigious task of doing Red Square and the Kremlin Gates, and with Alexander's help he created a dramatic scheme of red cloth and Soviet slogans that was widely praised.[34] However, this cost Victor his job. After the festival he went back to his work with the railway magnate von Mekk, son of Tchaikovsky's patroness, to find a dismissal note pinned to his drawing board. As Natalya put it, 'he was not a member of the Party but they said this involvement in the festival proved he was a Bolshevik.'[35]

Victor did not care. None of them did. Throughout the ensuing civil war his expertise in industrial buildings was in high demand on superphosphate plants, while Leonid went to build the Shatursk power station. Alexander, like several of his artist friends, worked in another of the few fields that were booming at that time: theatre design.

The worse Moscow living conditions became, the more the population thronged to the theatres for warmth and distraction (cinema was still undeveloped in Russia). In this field and in painting, Alexander became a central, if older, contributor to the burgeoning avant-garde and through this encountered Alexei Gan. In June 1918, Vesnin's abstract paintings were described as 'too material' by Malevich in one of the last issues of *Anarkhiia*.[36] On 14 January 1919 he was one of those artists, with Rodchenko, Stepanova and Popova, in the show being discussed in Gan's lodgings, when he contrasted their factiousness to his ability to work simultaneously 'with the anarchists, the maximalists and the bolsheviks.'[37] In April 1921 the same group showed together in the famous little exhibition called '5×5=25'. Moving to the supra-architectural scale, Vesnin and Popova designed an extraordinary 'city of the future' installation for the Moscow-wide 'mass action' which Gan proposed to celebrate the

Third Comintern Congress two months later.[38] In all this, Alexander's architectural expertise fed into that artistic group a confidence in real space and a structural boldness which were not at the command of those who were purely painters. In the next year, equally fruitfully, his theatre design work fed back into architecture.

Figure 2.3 Alexander, Leonid and Victor Vesnin, competition entry for the Moscow offices of the newspaper *Leningradskaia Pravda*, 1924

Synthesis of a building organism

When the three brothers were all back in Moscow at the turn of 1922–3 and working together again for the first time on the Palace of Labour competition, it was from Alexander that the main organising idea for their scheme came. Looking at the drawings, and particularly at the section, one can see the origins of what Natalya called 'Shura's fantastic conception'.[39] Consciously or unconsciously, in the designer's typically incremental way, Alexander had mapped the functions of the Palace onto the great wooden framework that he was just then finalising for Tairov's delayed production of G.K. Chesterton's *The Man who was Thursday* at the Kamernyi Theatre up the road. With its two multi-storied 'towers' and their connecting ramps, this stage structure which was so articulate and dynamic as a freestanding model became absurdly confined behind the theatre's proscenium arch.[40] Transplanted into the open and enlarged to city scale, however, one can see it clearly transposed into the basic concept of the Palace building. The two blocks of vertically organised activity now stand on the long axis of the site, each addressing one of the urban spaces. They are separated by a new north–south cross street over which the ramps of the theatre installation have become the raked auditorium for Mossoviet's 2,500 councillors. Among the drawings it is only the section which properly reveals the auditorium's crucial linking function, but the accompanying notes described its technical and functional ingenuity:

> The Mossoviet auditorium adjoins directly to the auditorium for nine thousand, only separated from it by steel blinds. This arrangement makes it possible for the whole of Mossoviet to participate in special celebratory occasions in the general assembly without actually leaving their own accommodation.[41]

One can picture the project's evolution among their complementary talents in the studio adjoining their flat. Alexander has some first volumetric sketches done: 'I've got a scheme, Vikusha' (this was Tatlin's nickname for Victor and the family had long ago also adopted it). 'Can you try putting a structure on it?' So a real building emerges from the synthesis of the superphosphate plant with the theatrical set.

Two distinct sets of documentation on this project show us two aspects of it. The images actually submitted for the competition constitute the project to which public and profession reacted at the time. These are now only recorded in contemporaneous publications: the originals must have gone into the archives of Mossoviet, as the client, where presumably they were lost.[42] The drawings which are now in the Russian Architectural Museum and have been widely shown in the last decade are preparatory material that was kept in the family and donated by Natalya and the Vesnins' first sister Lydia in the 1960s. These ten sheets are rather faintly drawn in hard pencil on tracing paper. One of them, in Alexander's hand, documents an early conceptual stage. Others show different variants of its three-dimensional development and thus illuminate the working method which the Vesnins formulated on this scheme and maintained thereafter.[43] In their words:

> To concretise a meaningful form of the palace for the masses we worked on plans, sections, elevations, perspectives, axonometrics simultaneously, in parallel, not thinking of parts but of the volumetric and spatial composition as a unity, checking every change in the plan by a three-dimensional drawing.[44]

They saw this method as their means for generating the new spatial 'machines' of communism, and it became the basis of their design teaching. It was already being given a more theoretical underpinning by Moisei Ginzburg, in effect bringing together ideas from both Gan and Le Corbusier.[45]

The forty-six other Palace of Labour schemes were still overwhelmingly shaped by that taste-bound concept of 'monumentality' which Gan had declared 'cannot be the defining concept of new communist buildings' because it was basically about 'communicating a fantasy'.[46] The heroic myths being invoked included Byzantium, Imperial Rome and medieval Florence, but this is not yet Marx's conception of a proletarian culture that 'builds upon the achievements of past cultures'. These are merely floundering attempts to articulate enormous volumes. As one would expect from the eulogist of grain silos, the scholarly young Ginzburg had kept his volumes free of decoration but they were also inarticulate lumps. This was to be excused from one who had only built a few villas.[47] Like others who had begun to develop the programme of a new architecture but still lacked the technical experience to materialise it, he would have found the blinding lucidity of that Vesnin project unforgettable. As a person of the highest aesthetic sensibility, even in his own person (Natalya Vesnina recalled that he was 'always conspicuous because he moved very elegantly'[48]), he perceived immediately the leap of thinking it represented. Near the peak of his own building career four years later, its role was laconically summed up when he described it as being such a distilled response to its problem that 'It cannot be imitated. It can only be followed, along the thorny path of independent, thoughtful and creative work.'[49] Rooted as they were in practice, such empowerment was the essence of what the Vesnins contributed to development of a revolutionary practice in that first Soviet generation.

Notes

1 A.V. Shchusev, 'Ot Moskovskogo Arkhitekturnogo O-va', *Arkhitektura* 1–2, 1923, pp. 1–2.
2 V.N. Semionov, *Blagoustroistvo gorodov* (The Public Servicing of Towns), Moscow, 1912, p. 3.
3 V. Semionov, 'Ocherednye zadachi' (Priority tasks), *Arkhitektura* 1–2, 1923, pp. 28–30.
4 E. Norvert's 'Survey of Journals' in *Arkhitektura* 1–2, pp. 42–4, welcomed such journals as *Deutsche Bauzeitung*, *Le Génie Civil* and *The Architectural Review*, 'which

we have not seen since 1918'. Among these was 'an example of an entirely new type of journal related to the contemporary spirit in all forms of art called *L'Esprit Nouveau*' of which so far 'there are only a few copies in Moscow in private hands' but more were expected soon. Ginzburg's pieces were: 'Ot redaktsii' (From the editor) and 'Estetika sovremennosti' (The aesthetics of contemporaneity), no. 1–2, pp. 3–6, and Redaktsiia, 'Staroe i novoe' (Old and new), no. 3–4, p. 3.

5 'Estetika sovremennosti'.
6 A. Vesnin, 'Credo', presented to InKhuK April 1922; Russian text in S.O. Khan-Magomedov, *Inkhuk i rannii konstruktivizm* (InKhuK and early constructivizm), Moscow, 1994, pp. 224–228 with illustration of original manuscript; English translation in C. Cooke, *Russian Avant-Garde: Theories of Art, Architecture and the City*, London, 1995, p. 98.
7 I. Grabar, 'Na povorotakh ostorozhnee' (More cautious at the changes of direction), *Sredi kollektsionerov* (Amongst the Collectors) 6, 1923, pp. 46–7.
8 Gan to Rodchenko and Stepanova, 7 January 1919, in V. Stepanova, *Chelovek ne mozhet zhit' bez chuda* (A Person Cannot Live Without a Miracle), Moscow, 1994, p. 92.
9 For the work of Ladovsky, Krinsky and colleagues in Zhivskulptarkh and the Vkhutemas school during 1919–24 on themes like 'Communal House', 'Temple of Communion between Nations' and 'Headquarters for the Soviet of Deputies', see S.O. Khan-Magomedov, *Pioneers of Soviet Architecture*, London, 1987.
10 M. Ginzburg, 'Itogi i perspektivy' (Achievements and prospects), *Sovremennaia arkhitektura* (Contemporary Architecture) 4–5, 1927, pp. 112–18. For a full English translation, see T. Benton, C. Benton and D. Sharp, eds, *Form and Function: A Source Book*, London, 1975, pp. 156–60.
11 P. Antipov, 'Khronika' (Chronicle), *Arkhitektura* 1–2, 1923, pp. 47–9. In a revealling indication of the 'retreat' to private enterprise under the NEP they 'established new fee norms and published them in a special pamphlet'; I. Mashkov, in *Ezhegodnik MAO* (MAO Annual) 5, 1928, p. 13.
12 Antipov, 'Khronika', pp. 47–9. Their competitions were explicitly contrasted to those hitherto conducted since the Revolution which were 'of purely academic character'. The combined brief for the two housing competitions on sites in the Simonov and Serpukhovskaia districts is published as Document 46 in V. Khazanova, comp., *Iz istorii sovetskoi arkhitektury 1917–1925 gg: dokumenty i materialy* (From the History of Soviet Architecture 1917–25: Documents and Materials), Moscow, 1963, pp. 51–2.
13 Winning schemes were published in *Arkhitektura* 3–4, 1923, pp. 35–45.
14 The full brief is published with site plan from an archival copy of the 'printed pamphlet' as Document 174 in Khazanova, *Iz istorii 1917–25*, pp. 146–7. Elsewhere she names the six-man 'commission' which compiled it, from the same archival source. The other three members were Roman Klein, Ivan Mashkov and one D. Sukhov: V. Khazanova, *Sovetskaia arkhitektura pervykh let Oktiabria* (Soviet Architecture of the First Years after October), Moscow, 1970, p. 15. Shchusev had written a first draft in September and this 'commission' was appointed by MAO on 1 October; see *Kommunal'noe khoziaistvo* (The Communal Economy) 8–9, 1922, p. 24 and 12, 1922, p. 21.
15 The submission date is in the brief but was later extended to 20 February. Antipov, 'Khronika', p. 49, states that Palace and housing competitions were announced on 5 November and Kazus reports three 'announcements with explanations' appearing in *Izvestiia* on 5, 7 and 9 November: I. Kazus, 'Allrussischer Wettbewerb zum Projekt "Palast der Arbeit" in Moskau (1922–1923)', in R. Graefe *et al.*, eds, *Avantgarde 1: 1900–1923*, Stuttgart, 1991, pp. 118–27.
16 This speech to the First Congress of Soviets of the USSR (as it became on that day) appears in S.M. Kirov, *Izbrannye stat'i i rechi 1912–1934* (Selected Articles and Speeches 1912–1934), Moscow, 1957, pp. 150–2. For the passages about 'a palace' see Document 176 in Khazanova, *Iz istorii 1917–25*, p. 148. Kirov had led the

Bolshevik side in the Civil War in North Caucasus and at this time was Secretary of the Party Central Committee in Azerbaidjan. It is therefore quite possible that he did not know about the architectural competition then running in Moscow.

17 Their letter of 14 December 1922 to the editor of *Pravda* is quoted in Kazus, 'Allrussischer Wettbewerb', p. 120. See also V. Khazanova, 'ASNOVA', in Khazanova, comp., *Iz istorii sovetskoi arkhitktury 1926–1932: dokumenty i materialy*, Moscow, 1970, p. 40.

18 A.G. Chiniakov, *Brat'ia Vesniny* (The Brothers Vesnin), Moscow, 1970, p. 84.

19 Report on the opening, *Pravda*, 3 March 1923, published as Document 183 in Khazanova, *Iz istorii 1917–25*, p. 152; Antipov, 'Khronika', p. 49.

20 A.V. Shchusev, 'O printsipakh arkhitekturnogo stroitel'stva' (On the principles of architectural building), *Stroitel'naia promyshlennost'* (The Building Industry) 12, 1924, p. 760. He referred to it again ten years later in 'Uroki maiskoi arkhitekturnoi vystavki' (Lessons of the architectural exhibition in May), *Arkhitektura SSSR* 6, 1934, pp. 14–16.

21 Report in *Pravda*, 19 May 1923, published as Document 184 in Khazanova, *Iz istorii 1917–25*, p. 152.

22 These and other schemes can be found in Khan-Magomedov, *Pioneers*, figs 177–9, 261–4, 488, 532–4, 1050–3; C. Cooke, 'Mediating creativity and politics: sixty years of architectural competitions in Russia', *The Great Utopia*, Guggenheim Museum, New York, 1992, pp. 680–715; Kazus, 'Allrussischer Wettbewerb', which also includes the site plan.

23 Announcement in *Pravda*, 24 May 1923, published as Document 185 in Khazanova, *Iz istorii 1917–25*, p. 153; 'Konkurs proektov rabochego dvortsa truda', *Prozhektor* (Searchlight) 8, 31 May 1923, pp. 16–17.

24 For recent photographs of this complex, see E. Kirichenko, *Moskva: Pamiatniki arkhitektury 1830–1910 godov* (Moscow: Architectural Monuments 1830s–1910s), Moscow, 1977, plates 205, 206.

25 'Konkursnyi proekt "Dvortsa Truda", deviz, ANTENA, arkh. B.(sic) A., V.A., A.A. Vesninykh, 1923g' (Competition project for the Palace of Labour, pseudonym ANTENA, by architects B.(sic)A., V.A., A.A. Vesnin, 1923), in *LEF* 4, August–December 1924, pp. 59, 62.

26 A. Gan, *Konstruktivizm* (Constructivism), Tver, 1922, p. 60.

27 Vesnin, 'Credo'.

28 Gan, *Konstruktivizm*, p. 60.

29 Natalya Vesnina, 'Moi vospominaniia ob arkhitektorakh brat'iakh Vesninykh' (My reminiscences of the architect brothers Vesnin), *Panorama iskusstv*, vol. 8, Moscow, 1985, pp. 152–72.

30 The most detailed account of their early life is the first half of Vesnina, 'Moi vospominaniia', and on their early careers, Chiniakov, *Brat'ia Vesniny*, pp. 10–48.

31 Vesnina, 'Moi vospominaniia', p. 156.

32 Vesnina, 'Moi vospominaniia', pp. 156, 159.

33 Vesnina, 'Moi vospominaniia', p. 160.

34 Original drawings in colour appear with installation photo in V. Tolstoy, I. Bibikova and C. Cooke, eds, *Street Art of the Revolution: Festivals and Celebrations in Russia 1918–33*, London, 1990, figs 1–6.

35 Chiniakov, *Brat'ia Vesniny*, p. 50; Vesnina, 'Moi vospominaniia', p. 161.

36 K. Malevich, 'Vystavka professional'nogo soiuza khudozhnikov-zhivopistsev. Levaia federatsiia – molodaia fraktsiia' (The exhibition of the Trade Union of Artist-Painters. Left Federation – Young Fraction), *Anarkhiia* 89, 20 June 1918, p. 4; republished in D.V. Sarab'ianov *et al.*, eds., *Kazimir Malevich: sobranie sochinenii v piati tomakh: tom 1*, Moscow, 1995, pp. 117–23.

37 Stepanova, *Chelovek*, p. 66.

38 Cooke, *Russian Avant-Garde*, pp. 23–4; D.V. Sarab'ianov and N.L. Adaskina, *Liubov Popova*, London, 1990, p. 258.
39 Vesnina, 'Moi vospominaniia', p. 162.
40 Drawing, model and installation are illustrated in: Khan-Magomedov, *Pioneers*, p. 175.
41 'Konkursnyi proekt "Dvortsa Truda" ', pp. 59, 62.
42 The site lay between Manezh and Theatre Squares on the site of the present Hotel Moskva. These competition drawings include the perspective from the direction of the Historical Museum (south), an aerial axonometric and elevation from the Theatre Square end (east). All are strong images and clearly 'finished' presentation drawings. Perspective and elevation were reproduced by Ginzburg in his *Stil' i epokha* (Style and Epoch), Moscow, 1924, plates XII, XIII. All three appear in Khan-Magomedov, *Pioneers*, figs 485–7.
43 The 10,000 Vesnin drawings in the Shchusev State Russian Museum of Architecture, Moscow, are listed in: K. Murashov, ed., *Katalog-putevoditel' po fondam Muzeia: Vesniny* (Catalogue-Guide to the Museum's Collections: The Vesnins), Moscow, 1981. The Museum has ten Palace of Labour drawings, RIa 6593/1–10 (*Katalog*, p. 41). No.10 is one of Alexander's early concept perspectives. Nos. 1–9 are plans, elevations, a section and one perspective, all plainly preliminary or 'setting up' drawings in very light pencil on tracing paper. North elevation and the sketch are reproduced in colour in *The Great Utopia*, figs 681, 682, with recent model made in Los Angeles, fig. 679. The same drawings with one elevation, the section and the perspective from the East (i.e. from the then government headquarters, the Second House of the Soviets, now and originally the Hotel Metropol), are reproduced in black and white in C. Cooke, *Architectural Drawings of the Russian Avant-Garde*, New York and London, 1990, figs 37–41.
44 Quoted in Chiniakov, *Brat'ia Vesniny*, p. 85.
45 As Ginzburg reported, the 'basic arguments' of his book *Stil' i epokha* 'were presented in MAO on 18 May 1923', i.e. at precisely the period when Palace of Labour results were being announced. 'The final text was read in RAKhN on 8 February 1924' (Ginzburg, *Stil' i epokha*, p. 7).
46 Gan, *Konstruktivizm*, p. 61.
47 Ginzburg printed two elevations and one perspective of his scheme in *Stil' i epokha*, plates XXVI–XXVIII. It was in fact entered with another architect, Alexander Grinberg, thirteen years older, but he did not save it from its pseudonym, 'Monolit' (Monolith). For the perspective see Khan-Magomedov, *Pioneers*, p. 182; Cooke, *Russian Avant-Garde*, p. 46.
48 Vesnina, 'Moi vospominaniia', p. 168.
49 Ginzburg, 'Itogi', p. 114.

3 Notes for a manifesto

Jonathan Charley

From the safe haven of relativism

Permission to speak of revolution is granted on the precondition that the protagonist does not transgress the rules of historical relativism. This is the defeat of reason when no history can claim authenticity and truth.

A revolution against the aesthetic of the political replaces the concept of political revolution itself. Locked in the field of representation, the aesthetic finally achieves autonomy, not from capital within which it remains wholly locked, but from the critique of capital.

Imprisoned in the embrace of utopian reason, discussions of revolution became confined to the shifting games associated with representing objects. Neither the object nor the social relations they mirror are any longer worthy of consideration. The soft critique of the bourgeois world is operative in this safe haven, unconscious of the fact that however menacing, it can rarely escape assimilation.

The dilution of meaning

Far from having been removed from the late twentieth-century political lexicon, the word 'revolution' made an unexpected comeback. The years from 1980 to 1995 were peppered with talk of revolutions in Africa, Eastern Europe, Latin America, the Middle East and the old USSR. There were Velvet, Thatcherite, Reaganite and even 'Blairite' revolutions, and under the guise of postmodernism we were led to believe that a revolution had occurred in ways of thinking and seeing.

Anything that denoted some kind of change could be labelled revolutionary, and alongside the digital revolution sat revolutionary perfume, cars and washing machines. As the true heirs to Debord's spectators, we were saturated with a daily media diet of revolutionary activity, the high point being the live filming of a gun battle around the Bucharest Television station during the Romanian uprising of 1989.

Haunted by the scars left by fascist and state capitalist dictatorships, the European adapted to the ideological trickery of the slogans 'new consensus', 'new realism', 'new pragmatism' and 'new Europe', content to accept that we had finally entered a time that had no need for the 'other' big political idea.

Once the concept of revolution had been reduced to a banal discourse on aesthetics, the revolutionary critique of capitalist society was deposed by the self-evident truths of bourgeois common sense. The main contradiction of capitalism was not to be found in global and institutionalised forms of inequality, exploitation and repression, but in its ugliness and lack of efficiency, contradictions that could be solved through plastic surgery and sexier machines. All revolutions from now on would be simply technological.

The revolt against capital was left on the periphery, an interesting but unnecessary romance from a previous epoch, and as tragedy replaced romance, so the revolutionary became the nineteenth-century idiot, the different became a deviant, the rebel an outcast, and the dissenter a marginal.

The rebirth of the bourgeois utopia

Two hundred years after the publication of the *Wealth of Nations*, the idea of a world governed by legitimate self-interests found its fiercest advocates amongst the cost accountants, management consultants and political guardians of rampant individualism. Fortified by the collapse of the Soviet Empire, and by the successful identification in popular culture of such a regime with socialism, these troopers of the new utopia set about dismantling the bonds and institutions of collective solidarity, privatising state and social services, and forcibly introducing commodity–money relations into all sectors of public life.[1]

Accompanied by a government-led crusade to construct a new model citizen fiercely heterosexual and loyal to the institutions of the market, god, nuclear family and white nation-state, this version of the bourgeois utopia was presented as the natural end to human achievement, an historical reprise of the claim of Adam Smith and the physiocrats that free economic competition corresponds to the principles of natural right. The concept of freedom was high-jacked and restricted in meaning to the intensification of capitalist social relations, but in a manner that made the late twentieth-century bourgeoisie a poor relative of its revolutionary ancestor.

In this world of apparitions, where exchange value is held to be the final judge of necessity, there are no plans, only markets; no tenants, only homeowners; no socially contracted labour, only self-employed workers; and there is no ruling class, only shareholders and stakeholders.

Reconstructing capital

The construction industry was an ideal platform on which to mimic such aspirations. One of the main objectives of the neo-libertarian project was to dismantle the legacy of post-Second World War social democracy. Within the built environment this had possessed three main features: the greater role assumed by the state for the social and economic regulation of the construction industry; the increased priority given to social need in the development of plans for national construction; and the expansion of public sector ownership and control.

As an ideological inversion of this historic attempt to shift the balance of commodity production in favour of the use-value of buildings and land, a programme emerged, symbolised by the abolition of the Greater London Council, to privatise the use of public land and buildings and to transform the construction industry into a giant free enterprise zone. With the sale of state property and the minimisation of its direct participation in economic activity, this plan paved the way for the creation of a built environment overwhelmingly owned, produced and managed by the private sector.[2]

The subsequent campaign to discredit the concept of a socialised economy in which residential, educational, health and cultural buildings are produced and managed by democratically elected institutions was symptomatic of a general erosion of belief in the very idea of social and environmental planning. This was mirrored by the deterioration in building workers' rights that followed the abandonment of directly employed labour, the marginalisation of construction trade unions and the escalation in labour-only sub-contracting. Leaving no corner of the old 'public' economy intact, the process of collective obsolescence was capped by the poverty and closure of social and community organisations, a consequence of the withdrawal of state capital and revenue funding.

Although the catalyst for this restructuring of capital had been the economic crisis of the late 1970s, it was a project driven by three deeply ideological assumptions: the identification of freedom with the universal operation of a 'free' market; the identification of the self-interest of the unelected management contractors controlling the construction industry with the general needs of society; and the representation within law and language of building workers, architects, tenants, users, landowners and capitalists as equal subjects.

Seen by some as the victory of a new pragmatism, for others this 'market idealism' represented a utilitarian tragedy of epic proportions, one that had dragged an already weakened social programme for construction to the verge of disintegration. Despite the partial disguise of this assault on the public sector in the jargon of realism, efficiency, property and choice, the twenty years from the late 1970s will be remembered by many as a period of profound social atrophy.

The power of ideology to camouflage social reality can never be total. For all the conviction with which self-employed homeowners were projected as ideal subjects, they were only ever a breath away from the repossessed home, the vagrant, the bankrupt small builder and the wandering 'free' wage worker of Marx, queuing at train stations for access to casualised labour markets, free of all property but the power to sell labour.

The architecture of capital

To commemorate this era, the British skyline was punctured with four symbols of the state and market, edifices that came to function as icons of 'Thatcherite' ideology. These were the Lloyds building, a monument to technological fetishism and fictitious capital; Canary Wharf, a shrine to global finance capital;

the DHSS Kremlin in Leeds, a testament to the institutionalisation of poverty; and the MI5 headquarters in London, a bunker to order and servility.

In the shadows of these bastions of administrative power, the architectural commodity was to find its most vivid expression in the explosive mass production of speculative suburban utopias, retail parks, leisure complexes and fortified offices. From the fragments of de-industrialisation and economic restructuring proliferated new urban and suburban landscapes adorned in a prefabricated formal language, that accurately described the symbolic and practical function of such building types as historic idyll, advertising hoarding, fortress and monument.

Materialising beneath the chimera of heterogeneity through which such buildings were marketed, the production of the built environment assumed an increasingly homogenous form, a mimesis of the process of rationalisation and commodification by which labour in the epoch of industrialisation tended to acquire an equivalent abstract homogenous character. By the late 1990s, this process of exchange-driven commodity production accounted for the majority of new building work, in which technological innovation was driven by the competition to accelerate the turnover of capital, and in which the use-value of a commodity was primarily defined by its function as an object to be represented, desired, bought and sold.

Under the conditions of this market dictatorship, concepts of need, and questions of qualitative material and spiritual change became aestheticised and only understood through their object commodity forms. Minimum space standards were sold as luxury, uniform replication as status and choice, myth as history, and no time as free time. The architect, if used at all, had a role in piecing together the bits of a prefabricated discourse, not just of timber, brick, steel and concrete but of the language of historical myth, nostalgia and power.

To guard this process, a new panoptican project emerged, this time backed up by information technologies borrowed from the defence industry. A violation of human rights hailed as a freedom, the introduction of a carceral culture, of cameras, security guards, more prisons, neighbourhood watch and electronic surveillance was the price paid for the negation and privatisation of public space.[3]

With the advent of the digitally tracked subject, the militarised city moved beyond the direct physical barriers of nineteenth-century space government. In this world of perpetual observation and discipline, the concept of free space shrunk to the cracks left untouched by the commodity, and free time to what was left after twenty-four-hour non-stop commodity consumption.

The persistence of inequality

The massive social and spatial disparities in wealth and resources that distinguish the built environment at the end of the twentieth century represent a new phase in the defining spatial metaphor of capitalism's history, *uneven development*. It is this fundamental spatial division of power and property that reproduces the complex matrix of dependent and exploitative relations between home, street, locality, metropolis, region, nation, continent and globe. It is a process that separates north from south, removes the fortified edge suburb from the no-go ghetto, white from black, and the happy shopper from the banished proletarian.

Its production along with all of its accompanying discourse remains similarly locked into the historic trinity of commodity production (speculative house and office building), Hegelian aesthetics (the pursuit of the ideal) and absolutist dreams (the expression of power and status). It is a familiar structure that despite the claims of post-modernity is firmly located in the bourgeois ideals of the nineteenth century.[4]

What we have not seen is a revolution against capital. We face instead a new phase in its historical campaign to maintain the rate of profit, by switching to a more flexible pattern of accumulation, diversifying into other sectors, crossing borders to seek out cheaper labour power, and penetrating areas of social life that are as yet unbound by the commodity form.

Away from the abyss

It is at times of such crisis that people turn to illusion, artifice and utopia. Here, the weight of bourgeois ideology hermetically seals the western European gaze, trapping a view of a social world constructed through the lens of international capital.

While this renders knowledge of the political realm elusive, no such regime dependent as it is on a primary mythology, that of the bourgeois utopia, can ever be permanent, and throughout the development of capitalism there streaks another history, occupying the interstices, fractures and horizons. Exiled but lodged in the memory of the twentieth century is the revolution that seeks not just the overthrow of structures of economic and political power, but the overthrow of the class origins of power itself.[5]

Within the built environment, this is the history of architectural avant-gardes, building workers strikes, rent strikes, land occupations, tenants campaigns, communes, collectives and urban uprisings. It is the history of people bound together within the built environment as the producers and consumers of use values, as non-owners of property, and as social groups and classes engaged in struggle both through and over space. It is through the lens of this other historical tradition that we can begin to counter the lure of pessimism and make links between what appear to be disparate patterns of resistance to the capitalist organisation of space, time and labour. To locate ourselves within this other history is the first step in the imagination of a different future.

1917

In the history of the rebellion against capital, it is the Russian Revolution of 1917 that represents the most comprehensive attempt to demolish the commodity form of labour and space. Any talk of the development of non-capitalist forms of labour and spatial organisation must confront its legacy.

The popularly organised western memory makes little or no distinction between the different periods of Soviet history. But the utopianism through which Soviet history is universally dismissed lies not in the programmes of the workers movement and architectural avant-garde of the early 1920s, but in the counter-revolution from the late 1920s onwards that destroyed the political authority of the working class, reintroduced capitalist forms of industrial management, abandoned internationalism, and returned to an absolutism of government, culture and spatial organisation.

Social ownership of property and workers' control of building production were replaced by state ownership, one-man management, Taylorism and piece rates. In place of the social condenser and *sotsgorod* appeared the imperial city. Critical realism and the critique of bourgeois culture degenerated into a patriotic neo-classical idealism, and the revolution of everyday life at home, at work and at play was substituted by the state administration of time and space.

But the lesson of the revolution lies not only in its negation, but in the memory of the collective strength of people when mobilised in a common struggle. It is for this reason that the decade from 1917 occupies a unique place in the history of the built environment, a brief moment in time when in all sectors of economic and social life, workers were involved in parallel revolutionary activities. The building workers union debated wage equalisation, architects designed workers clubs, planners attempted to map democratic space, the homeless occupied buildings, and the theorists talked of global revolution, socialist accumulation, Soviet power, reification and the emancipation of women.[6]

While these programmes were killed in their infancy, the questions posed remain. What is the alternative to wage labour? What are the alternatives to the capitalist labour process? What might the liberation of labour and space mean? What would a contemporary revolutionary programme for the transformation of the built environment have to say? As a conclusion, here are some notes for a manifesto.

Liberating labour

1   No longer restricted to demands for a more equitable distribution of the social surplus, a strategy for the liberation of labour calls for the social ownership of the means of production and communication in all large firms and institutions.[7]

2   This should not be understood in terms of nationalisation and the creation of unwieldy state-owned construction and design combines, but as the development of non-statised workers' collectives organised on the basis of self-management. This is a precondition for the introduction of democratic workers' control of production in design offices and factories and on building sites.

3   Beyond political emancipation from institutionalised class, gender and racial discrimination, the final liberation of labour lies in the transition from alienated work to 'free creative self-activity'. After the alienated labour of the slave, serf and wage worker comes the producer revolutionary, reclaiming

workers' rights, transcending trade union politics, liberating technology and abolishing work as we know it.[8]

4   This signifies a revolt not only against the institutions of wage labour, but against the legacies of Taylorism, Fordism and all other techniques of capitalist accounting and quantification; a resistance to all forms of instrumental violence that alienate the worker not only from the means and ends of production but from work itself.

5   Step one is to break the capitalist control of the global division of labour and to develop new patterns of international solidarity. Step two is the development of programmes for direct worker creativity and control. Step three is to redefine on a collective social basis the whole concept of productivity and work incentives. Step four is the production of socially useful building technologies that are genderless and non-destructive of humans and nature.[9]

6   On the horizon of anticipation is the concept of free labour itself, free, that is, of exchange value and exploitation.

Liberating space

1   Beyond the limits of a politics of participation, a strategy for the liberation of space would seek to break the commodity status of land and buildings by taking them into social ownership. This should not be confused with the state nationalisation of property, but understood as the decentralisation of political power and economic ownership to non-statist workers' councils.

2   This implies a spatial redefinition of the urban as a network of self-governing collectives with the power to reassert common rights of access, and to control the development of land and buildings. The task for planners and urbanists is to think on the spatial and physical consequences of this global, territorial and local redistribution of power and resources.

3   One of the main tasks of the architect is to break the connection between spatial organisation, building form and social power. This signifies a critical return to one of the traditions of the avant-garde, the projected synthesis of revolutionary social and spatial goals. It is marked by the reassertion of the primacy of human and social need in building design, and by the exploration of the formal possibilities opened up by new technologies and social programmes. Before the White House is turned into a nursery and skateboard park, it will be painted black.[10]

4   The rehabilitation of our relationship with nature is the third task in Marx's triangle of self-estrangement. This calls on all built-environment workers to engage with the environmental protest movement so as to shatter the mythology of infinite natural resources. In this arena of conflict, the greatest impediment to the development of a sustainable city remains the exploitation of both human and natural resources by democratically unaccountable capitalist and state bureaucracies.

5   The appropriation and reclamation of the spaces of everyday life is a fourth dimension to the struggle. This concerns the pursuit of autonomous mini-republics outside of the camera. Even in the depths of twentieth-century dictatorships, associations of the marginal, deviant by virtue of class, gender, race, ethnicity and sub-culture, have always mapped different spaces, cutting through the institutional fabric of the city in communes, raves, shebeens, street protests and lock-ins, constructing lives that stand in opposition to the dominant culture. The defence of these rights to space should lie at the heart of any programme.

6   On the horizon of anticipation is the concept of free space itself, free that is of exchange value, surveillance and state dictatorship.

1789, 1848, 1871, 1905, 1917, 1918, 1949, 1956, 1959, 1968, 1981

For all the belief in the inevitable identity of capitalism and nature, there is no teleological certainty to history, bar that of revolution.

Notes

1   This was the rebirth of a dream to legitimise a bourgeois utopia that sprang not just from the work of Adam Smith and David Ricardo, but Quesnay and the French physiocrats in the late eighteenth century. It is in the works of all three that we first encounter the bourgeois ideas of individual and economic freedom. But it is important to note how these notions of freedom, that is, personal freedom (from serfdom), freedom of private property (that is freedom from feudal obligations) and freedom of competition (the abolition of guild restrictions), were born in the midst of a revolutionary struggle against feudalism. For one of the best histories of the philosophical foundations of economic thought see Isaac Rubin, *A History of Economic Thought*, London: Pluto, 1989.

2   While there are limits to the total privatisation of the built environment, due in part to its intrinsically collective character, there was in Britain a wholesale shift away from the public sector, signalled by the sale of council housing and severe reductions in capital grants to local authorities. Although many nationalised areas of the economy reproduced many of the contradictions to be found in private industry, nationalisation for many still represents a necessary step towards to the full socialisation of the built environment. Between 1969 and 1988 as a proportion of new house building, the public sector share declined from 51 per cent to 13 per cent, with new orders for all types of building work in the public sector falling from 48 per cent to 23 per cent. By the end of the 1980s, 92 per cent of total national building output and 98 per cent of new public sector housing was produced by private contractors (Housing and Construction Statistics, 1969–79, 1978–88).

3   The militarisation of Glasgow is a case in point. A project carried out with post-graduate architecture students at the University of Strathclyde to map forms of surveillance and space control, show that within the urban grid in the centre of the city there is virtually no space remaining that is not governed either physically by police, security guards, and bouncers or electronically through cameras and swipe cards. Free public space has vanished from the centre.

4   The analysis of the specifically capitalist production of the built environment and of the history of the resistance to it is the primary subject of a new book for Routledge

to be published in 1999. Working title *Architectures of Resistance: History and the Production of the Built Environment.*

5   For those unfamiliar, it is Marx in the much repeated passages from *German Ideology*, the *Manifesto* and the *Preface to the Critique of Political Economy*, who introduces us to the idea that the class struggle is the motor of historical change. See for instance Karl Marx, *Preface to the Critique of Political Economy*, London: Lawrence & Wishart, 1981, (first published in 1859) and Karl Marx, *German Ideology*, London: Lawrence & Wishart, 1985, written between 1845 and 1846.

6   For an analysis of the history of the Soviet built environment from the revolution up to the end of the 1980s, see J. Charley, 'The Dialectic of the Built Environment: A Study in the Historical Transformation of Labour and Space', Ph.D. thesis, University of Strathclyde, 1994.

7   In the declaration of 14 November 1917, Bolsheviks called for the introduction of workers' control of production in all construction enterprises employing more than thirty people, a programme adopted by the All Russian Union of Construction Workers in May 1918.

8   This recalls not only the critique of the commodity by the early Soviet theoreticians Evgeny Pashukanis and Isaac Rubin, but Trotsky's analysis of the Soviet bureaucracy and the development of new ideas on labour from groups like the Worker's Opposition led by Shliapnikov and Kollantia in the Soviet Union in the 1920s. It also draws on the Frankfurt critique of 'instrumental reason', and the radical rethinking of 'work' conducted by a distinctly French group of writers such as Debord, Baudrillard, Guattari and Gorz that followed 1968.

9   In Britain, one of the most famous examples of this was the workers' takeover of Lucas Aerospace and the plan to develop socially useful technology. See Mike Cooley, 'Drawing up the corporate plan at Lucas Aerospace', in MacKenzie and Wajcman, *The Social Shaping of Technology*, Open University, 1985.

10   This would include famous innovators of the 1920s and 1930s like the constructivists, the German avant-garde of Ernst May and Hannes Meyer, MARS and ATO in Britain, but also the architects throughout the industrialised world who have sought to maintain a social programme of construction during the absence, emergence and subsequent decline of the concept of a welfare state. This has more often than not required the architect to become directly politically engaged and has seen architects work inside the state system, alongside it in cooperatives, directly with users, and at times outside it in the role of design subversive.

4 A postmodern critic's kit for interpreting socialist realism

Augustin Ioan

Figure 4.1 Publishing House, Bucharest, an example of Stalinist architecture

In comparing Soviet socialist realism, which was popular between roughly 1932 and 1954, and postmodernism, which flourished and then largely faded away in the 1980s, one is forced to address certain points in common which shed a certain reciprocal light on their individual characteristics.[1] This text will focus on their opposition to the avant-garde and modernism respectively, as the possible primary generator for both 'styles', an opposition which is based on the question of 'identity'. Their common antipathy to modernism, and their shared use of the classical language of architecture, and of realism from the world of art, will then be analysed as mechanisms for reviving a popular adherence to certain systems of values and power which underpin both discourses. As a large amount of contemporary literature exists on postmodernism, our primary interest will lie in socialist realism. The latter will be read through the lens of concepts usually associated with the former. This will inevitably lead to a slightly imbalanced study which gives more space to socialist realism than to postmodernism.

The issue of identity which underpinned both Reaganism in the United States and Thatcherism in the United Kingdom claimed to offer a remedy against the dissolution of any sense of real ideology. By reactivating a rhetoric of ideology and pumping it through the dry veins of the power system, these conservative revolutions awoke the latter's dormant inner strength, reaffirming values associated with tradition, and implicitly offering a different aesthetic to an exhausted, redundant modernism, already drained of its last drop of expression.

Fragmentation – pastiche – collage

In observing the aesthetic discourses of socialist realism and postmodernism, one has to note that both were cultural expressions of fragmentation, collation and pastiche, though each for different reasons. Postmodernism rejected the unified set of values promoted by modernism, claiming that there were many other equally valid systems that deserved to be recognised, no matter how varied or even contradictory. Any mechanism that might render a building more popular deserved to be recognised. As a way of enhancing the appeal of a certain building, it made sense to open up a range of references within the 'text' of its facade, to reflect the diversity of culture itself. Pastiche was a way of 'quoting' other 'texts', and therefore a tool for expanding the horizon of meanings, references, sources and related layers of interpretation for a given 'text'.

Socialist realism likewise used pastiche, collage and fragmentation in the facades of its buildings as a way of re-affirming its identity. Yet this identity was a radically different identity, defined by contrast, by manicheistic dichotomies; inclusivist, yes, but only to the extent that it had to conform to the dictates of the socialist realist censors. History, in this context, was divided into 'revolutionary', 'progressive' epochs, and 'retrogressive', 'conservative' ones. The criterion used to differentiate history was a Bolshevik one: according to Marxist theory, art came to embody the social and political agenda of a particular epoch. And so for socialist realism, Greek classicism was 'progressive' because it belonged to a 'democratic' society. The Italian Renaissance was admitted to the post-apocalyptic 'members only' club of Stalinist culture because it accounted for the rise of the advanced social force of the bourgeoisie. In the fine arts, the *Peredvizhniky* realist movement of nineteenth-century Russia was yet another select guest, for both national and social reasons, while in architecture, Russian neoclassicism and baroque offered a reliable source of vocabulary. In drawing upon this large range of discourses, all of them 'politically correct', artists were not only allowed and entitled to select their own melange of historical forms, but they were morally (in other words, ideologically) obliged to do so. Yet one could hardly claim that, provided they remained within the approved style, architects had perfect freedom. There were further rules which governed, for example, the 'severity' of a building, and so on. Furthermore, local and traditional ornaments had to be included, according to the Stalinist thesis of a compulsory 'socialist content and national form'.

A socialist realist building would therefore come to stand for trans-historical class solidarity, a living proof that history had finally rewarded the 'good' citizen who could now enjoy the Bolshevik heaven. Since socialist realism inherited this treasure of 'purified' discourses, its identity could be best expressed by being associated with the range of moral virtues imbedded in this 'left' half of humankind's history. Consequently, any further research into 'new' vocabularies was unnecessary. Communism was the happy end of history, and Socialist Realism had to be the ultimate style, which recycled, and, in so doing, dramatically improved the meaning of the 'chosen ones'. To search for new forms meant to reject the positive message encompassed by previous discourses, and to refuse the aura of continuity, legitimacy and, consequently, identity, that could be drawn upon by using the 'reliable' pool of rhetoric. For an ideology centered around historical manicheism and social teleology, the failure to take advantage of these references – as in the case of the Constructivist avant-garde – was a capital offence, a heresy to be severely punished. Thus, instead of the unified aesthetic of the avant-garde, social realism opted for an eclectic play of fragments and pastiches of previous buildings, or of past vocabularies.

Decorum and classicism

There would seem to be a contradiction in a unitary totalitarian regime expressing itself in a plurality of different discourses, allowed to play, as in postmodernism, or conforming to a certain set scenarios. Yet the contradiction is only apparent, since the play remains both artificial and superficial. The buildings are decorated in rich but nevertheless superficial skins. The decorum that enveloped both socialist realist and postmodernist buildings served to dress up an austere expression of power. It was meant to relate to popular culture by making the edifice 'user-friendly' and theatrical, and by apparently sharing with the average citizen the 'secrets of the gods' which reside in the form. Consequently, populism became an important issue, and official propaganda advanced either the 'Soviet people's right to have columns' (Lunacharsky), 'popular capitalism' (Thatcher), or 'Versailles for the people' (Bofill).

The buildings of socialist realism made an elaborate gesture to the people with squares in front of their main elevations for mass gatherings and marches – as in the case of the Palace of the Soviets, Lenin's Mausoleum and all regional party headquarters – and tribunes for party officials also within the main elevations. Since the masses never had any real access to the 'Winter Palaces' of the Soviet regime, the square in front offered a token gesture of participation by suggesting that the top leaders were somehow accessible, at least visually. Conversely, within the postmodern era, by designing supermarkets and company headquarters as luxurious, rich and highly symbolic buildings, the corporate world attempted to suggest that consumerism and business were meaningful activities in today's society, and had to be celebrated as such.

In that context, the 'popular palaces' of socialist realism and postmodernism represented a method for making the elitist, closed world of modernism more accessible and open. They were 'decorated sheds'. Both simulated the grass-roots origins of their respective power systems that stood for, and were generated by, the people themselves, and through their richness of representation celebrated the common values of an homogenous, supposedly classless society. The best way to assert and celebrate those values was through a classical language. Classicism could decorate the offices of the State Department, at the top of the social hierarchy, city halls and corporate headquarters somewhere in the middle, and consumerist institutions at the base. Its language could be both elitist and popular; both utopian and forward-looking as well as realist and retrospective.

Both discourses addressed the question of origins. But whereas socialist realism 'inherited', and consequently 'displayed' its stylistic 'ancestors', which could be identified according to ideological criteria, postmodernism attempted in a nostalgic fashion to recapture a lost tradition ranging from the 'primitive hut' to the 'golden' classical age, and the values that were forever engraved in their forms. In both discourses, not only did classicism hold a certain popular appeal and therefore prove more meaningful than the alienating forms of modernism, but it also imposed a sense of order and hierarchy on the urban condition. It lent its buildings a certain monumentality, and as a style, unlike modernism, it served as a 'readable' and hence 'understandable' text.

The contradiction between the 'irony' of postmodernism and the 'serious-ness' of socialist realism's use of classicism dissolves in the concept of 'play'. Postmodern architects tended to be ironic and sarcastic about the values celebrated in their buildings, but did not utterly reject them. Postmodernism thereby acknowledged the central structure of power while attempting to 'play' with its outer surface, the interface between power and society, in a sort of semiotic schizophrenia. It did not attempt to disrupt or resolve the internal contradictions of an architecture that is merely decorative. Socialist realism was also allowed to 'play' with synonymous languages within a unique framework of (ideological) meaning, without questioning it. This play was a highly regulated play: the meaning, no less than the range of building forms, was controlled by the party. The artist had only to consult the officially approved portfolio of architectural language, and select the best combination of forms to articulate that meaning to the masses.

Both postmodernism and socialist realism attempted to embellish reality, and to transform the state into a work of art. Yet as styles they remained fragmentary, eclectic and superficial. Playing with forms, without any deeper agenda beneath their supposedly beautiful facades – because either there was allegedly no such agenda, or else the artist/architect had no influence over it – neither of these styles had much influence. By 1953, socialist realism was a corpse, an embellished one perhaps, but a corpse nonetheless. But was it really no more than a moribund style? Perhaps the strongest arguments against dismissing socialist realism too soon are that, firstly, at least in name socialist realism remained the official Soviet style up until the Gorbachev era, and, secondly, even immediately after it fell out of favour and a form of modernism came back into vogue, many of the buildings constructed were in fact merely socialist realist designs, stripped of their ornamentation.

Despite the grandiose visions and utopian plans for Moscow and other major Soviet cities, socialist realism was only realised in a local and piecemeal form. Those nostalgic utopias, those 'communist Jerusalems', were so visible in international exhibitions and posters and maps that they did not actually need to be built. Those which did get built – fragments of this larger vision – allude to an immanent and imminent vision of total coherence. Like socialist realism, postmodernism has manifested itself in fragmentary, disjointed forms, such that it is hard to identify any coherent vision from an urban planning perspective. Rather, one can speak of local and piecemeal interventions in the form of individual buildings or groups of buildings as a way of healing the damaged fabric of the built environment. Postmodernism has proved a form of architectural DIY for the average citizen.

Notes

1 Postmodernism should be understood here in the strictly architectural sense in which Charles Jencks, in particular, has used it to refer to a style of architecture which relies heavily on the application of historicist motifs. In cultural terms it relates to the largely conservative 'postmodernism of reaction', as opposed to the 'postmodernism of resistance' as outlined by Hal Foster in his introduction to *The Anti-Aesthetic*.

II

Architecture and change

5 History lessons

Fredric Jameson

Our assignment here seemed to be twofold: to think possible reconstructions of the city, and to reflect on the situation that obtains 'beyond the wall'.[1] This last is deliberately ambiguous, since it can signify the temporality of the post-communist period, or on the other hand the specificities of the 'East', in particular of Romania and of Bucharest, our host space. The second term, then, is more than merely specific; it is radically self-specifying, and leads us on more and more into historical and social difference and uniqueness. 'The city', on the other hand, is uniquely general: no one doubts its correspondence to a concept, or boldly demands the suppression of this meaningless and totalizing generality, even after the historical death of so many classical cities and the careful notations of their wholesale dissolution into megalopolis or something post-national. Yet 'the city' always seems to be a term more meaningful for those coming from the countryside (or the suburb): from one 'city' to another, the movement is rather different, and the comparisons that ought to generate a usable abstraction (of 'good city form', for example) become more aimless and agitated, their common reference spilling out into sheer geographical difference, or a search for trivializing abstractions of problems only too concrete (the transportation system, specialization into sectors, daily life and 'the street'). Nominalism becomes a tempting if desperate resolution to these conceptual frustrations, when we decide to put an end to them with the affirmation that there is no city: there is only Stockholm, Bremen, Seoul, Zürich, Ljubljana, Budapest, and Bucharest, to limit myself to the cities I have briefly visited in the past month. Nominalism is, however, a harsh taskmaster, a corrosive and demystificatory process not so easily arrested as it is initiated: in this case, it comes to mean not even these names, but the ephemeral experiences associated with them. It is true that these experiences can be planned, extended and deepened, by information and history, by testimony of the people included in them: the period in which an essentially lyric impressionism was felt to be radically incompatible with conceptual interpretation or analysis has ended, one would hope, but perhaps by a pyrrhic victory in which interpretation has itself become a 'mere' impression.

I can at least begin with the useful notion of 'reconstruction', which will at once make plain how distinct and incomparable all these names turn out to be.

Arriving, dwelling, in Seoul in the space between two catastrophes – the collapse of the Seongsoo bridge last summer, that of the Sapoong department store a week or two ago – my impression is nonetheless not one of buildings suddenly disappearing into a mined soil one after the other, but rather, alongside the prodigious construction in course everywhere, that of a city closer to Taipei than to Tokyo. Is this only because I know about the Japanese occupation, over so many years? Is it the interference of knowledge with perception? Or does it merely reflect the obvious fact that nothing is comparable to Tokyo, and that the absence of any privileged vantage point, of any handle on a perceivable exterior, of any survey or profile of a cityscape, can scarcely characterize any other place? Yet Taipei was not a great deal easier to visualize, although a great deal smaller; whereas there are certainly places from which you can see all of Seoul. The immense golden skyscraper, the Yook-San Building, however unlovely, is certainly a marker, while the river organizes this space, demarcating the new and booming southside with its Olympic stadium, its hotels and financial institutions (along with the ill-fated department store). It reminds us of the remarkable natural site in which this city developed, between the mountains, in a plan guided, as several lecturers explained to us, by a geomancy that becomes self-evident on the maps with their mythic systems of coordinates, even though it loses all its suggestive and organizational power in the hot and dusty phenomenology of the streets themselves.

Now, however, we can mobilize our topic word, 'reconstruction', and turn it into useful and probing questions. For Seoul has already been reconstructed several times over, most recently since the almost total destruction of the great civil war of the 1950s. What can reconstruction still mean today in this only too-reconstructed context? It would only seem thinkable historically, as a going back to something more primordial: if not nature in any unmediated sense, then at least the nature of the great geomancers and of the sacred coordinates. Yet oddly, it was rather in Bucharest that our hosts insisted over and over again on the fundamental axes, the great north–south and east–west boulevards that articulate the city and distribute our fragmentary experiences and impressions of it into the space of great quadrants. In East Asia, however, where the (often elevated) cross-city highways are a fact of life and a fundamental starting point (rather than an organization you lay on afterwards to help you clarify your thoughts and determine your directions), the more instinctive movement of primordiality emerges in exotic motifs and a folkloric distribution of the spaces of this or that new building: in other words, Disneyland (to which we will return below).

So a reconstruction of that kind – what the Japanese meant by 'overcoming modernity', a thoroughgoing 'overcoming' of the West itself and modernization – is not really in question here. But if on the other hand, modernity (and along with it modernization) was felt to be not so much Western as rather Japanese: then, perhaps, something might still be overcome. But this immediately opens up the question of historicity, of what survives from the past and what can be retained of it. You can cross around Shinjuku station from the now dehumanized administrative and bureaucratic zone of this quarter, dominated by Kenzo Tange's baleful Tokyo Metropolitan Government, to its other half, devoted to department stores when not to night life and red light activities, by following a little tunnel under the railroad tracks in which the old zinc shacks and shop counters are still preserved. I think of it as the last remnant of a Tokyo emerging from its year zero, at the end of the war, as in similar hastily built structures in the German cities of the 1950s. If so, one could at least preserve *that*, as a surviving remnant of whatever past (in Seoul, we look down alleys off main traffic thoroughfares, in which a palpably premodern city still continues its life). But apart from the cost (since land speculation is the fundamental motor of urban development today, and the real estate in Shinjuku in particular is counted among the most valuable and costly in the world), we must nonetheless stand perplexed before this operation: if some premodern economic activities (or rather, to be more accurate about it, some pre-postmodern economic activities) still persist within the newer city fabric, then they will preserve themselves, by virtue of unequal and uneven development. If they vanish, then we face a situation of enclaves and 'reservations', and wonder whether the inhabitants should be paid a salary to dress up and go about their outmoded tasks, as at Mystic Seaport or Dearfield Village.

Indeed, Dolores Hayden reminds us in her new book, *The Power of Place*, that the outsider characteristically represses a wealth of ethnic realities from a henceforth schematized urban life, inevitably mapped out by the victors and the hegemonic power structure: she speaks out for the pedagogical and historicizing value of the past to preserve these monuments of the other classes, and for their use in on-going history lessons (reinforced by city walks and literature) which are, at least in the American and more specifically southern Californian situation which is her reference point, inevitable tactical moves in very contemporary political struggles. To what degree her references, which are racial and ethnic, are transferrable to other societies altogether, as in East Asia, is unclear to me; my own impression is that the equivalent in working-class history (as in labour tours of Pittsburgh, for example) emerges only after industry has disappeared, and along with it, the most vital milieu for the working classes in question. But in all these situations, the relationship to a spatial past seems to have two relatively distinct dimensions: the one is the pedagogical value in the present of the urban traces of the past; the other is the relationship between space and current production as such. It is not quite a division between theory and practice, but risks suggesting an opposition or at least a tension equally dramatic, and should perhaps rather be thought of as two essential and inseparable dimensions of the sense of history which we are in the process of interrogating here.

The Seoul National Museum, however – the former Japanese Colonial Government Office – has a rather different message for us. Built by the Japanese in an architecture as characteristic of their colonial possessions (it can be found again in Taiwan) as the not unrelated British colonial architecture of a much vaster geographical area, it has been the symbol of Japanese imperialism and, long after liberation, a painful and embarrassing historical reminder of the shame of colonization. Indeed, it is said that this building played a role in the Korean War, and that in three separate offensives the North Korean army drove into Seoul with the explicit intent of destroying it. But it was only in 1995 that an official decision has been taken by the current South Korean government to tear down the building, which had hitherto been protected by its transformation into a museum.

The relevance for Eastern Europe is obvious: 'reconstruction' must at this point be recognised not merely as a matter of rebuilding but also as a matter of strategic demolition as well. The renaming of streets, sometimes of whole cities, the removal of statues and monuments, are conventional marks of triumph over your enemies and cannot be gainsaid by the victors. Indeed, in a way the memory of an older, now vanished, street name (the rue Michelet, the Stalinallee) ensures a moment of the past a certain definition and identity it might not have had so striking a vehicle for. As for statues, perhaps the question is not so much who misses them, as who notices them in the first place. The statue often seems to stigmatise its moment of the past with a greened and bespattered boredom and stifling dustiness that unmarked glories do not have to contend with. On the other hand, the commemorative statue, in representational or allegorical form, is so foreign to the contemporary aesthetic that it may well be the style of the art rather than the content of the memorial that drives this dreariness and death of the past so strongly home.

As for a specific building, like the Seoul National Museum, it raises the more general question about history lessons and the sense of history generally, along with its specific aesthetic corollary, the question as to whether the work of art – in this case, the building as such – has any intrinsic power to enforce any kind of aesthetic response, let alone the one planned or foreseen by its maker. Left-wing thinking on this matter has tended predictably enough to fall out along the lines of a continuum running from positive to negative, or more precisely, from a conception of the utopian function of the individual work to a conception of its mission to subvert or undermine the established order in some way or other. These two conceptions then are also accompanied by the relatively modern gap between the referential spheres of the work of art in modernity, which Terry Eagleton has characterized in terms of their effects in the realm of general ideology as opposed to those – more autoreferential – in the realm of aesthetic ideology as such. So, for example, a work might wish to be subversive of the social law or the general social order as such, and in particular to undermine its various social ideologies: but it might also wish – indeed, in the modern movement, it has frequently also wished – to take as its sphere of action aesthetic ideology and in particular the dominant conceptions of art and its works, closed or culinary notions of the aesthetic, conceptions of classical form, existential or bourgeois notions of how the work is to be used in private life, or of the transcendental value of the aesthetic as such. Here it might be said that what subverts these inherited or hegemonic aesthetics also wishes to be in some sense allegorical of the subversion of the social order as a whole. But in fact, these two poles have been in tension at least as far back as the beginnings of the modern movement, and have conventionally set the henceforth stereotypical terms for an antagonism between a properly political art (that set out to deal in some unmediated way with general ideology, whether from a utopian or a subversive perspective) and that which 'self-referentially' seems to confine itself to the aesthetic and at best to produce its effects there (where the Utopian function is less visible, unless it be that of the great work itself, while the subversive one is only too evidently called for by an environment of non-aesthetic objects, very much including the 'political' works of the first category). In fact, in the greatest works of the modern period, such as those of Brecht, these tensions are addressed and overcome in a variety of often ingenious ways, so that we probably have an interest, in any historical consideration of the modern period, in calling them back into question as stereotypes.

But then in any case, two further problems arise in our current context. First of all, how satisfactory do these categories turn out to be when we have to do with architecture (let alone with urbanism as such)? Second, and even more serious, will they still obtain after the end of the modern and the universally recognized emergence, if not of postmodernism as an aesthetic movement or style of some sort, then at least of the postmodern situation as radically different from that of the older modernism?

Adorno's thought – that the building must always stage a kind of life superior to our own, and thereby keep our Utopian demands and expectations alive – presupposes the possibility of grasping the work allegorically, that is, as a figure for Utopia, as itself and at the same time more than itself. Yet the truth of the matter – the guilty secret of all aesthetics – is that the individual work can never impose a privileged reading on its viewers or spectators ('it cannot argue back,' as Plato said millenia ago about the written text). Yet without such an allegorical dimension, the utopian demand risks relaxing into a mere ethical imperative, into an apologia for the status quo, on the basis of possibilities claimed to be already present and inherent in this particular experience of the work of art. Thus the utopian dimension of phenomenology, which describes the experience of space and the body we ought to be having – in a transfigured space and a transfigured body – folds back under its own weight into the claim that it is up to us to lift ourselves to the level at which we are capable of experiencing built space 'properly', that is to say, 'phenomenologically'.

Meanwhile, the 'subversive' building – the other option of the modernist aesthetic politics – may well, in a given situation (but is that situation still ours?), subvert the hegemonic tastes and standards of the current role assigned to space in the current system: but its negativities are threatened by its very positivity as a building. Insofar as it comes into being, slowly exists in the material world, and joins the other components of what currently is, it would seem that it must cease to threaten that massive being, of which it is henceforth part and parcel. This can be said another way round, in terms of the sheer force of habit, which tames and domesticates the worst transgressions, pulls the sting of the most intensely therapeutic shocks, and leaves us standing before the new building in that numbness of the everyday, that forgetfulness and repression of all aesthetic 'distance', which the Russian formalists saw as the fundamental enemy and the defining situation of all genuine modern art in the first place. But this is itself a problem, if not a contradiction: what is the more fundamental opposite of the great work? The bad building, or the commercial, vernacular, mass-cultural junk building? Or simply the building we can no longer feel, see, or experience? Meanwhile, even if you were able somehow to restimulate aesthetic response, to jump-start the alienated blocked senses and to painfully reawaken the numbed feeling and circulation of the blood in the dead aesthetic member, how would it react to the mass-cultural environment? Would it reconquer some new sense of ugliness, some renewed aesthetic revulsion – as for the older moderns – or would it on the other hand insinuate itself into the pores of that vernacular (as with a Venturi) and find itself bedazzled by unexpected effects and possibilities (thereby passing over into the postmodern as such)? The great work of high culture seems at any rate to have not one, but two opposites: it negates the bad work of high culture, but also low culture as such mass culture, popular culture. But in architecture, surely, a different dimension – a possibility of *Aufhebung* or Hegelian diremption, of the radical restructuration of the problematic itself and all its terms – is given by something that looks like yet a third opposite of the great individual architectural work as such, namely the city and the urban.

Returning to the dilemmas of all political aesthetics (the subversive fully as much as the utopian), it has to be concluded that such aesthetics can work only if it can be at one and the same time transaesthetic (and this is the sense in which the problem is wedded to the values of modernism as such, which affirmed the heightened aesthetic status if its indispensible transaesthetic dimension). The building can, in other words, only serve as a history lesson if its public and its viewers still have a sense of history; it cannot provide them with one if that organ has atrophied (as is the case in the advanced countries, or at least in the postmodernity of the USA, the laboratory of the postmodern). It can only flex and exercise its Utopian or subversive distance if at least part of that public is still capable of feeling a certain distance from the status quo, from the massive ontology of what is: here too the United States remains an object lesson in what the eclipse of distance looks like, what a society and a population look like who are so deeply immersed in the sheer being of things and commodities that the very memory of distance is effaced, like a word on the tip of your tongue which is fading too rapidly for voluntary recall. One cannot imagine that this repression of historicity is fully achieved in the East, no matter how passionately it may be sought after by any number of sectors of the populations; nor do we have the means to speculate on its realization in the former Third World either, itself equally thrown open (but in different ways) to the forces of privatisation and the hot breath of the current 'end of history'.

As far as the Wall that divided East and West is concerned, however, surely a conference of this kind, which somehow wants to build on its disappearance, needs to be spatially and historically commemorated a little more dialectically than anyone seems to have been willing to do here so far. The Wall has so far been read only as a monument to tyranny and oppression, to segregation and enforced uniformity: thus, Neil Leach's defence of 'difference' seems on the face of it relatively perverse, where we have to do with what has been affirmed as the absolute systemic difference of the Cold War between two ostensibly radically different systems. (See Neil Leach pp. 150–62, this volume.) The argument in favour of the coexistence of radically different social groups, meanwhile, would seem to ignore the lesson of Renata Salecl's analysis of the inevitable imaginary hostility between groups as such: in other words, the dialectical lesson here is that the opposite of a negative – in this case, the repudiation of the oppression of one group by another – is not often likely to offer a positive alternative. It is the scandalous old lesson of Marx's early essay 'On the Jewish question', in which he affirms that oppressive difference can only be overcome by the transcendence of all group distinctions as such, and not by their coexistence in liberal and 'tolerant' legislation (a position which has predictably earned Marx the reputation of anti-semitism).

'Tyranny' is at any rate an eighteenth-century Enlightenment concept, alongside which a different kind of historical narrative might well be placed, if only for variety and 'difference'. For there was an official defence of the building of the Wall, at the time, that needs to be remembered, whether it is judged to be mere propaganda or not. The leaders of the East German state reminded the world that their system involved the free education of generations of younger professionals, at the expense of the working population itself. Doctors, lawyers, architects, scientists, teachers in a variety of professional fields, all paid for by the state through graduate school. What the DDR found increasingly at the end of the 1950s and the beginning of the 1960s was that a veritable brain drain (after the promising sputnik or Krushchev moment of Soviet communism) led increasing numbers of these professionals to cross the border and seek their fortunes in the West. The phenomenon seems to have been far more massive than in the actual working classes: a fact for which there can always be two explanations as well, the one from sheer opportunity, but the other one from the disillusionments of a Western system in which capitalist 'efficiency' demanded a far greater productivity, and thus a more intensified working day, than anything that obtained in the slacker conditions of the 'workers' state'. At any rate, this immense haemorrhage of collective investment was according to some versions the official justification for the building of the Wall in the first place. Nor is it clear to me how the current spokespeople for competition and the free market could without contradiction repudiate this particular version of things (although certainly political liberals – in the US sense – would be able to by virtue of a displacement of the argument from economics to politics, and from the market to social freedom).

Perhaps, however, the argument in favour of difference can be rewritten more strikingly in terms of space itself. Readers of Heidegger will no doubt remember the moment in 'Building, Dwelling, Thinking' in which building, 'by virtue of constructing locales', is defined as 'a founding and joining of spaces':[2] this relatively unusual Heideggerian inflection towards heterogeneity offers at least one possible way of bridging the gap between architecture and urbanism, between the individual building or work and the urban fabric or text. For the coordinates of the city, and its inevitable divisions of labour, traverse the individual building and, transformed, re-emerge in the microconstellation of rooms and spatial relationships within the house, which then becomes the allegory of the larger social conjuncture generally (very much including its telltale silences and absences). Yet it is precisely this conjunction of radical differences that characterizes not merely the city as a totality, but also the city as a superimposed layering of divers historical pasts. Thus, alongside the will to transform the pre-existing city into a homogeneous style – something triumphantly achieved in the grand, henceforth normative, reconstructions of nineteenth-century Paris and Budapest – one can perhaps posit a different urbanizing strategy in which 'difference relates', and the incompatible styles of different quarters, classes and modes of life enter into an active critique of one another by way of a juxtaposition that is read as a figure or trope, and not merely as the fallout of sheer Cartesian extension.

Bucharest would no doubt be one of those cities, its multiple pasts still vividly enscribed in a multiplicity of built styles through which, as through heavy curtains of rain, the touring vehicle penetrates. The oldest precapitalist traces of ancient painted churches and of gypsy tracery and decoration stand shoulder to shoulder with the monumentalities of a European nineteenth century, and then the villas of a specifically Romanian art nouveau herald the successive waves of a specifically Romanian modernism or 'international style', virtually simultaneous with a specific 'neo-Romania' and a Romanian version of the equally international 'fascist art' of the period, then followed shortly by the international 'Stalinist art' of the immediate postwar. Indeed, Romania is not a bad place to study this last, whose principal monument – the great Publishing House building (Figure 4.1) on the outskirts of the city, reminiscent of Moscow's Lomonosov University – can be seen to float magically above Lake Herastrau from a certain privileged point of view, weirdly foregrounding the otherwise invisible utopian dimension of these Stalinist birthday cakes, which now for the briefest instant rejoin the spires of fairy-tale cities.

Yet the more recent architecture of Bucharest is not that international-Stalinist type, but rather a mass housing development 'style' (or lack of it) often characterized by Romanian architects and architecture historians as merely 'socialist'. On this follows the most distinctive if not infamous moment of Romanian architecture and urbanism alike, namely Ceausescu's grand city projects, which, beginning with the rebuilding of the National Theatre and the redesign of Revolution Square in the 1980s, then bear their unexpected and ominous fruit in the massive 'urban renewal' of a whole quarter of Bucharest, filled back in by an extraordinary larger-than-life boulevard of immense facing apartment structures, adorned by a little river in the midst and climaxed by Ceausescu's well-known palace at the artificially razed other end – the second largest built structure in the world (after the Pentagon), and one of the largest surface areas, along with the various Egyptian and Mayan pyramids and any number of other 'wonders of history' which it is conventional to enumerate in such contexts. No longer Stalinist, the detail of this pseudo-classical building, often unnecessarily random and mediocre, is only partially redeemed by the precious and authentic, genuinely Romanian, materials of which it is composed, so that this building, next to which Versailles and the Stalinallee are but doll-houses and which is now used for various UN-style international conferences and meetings of foreign ministers or heads of state, can be allegorical of the nation's 'natural wealth' at the same time that it incorporates year upon year of the national collective surplus value. It has indeed been suggested (by Ioan Andreescu) that Ceausescu's unique spatial and urbanistic ambitions were stimulated – if not triggered – by the great Bucharest earthquake of 1977, which showed the signal opportunities thrown up by sheer natural disaster and the radical effacement of the past. Americans will think of the example of Robert Moses' catastrophic 'urban renewal' projects in New York (documented in Caro's *The Power Broker*), equally monuments to that 'window' in history during which, owing to the uneven developments of modernization, a single individual can briefly hold the impersonal and collective reins of history in his hands and imagine that he is in the process of leaving his personal mark on space and the city alike. To be sure, it was among other things precisely this crystallization of Ceausescu's fantasies around the spatial expression of the palace project that gradually reduced his personal power over the country at large and became the pretext whereby a certain ruse of history and of revolution – as his personal fortune became institutionalized and the objective field of management and exploitation delegated to the younger staff of the Sekuritate – could sweep him away as an historical actor who had already fulfilled his objective mission.

The question of 'reconstruction' then takes on very special content in this unique situation: is the Palace then to be thought of as one of those reminders of an unpleasant past – like statuary or Japanese colonial architecture – in the face of which the most consequent 'symbolic act' might well consist in their thorough-going elimination and cauterisation? But the investment of labour and social value in this project is too enormous to waste in a gesture that could in any case never restore the spatial past and the authentic spaces of an old Bucharest which the modernizing project (like Moses's Bronx Expressway, but also like Haussmann's reconstruction of Paris) has swept away forever. (We must finally add, for the sake of historical and stylistic completeness, the sudden emergence in the Bucharest of today, fully grown and less postmodern than transnational, of the architecture of late capitalism as such, dramatized by the immense closed world of the Sofitel Hotel and Bucharest's World Trade Centre.)

But is a past one does not wish to memorialize simply to be forgotten, even 'strongly' forgotten in the therapeutic Nietzschean sense? Indeed, if forgetfulness as such is to be considered a relationship to the past in its own right and a possible option among others (whether the forgetfulness is a form of repression or not), then, particularly in the postmodern age, the ominous possibility arises that forgetfulness might become the final solution for the past as a totality, in its variously radical differentiations from our post-historical present.

One does not often associate modernist positions in architecture and urbanism – that is to say, predominantly functionalist ones – with this kind of historicist problematic. A certain modernism, indeed, follows Nietzsche in repudiating the past and in celebrating the gleaming (and mostly technological) novum of the absolute present as strenuously as does a certain postmodernism, which however sees in its conviction that 'tradition' is a construct of the present the pretext for a deployment of empty and decorative 'historicist' allusions of all kinds. Yet Siegfried Giedeon's influential ideological 'manifesto', *Space, Time and Architecture* (if one can use that word about so extensive a tome), very specifically positioned a properly historicist urbanism at the centre of its arguments for architectural modernization:[3] this was his reading of Sixtus V's plan for a baroque reconstruction of the Eternal City, even more fully developed in Norberg-Schulz's classic analysis, *Baroque Architecture*, from which we will quote in what follows.[4]

On this interpretation, Sixtus' opening up of Rome and his articulation of its fundamental traffic arteries, while comparable in its effects to the more familiar Haussmann restructuration of Paris – some of which is, unlike the Italian city, still as emergent as the rest is residual – is predicated on a logic of memory fully as much as on a logic of use and function. For Sixtus V, and following him for Baroque urbanism in general, the totality of the city is to be grasped as one of those 'memory palaces' (Frances Yates) in which the public, the participatory faithful, are to commemorate the meaning of a set of shrines whose spatial interrelationship will now begin to produce a new and heightened meaning-relationship in its own right. Sixtus's chief architect puts it this way:

> Our lord, now wishing to ease the way for those who, prompted by devotion or vows, are accustomed to visit frequently the most holy places of the City of Rome, and in particular the seven churches so celebrated for their great indulgences and relics, opened many most commodious and straight streets in many places. Thus one can by foot, by horse or in carriage, start out from whatever place in Rome one may wish, and continue virtually in a straight line to the most famous devotions.[5]

This emergence of a dynamic network, from what had hitherto been an inert set of places lost within a dense city fabric, now has consequences for those spaces themselves and the buildings associated with them:

> in the Baroque city...the single building loses its plastic individuality and becomes part of a superior system.... In general, we may say that the Baroque city converges on (or radiates from) monumental buildings which represent the basic values of the system. 'The monument constitutes a focal point of the very greatest prestige within the framework of a city and is generally placed in the centre of a vast area, planned so as to enhance the monument's aesthetic values'....[6]

To which quotation from G.C. Argan, Norberg-Schulz significantly adds this note: 'The word "monument" is used here in its original sense, that is, something which makes us remember'. He goes on to conclude: 'In fact, Baroque Rome does not form a systematic totality of a geometrical kind. The seven basilicas, taken as the main point of departure for the plan of Sixtus V, are placed in relation to historical events rather than topographical or urban reasons.'[7] Such an analysis authorizes us to follow the historical slippage from a Christian historicism to a later secular one, and to draw at least an active analogy between the uses of the Baroque city plan and those that might be developed in order to articulate the historical layers of distinct styles that make up the richness and complexity of a city like Bucharest. Indeed, the discussion of the role of the obelisque by Norberg-Schulz – a systematic placement, and not only in Baroque Rome, of even more ancient preclassical markers in order to articulate this new set of urban connections – suggests the fundamentally allegorical nature of the new space, which the vertical marker links to a new inner-worldly transcendence (the Baroque ceiling, the Baroque sky as such, now a Copernican pretext for inner-worldly ecstasy, rather than a designation of an other-worldly medieval cosmos that escapes all figuration), thereby demanding of the viewer a counter-reformation, Loyola-related exercise in controlled fantasy and the transformation of the spatial datum into a fully developed and semi-autonomous imaginary representation. But that is precisely what our own historicism demands of us, when we attempt to transform the surviving shreds of an older city space into fitful visions of a distinct layer of the past, of an historical periodization that aesthetic reception wishes to exercise.

In conclusion, however, we need to admit the contradictions of this urbanism as well, and to remind the reader that in some such direction Disneyland also lies. EPCOT is the more accurate designation for reconstructions of great technical quality (or so we are assured), whose explicit purpose lies in the literal spatial evocation either of exotic cultural otherness (Sinity, Mexicanity, Francity, as Barthes might have put it) or of distinctively and stylistically differing moments of the past. At a certain moment in the postmodern – one assumes it is at the moment in which the residually pre-modern lifeways and spaces have finally been completely modernized – the appeal to the past becomes a matter of sheer images, whose existential or social substance has been lost. In *The Seeds of Time*, I suggested that one of the features characterizing the situation of postmodernity (as opposed to those modernities evidently so closely related to it) was the operation of a series of unresolvable antinomies, in which space becomes time and time becomes space, and in which the critique of nature turns around into a new kind of appeal to natural groundings.[8] I am tempted now to add to these antinomies (but I feel sure that it was already implicit in them) a new formulation that has to do with authenticity, namely, the proposition that in our time all thoroughgoing evocations of authenticity as such (like those of the Disney architects and historical experts) is necessarily as inauthentic as the Disney logo suggests. This means that all attempts to reconstruct the past, or its markers – such as the rebuilding of the old city in

Warsaw – are Disney-related operations which have as little to do with any "authentic" sense of history or relationship to the past as that henceforth emblematic operation whose signature will be central in any analysis of our own (postmodern) moment of history, or of the current situation.

The reverse is presumably also true, and that the celebration of the inauthentic can under certain circumstances take on a certain authenticity is evident implicit in the paradigmatic Venturi–Brown–Rauch manifesto about the altered relationship to the American vernacular (Las Vegas).[9] This antinomy does not, however, have as its consequence that utter repudiation of the past and of historicism so often claimed by postmodern ideologues; but rather only a careful dissociation between the categories of historicity and authenticity. This dissociation sets new tasks for any North American cultural politics, tasks in which the problem of the reconstruction of post-socialist cities can be most instructive indeed.

Notes

1 This paper was written for the 'Beyond the Wall' conference held in Bucharest in July 1995.
2 Martin Heidegger, *Basic Writings*, ed. D.F. Krell, New York: HarperCollins, 1977, p. 360.
3 Siegfried Giedeon, *Space, Time and Architecture*, Cambridge, MA: MIT Press, 1942.
4 C. Norberg-Schulz, *Baroque Architecture*, New York: Abrams, 1971.
5 quoted by Norberg-Schulz, *Baroque Architecture*, 1971, p. 15.
6 ibid., p. 18.
7 ibid., p. 64.
8 Fredric Jameson, *The Seeds of Time*, New York: Columbia University Press, 1994.
9 Robert Venturi, Denise Scott Brown and Steven Izenour, *Learning from Las Vegas*, Cambridge, MA: MIT Press, 1977.

6 Policing the body

Descartes and the architecture of change

Andrew Benjamin

Perhaps the most remarkable legacy of the regime in Romania is the architecture of Bucharest. The complicated problem of what to do with this legacy is the subject of this paper.[1] The problem is both architectural and philosophical. Repeating the destruction that created the present city by a further act of destruction is not an intervention. What must be done involves developing ways of understanding the regime's own urbanism and thus ways of countering it. Fundamental to both is thinking a conception of the new or the other which demands the abeyance of destruction on the one hand and the refusal of a nostalgic sense of recovery on the other. (The latter would be the new as the rediscovery of a lost tradition.) Approaching this issues via Descartes may seem aberrant; but the real strength of the Cartesian formulation of the interplay between the philosophical and the architectural is that it is premised on the interconnection between destruction and the new. The limits of Descartes therefore are central to thinking the limits of this conception of modernity.

One of the problems confronting any attempt to present conceptually, let alone enact, fundamental change will be the housing of that which occurs in the process and as the consequence of such change. While it will always be essential to hold to particularity, it remains the case that this problem will endure within philosophy as much as it will within architecture. Not only must there be the possibility that change can be registered, given the impossibility of sustaining a successful link between change and either the utopian project or a metaphysics of destruction, it must also be the case that there will be a form continuity. What this means is that an integral part of the problem stems from having to give formal presence to a discontinuous continuity. Within the context of the countries comprising the former Eastern Europe, part of the challenge to be faced if the authoritarian regimes that characterised their former existences are no longer to be politically or architecturally present, is how to house the future. (This is, of course, a question concerning the present and not an imagined future.)

Engaging with the issues that arise will demand the resources of architects, political scientists and philosophers. Philosophy is positioned by such questions because philosophy has consistently concerned itself with the problems of cessation and continuity, and inclusion and exclusion.[2] Analysing the way these problems are taken up will open up differing ways in which the interplay between change and its housed presence can be thought. Rather than giving this problem a purely abstract determination, it will be given the setting provided by a consideration of the domestic and the body within the work of Descartes. The importance of this setting is that Descartes' writings bring the architectural and the domestic within the setting of an attempt, albeit one undertaken within philosophy, to think radical change.

Philosophy and the domestic

Two well-known motifs in Descartes' work will allow these philosophico-archi-tectural considerations to be opened up. Descartes' reference to the possible renewal of a city and its buildings as presented in the *Discours de la method* will comprise the first. The second will be the investigation of the nature of the distinction between the human and the animal, and the human and the machine, staged by Descartes both in the *Discours* and in *Le Traité de l'homme*. In general terms, what will emerge from an analysis of these two motifs is the insistent necessity to judge mastery, or rather to judge the desire for mastery. While the choice will not be positioned around an either/or in any straightfor-ward sense, it remains the case that the critique of the conception of mastery within Descartes' writings opens up the possibility of a conception of subjec-tivity and thus of architecture that will be positioned around the incomplete. Rather than the incomplete being the sign of lack, it will register the impossi-bility of there ever having been the unity and thus the already present self-completion demanded by a self-enclosing and thus self-giving conception of architecture or subjectivity. In the place of a politics of lament, there will be a political and thus an architectural configuration that will continue to work within and through the incomplete. Strategies of working with the incomplete – of the always already incomplete – will, in the end, demand another form of universality and therefore another thinking of the absolute; it will be an abso-lute admitting of an original complexity. The demand would be different; it would involve a founding ontology of the incomplete. What this will mean, philosophically, is that the always already incomplete is an ontological set-up and not the consequence of a semantic undecidability.[3]

Even though the Cartesian formulation is well known, it is worth allowing the detail of his position to be cited:

> there is not usually so much perfection in works composed of several parts and produced by various different craftsmen as in the works of one man. Thus we see that buildings undertaken and completed by a single architect are usually more attractive and better planned than those which several have tried to patch up by adapting old walls built for different purposes. Again, ancient cities that have gradually grown from mere villages into large towns are usually ill-proportioned, compared with those orderly towns which planners lay out as they fancy on level ground. Looking at the buildings of the former individually, you will often find as much art in

them, if not more, than in those of the latter; but in view of their arrange-
ment a tall one here, a small one there – and the way they make the streets
crooked and irregular, you would say it is *chance*, rather than the will of men
using *reason*, that placed them so. And when you consider that there have
always been certain officials whose job it is to see that private buildings
embellish public places, you will understand how difficult it is to make something perfect by working only on what others have produced (l. 519).[4]

Held within these lines is an implicit conception of historical time. It defines
the nature of change by providing it with its philosophical possibility.
Furthermore, what characterises this particular conception of change – indeed,
what would count almost as an architecture after the enactment of destruction –
is that it is structured in terms of the opposition between chance and reason.
It is the conception of historical time that is at work with this passage and which
in turn holds in place, and is held in place by, the opposition between chance and
reason, that will become central. Any attempt to think the through the question
of change is constrained by the ineliminability of temporal concerns.

The ostensible point of Descartes' example was to indicate why it is better
for a single philosopher to recast philosophy – to provide it with new foundations – than attempt to refurbish what the Scholastic tradition had given as the
philosophical, and thus as that which set the conditions for truth. Employing
the language of the *Meditations*, what was necessary was 'destruction'.
Moreover, it is an act of destruction that will have to be singular in nature. Its
singularity will, of course, lend itself to a necessary universalisation. Reason will
provide the basis of universality, since the act of destruction and the subsequent
philosophico-architectural activity will have been acts of reason. The project of a
new philosophy, as with that which would pertain to a new house or a new city,
is not to have to work on 'what others have produced'. A real departure – be it
architectural or philosophical – must involve the interplay of destruction and
the new, with the former being the precondition far the latter. In other words,
the presence of the new is premised upon the destruction of the old.

While the full force of the Cartesian project may not have been apparent to
Descartes, what must be maintained is that with Descartes there arises that
version of the modernist project which works by maintaining and articulating a
metaphysics of destruction. What characterises such a metaphysics is that it is
given within a destructive possibility in which alterity – an-other philosophy,
architecture, *et cetera* – arises out of a destruction of the given. Here, not only
is time such that it is possible to intervene within it in order to establish the
new, but memory will not work against this particular construal of renewal. In
the end, this position will become more intricate. Nonetheless what emerges at
this stage is the opposition between destruction and memory. The latter term
needs to allowed to have both its positive and negative determinations: in other
words, it must be allowed to be present as either remembering or forgetting.
Destruction is premised on either an enforced forgetting or the attempted elimination of traces, thereby trying to obviate memory's possibility.

The setting given this passage in the text is located within what could be described as the straightforwardly domestic. Immediately prior to making this claim, Descartes writes that it had occurred to him after spending the day 'shut up in a stove heated room'. In other words, the comfort of the domestic setting – a warm room within the house – determines the need to engage in an argument about philosophy and the development of philosophy which is itself advanced in terms of an analogy whose concerns touch on architecture, urbanism and forms of restoration. Moreover, the precise nature of the engagement will necessitate a destruction of the edifice that comprises the philosophical tradition – as construed by Descartes – and thus, to the extent the analogy is maintained, it will also demand a sustained rebuilding and redevelopment on the level of the architectural. It is this set up that demands to be thought in terms of the implicit conception of temporality that inheres in the formulation of the architectural analogy.

What attention to the details of Descartes' formulation reveals is not the presence of a foundering moment within the text as such, but a complication given by the temporality proper to the analogy's own work. Inherent in it is the proposition that the time of historical development – the temporality of the philosophical tradition and equally the tradition of building – while continuous or sequential allows for an emphatic intervention in which the content of the tradition can be destroyed, and the philosophical project is able to begin again 'all anew from the foundations'. There is, however, one fundamental additional detail. The 'stove heated room' seems to be outside that particular formulation. Before pursuing its details, the direct consequence of this positioning needs to be noted. The domestic – and here it is not just the domestic but the domestic as the site in which truth comes to be recognised – is lodged outside that domain to which truth refers. The domestic is positioned outside the city and thus as, in some sense, outside its buildings. Despite being placed outside, it comes to reveal the truth of that which takes place within the city. Furthermore, what will count as the domestic can be extended in so far as the 'stove heated room' has an almost inevitable ubiquity. Most sites will lend themselves to a domestic rendering. What this will mean is that if the domestic is the site in which the necessity for the enactment of a metaphysics of destruction will have come to insist, then it is equally the site that is not included within its own reworking. Reverting to the analogy, it would be as though the 'stove heated room' was not located within the old city – and if it were to be then it would be there by chance – and thus not in need of another set of foundations.

Indeed, it is possible to see that this is the position that is reinforced by the other major recourse to the language of architecture that occurs in the text. In the opening of the Third Section of the *Discours*, Descartes argues that it is not sufficient prior to the act of rebuilding – and note his formulation is 'to rebuild the place where one lives' (l. 591) – simply to prepare for the work. It is impermissible to be *irrésolu*. It is essential that 'one is lodged happily during the time that the works is being carried out' (l. 591). In other words, there is a necessity to be 'lodged happily' during the time in which the philosophical project is carried out. Part of what this entails, for Descartes, is 'obeying the law and customs' of the land in which he finds himself; not only is that essential, not engaging in activity, be it philosophical or otherwise, that was not part of the project of truth or which would lead away from the pursuit of truth is equally a fundamental part of being 'lodged happily'. What cannot come into the domain of reconsideration or re-examination, let alone refurbishment, is the initial setting in which this activity is undertaken. If designs are to be made – if 'one' is to become the architect, again a possibility identified by Descartes, the philosopher becoming the architect – then the sanctity of the home in which these plans are made and laid out is a fundamental condition; it is almost the *sine qua non*. Perhaps, here, it is possible to argue that the exclusion of the domestic – textually, the place of being 'lodged happily' – is the condition of possibility for the project of reworking the philosophical. Metaphysical destruction is constrained to leave the home intact. It will be essential to return to this point. What it sets in play is the possibility that strategies of destruction may end up conserving the place of the domestic, since the home cannot be subject to the same demands as that which is outside its walls, even though as has already been noted, this 'outside' is there in name only.

It is here that time needs to be reintroduced. What has arisen thus far is that time must have at least two particular determinations. In the first place, it must be such that intervention is possible in order that the project of philosophy can be reworked and thus given another foundation. Moreover, bringing about this situation must be the work of a solitary individual: the philosopher-architect. In the second place, while what appears to be public space – though in the end it will be no more than a private philosophical space – must be able to sanction this dramatic intervention, it must also be the case that what emerges as the domestic must fall outside the temporality that is, for Descartes, proper to the tradition of philosophy. What this means is that philosophy, thus conceived, is divorced from the everyday, and in being divorced from it comes to yield a conception of the everyday as untouched by philosophy. The everyday and the domestic – remembering the ubiquity of the domestic – are not just removed from the domain of the philosophical. It is rather that the concept of time that pertained to the unfolding of the philosophical – a temporality allowing for intervention and thus allowing, initially at least, the determining presence of a metaphysics of destruction – is not that in which the repetition of the domestic and the everyday are repeated. (And yet, as has already been suggested, there is a certain reciprocity at work within this set-up.)

The Cartesian project of renewal, therefore, in leaving the everyday untouched will leave its architecture untouched. While the use of architecture within the text works to indicate how a metaphysics of destruction would be enacted within philosophy – the new buildings, a new urban landscape springing from the originality of one mind at work – in the end there will be no change since the site of thinking, its home, the place in which one is 'lodged comfortably', remains outside the call for renewal. In this instance, architecture conserves the everyday and the domestic as they are untouched, necessarily, by philosophy. And it must be added that it is not just that they are untouched; they are equally not viewed as places warranting or needing the renewal that is demanded for philosophy by philosophy. What this means is that the place of bodies, the spatial relation that pertains between bodies and the place in which they find themselves and thus which is the locus of experience, are left out of consideration. Descartes has, of course, already made this point by withdrawing the domain of law and custom from the place of philosophical renewal. Despite the presence of the architectural within the text, despite the utilisation of explicitly architectural motifs, the architectural is not thought as such. The repetition of the end of architecture – its presence in terms of a building in which sheltering take place – occurs without consideration. Or, in fact the only consideration that is offered is the form that conserves the predetermined functions that architecture has been taken to serve. The question of lodging, let alone the question of what it means to lodge well in not being addressed, has to be assumed.

What is introduced therefore is not simply that which will check the Cartesian conception of the new, but the more demanding proposition that once the new is interarticulated with destruction, then what will be left out is the place in which destruction is conceived. What this means is that what comes to be advanced is a conception of the new that will leave the customs and the laws of the domestic untouched. Once again, assuming the ubiquity of the domestic, what is removed from consideration, and thus the possibility of its own renewal, is the everyday. This may have a number of different consequences. One will be that the presence of architectural urban destruction – renewal and thus the promulgation of the new as consequent on destruction undertaken in the name of the new, perhaps even in the name of progress – amounts to no more than a reiteration of the same domestic spaces, and thus the reinforcing of spaces with the same domestic politics as existed previously.

As architecture was in the end left untouched within Descartes' argument, this opens up the need to search for ways in which it may be incorporated in the possibility of thinking change. Architecture may be included once it is understood as being both the locus and agent of change rather than the neutral place of being 'lodged happily'. In fact, once it becomes impossible to avoid an analysis of what this state involves, then what would emerge is that the most sustained critique of forms of human activity – critiques that envisage the possibility of a type of transformation – would be critical engagements with the architecture that sustained the particular forms of activity in question.

Bodies, machines and souls

In order to investigate the operation of the human body and therefore as part of the attempt to establish what it was that defined the human, Descartes often used analogies with machines and invented animals which, for all intents and purposes, resembled humans in their actions. Descartes could 'suppose' that God had formed 'the body of a man' which, even though it did not have a soul, was nonetheless of a nature such that examining its operations would amount to examining the operations of the body of a human being. Descartes' immediate concession is that the human body is also an animal body. Indeed his own justification mirrors this set-up. Explaining that what he wants to establish is a link between the animal body and the human body, the link is presented in the following terms:

> I want to put here the explanation of the movement of the heart and the arteries, which, being the first and the most general that are observed in animals, it will be easy to judge on the basis of them what one must think *(ce qu'on doit penser)* of all the others (1. 819).

The 'man', like the human except for the absence of a 'soul' (*l'âme raisonnable*), will allow claims which, once generalised, will account equally for the operation of the human body. What governs this movement, indeed what allows it to have its explanatory force, are resemblance and imitation. In sum, there is a generalised mimetic economy that allows for the analogy to hold. The opening of the *Traité de l'homme* reinforces this point. Again, it begins with the supposition that the body is 'nothing other than a statue or a machine of the earth'. Investigating this other body – the body machine – will lead to an investigation of the human body since 'it imitates all of our functions which can be imagined to proceed from matter and which only depend upon the operation of the organs' (1. 379). Furthermore, after a lengthy description of the operation of the body, Descartes concludes that this entity – the automaton – 'imitates' perfectly the actions of man. Here, what he calls, 'this machine' is on the level of imitation indistinguishable from the human.

Now, the mimetic economy will only work if it is possible to establish the moments at which the human can be distinguished from the machine or the animal. Resemblance while productive is, for Descartes, equally an important source of error. The question therefore concerns how the mimetic economy is to be disrupted such that what emerges is, rather than a correspondence, a necessary non-correspondence between the machine or animal and the human. Answering that question will involve recognising that the argument advanced by Descartes in the *Meditations*, and elsewhere, is concerned to link the specificity of the human to the activity of thinking and thus not to the operations of the body. Nonetheless, what has to happen is that Descartes will need to describe the activities of thinking in such a way that they are automatically not reducible to bodily activities. It is this point that needs to be pursued. Pursuing it is equally to question the role of the mimetic economy in the formulation of the Cartesian position.

In the fifth section of the *Discours*, Descartes offers two stated reasons and what in the end will also count as a third reason, all of which will allow for a separation between humans and either animals or machines. This will be the case even though such machines (or animals) may resemble humans and imitate their actions. (It should be noted that it is Descartes who deploys the terms 'imitation' and 'resemblance'.) The first reason pertains to language. For

Descartes, neither animals nor machines use language. The specifically human activity is 'to declare to others our thoughts' (l. 629). The second is that animals or machines only operate in a determined way. Each organ has a dispo-sition that causes it to act in the way that it does. The comparison with human activity is described by Descartes in the following terms:

> For, in the place of reason which is a universal instrument, that can serve in all sort of encounters, these organs have need of some particular disposition for each particular action. From which it follows that it is...impossible that there is enough diversity in a machine in order to make it act in all occur-rences of life in the same way that our reason makes us act (l. 629).

The third reason is that present in the human is an element that is not comprised of 'matter', and which does not derive its power from it and more-over will not die with the body. This is the *l'âme raisonnable* (l. 631). What this means is that the mimetic economy that is opened up by Descartes is limited by the conception of machine and the introduction of the non-material. Central here will be how this non-material soul is to be understood.

The problem now is to try and find a way of linking the exclusion of the domestic and the failure to think placed activity to the concern that Descartes has with establishing self-certainty – where the latter is interconnected, neces-sarily, to holding the human apart from any reduction to either animal or machine. What this means is that the mimetic economy originally established must be effectively distanced. The *l'âme raisonnable* as non-material must be linked to the non-inclusion of the domestic and the everyday.

Fundamental to the Cartesian project is the attempt to differentiate the operation of the body for those which related only to the *l'âme raisonnable*. The soul, and this will be true equally with the understanding and the role of thinking, as construed by Descartes, brings with it an envisaged unity of the subject. On the level of the soul or thought the subject can be, and moreover has to be, self-identical. It is precisely this set up that is captured in Descartes' famous formulation that 'I think therefore I am'. The 'I' as that which thinks is indistinguishable from the activity of thinking; and thus in the formulation *cogito ergo sum* the self (the ego) affirms itself as being, being itself, in the process of its thinking. To the question what is the subject – who is the Cartesian self? – the answer has to be, that which thinks. Here the self is identi-fied with the 'I', with the ego. What is being staged in this opening therefore is a conception of the philosophical subject which, even though it may emerge in an act of differentiation and, even if it may hold itself in position by the conti-nuity of that differentiation, is nonetheless given as complete and thus having a self-completing finality. These two moments bring ontology – the existence of the subject – and temporality into conjunction. The latter, temporality, is given by the posited finality of self-completion. In the second place there is another possibility for thinking the self and thus for thinking its subjectivity.

Part of the difficulty with this position, however, is that while the Cartesian self was self-identical to the exclusion of its body, it could not eliminate the body. The body endured as an ineliminable remainder and therefore a constant reminder insofar as the body – operating as it does in terms feeling, pleasure, resemblance, etc. – remains as the continual source of error and deception. Having to maintain the body means that the Cartesian self is continually menaced by the possibility of deception and sin. It should not be forgotten that central to the project of the *Discours* is tying these two possibilities together. The pursuit of truth should not lead in any direction other than epistemological certainty and moral rectitude. And yet the body endures. Moreover, it endures as the unmasterable element in the philosophical home. Here the body cannot be at home with philosophy even though it has to be with the thinking subject. The body has an ambivalent status that turns the home into a site of surveillance, a site in which the wants of the body – bodily wants not wanted by philosophy – have to be kept at bay by the watchful eye of the self-certain subject. The house, therefore, is threatened by the presence of that which it cannot expel.

A consequence of this recognition of the place of the body and its inevitability is that certain regimes, be they architectural or philosophical, will become necessary in order to police the body. In other words, from what looks as though it were no more than a philosophical argument concealing the centrality and envisaged unity of the self, in fact is predicated on eliminating the body, a project that can only ever be partially successful, and thus with the body returning as the unruly element in what would otherwise a stable home, there emerges the necessity for a regime of control and thus the necessity for an organisational policy. The importance of this recognition is not the addition of this policy but that it has to have been there from the very start. The interarticulation of place and self – the interplay of shelter and the sheltered – was already the site that necessitated the imposition of mechanisms of control. Part of the way such controls work will be in the organisation of space.

It is not difficult to link what has been identified thus far as a metaphysics of destruction to the attempted elimination of the body. Of the many ways in which this topic can be approached, two of the most relevant concern the interconnection between memory and the body, and the relationship between the withdrawal of the domestic and the work of the soul. Memory and the body work in similar ways. The project of destruction encounters that which will mark the impossibility of that project once the insistent presence of memory is recognised. Memory, in this precise sense, can be neither controlled nor policed with any absolute certainty by the work of destruction. It will be present in the same way as the body will remain an ineliminable element in the attempt to establish self-certainty. However, what is significant is that in remaining it has to be controlled. In other words, as memory would have to be mastered the body will have to be managed in such a way that it was as though it had been eliminated. In both instances therefore there are versions of a metaphysics of destruction and attempts at mastery. As the body returns within an insistent presence that demands that consideration be given not just to its specificity –

the specific presence of the body and thus of bodily differences – but with equal importance to the housing of that bod?. After all, the body is that which is sheltered. Once it has to be allowed a place then the question that inevitably arises is what is the place for this body? There will, of course, be a similar move that has to be made in relation to memory, since with memory there will be the necessity to think through the complex repetitions; and they will be repetitions that pertain as much to housing and the architectural as they will to the philosophical and that which will allow the work and the presence of memory a place.

What is intended to control the body is located outside the body. Outside but inside, the rational soul has to legislate for, and over, the body. The site of philosophical activity, the place of the self-certain subject will attempt to exercise control over the body. However, control is also the impossibility of absolute control. Not only will the body remain the source of error, it will necessitate the hold of that which will legislate but which will fall outside the realm of philosophy. It is at this point that a connection emerges with the domestic. As has already been indicated the domestic while essential for the promulgation of the need for a philosophical revolution – articulated textually in terms of an architectural or urban destruction – was itself withdrawn from the necessity to which it gave rise. The domestic held back from the inception of complete change was merely to be subject to the unchanging repetition of law and custom. And yet, the domestic has a fundamental ubiquity. It has to be managed and controlled, or else it would upset the revolution that had been put in place, for Descartes, on the level of the philosophical. Apart from the possibility that such a conception of change locates it everywhere and yet nowhere, what it also entails is that to the extent that the domestic is held out of consideration – not positioned as a locus of radical change – it also has to be policed. The policing of the domestic will be fundamental both to maintain the possibility of the successful enactment of a metaphysics of destruction and because, as with the body, it is the domain which, while not falling under the sway of philosophy's rule, has to be ruled. This latter point – the necessity of its having to be ruled – means that the domestic, again as with the body, is the site that harbours the greatest potential precisely because it is the greatest threat.

Once it could be allowed that the body and the domestic fell within the domain of radical change, then to the extent that a metaphysics of destruction necessitates their exclusion, what would have to emerge is radical change as a consequence of their inclusion. Were this to be a possibility, then architecture becomes a central concern. Where, given the ubiquity of the domestic and the complexity of bodies, would such a conception of change come to be housed? It is only by allowing this question its full force that the limit of destruction can be chartered and with that limit a workable opening emerges.

Notes

1 This paper was initially a conference paper. It still bears the mark of an attempt to make a strategic intervention.

2 A number of the arguments advanced here have been argued in greater detail in my *The Plural Event*, London: Routledge, 1994.
3 I have tried to develop some of these concerns in *Present Hope*, London: Routledge, 1997. The reference to this distinction between ontology and semantics is an area of research that can only be addressed here in outline.
4 All references to Descartes are to R. Descartes, *Oeuvres Philosophiques*, ed. F. Alquié, Tomes I–III, Paris: Garnier, 1978.

7   The state as a work of art

The trauma of Ceausescu's Disneyland

Renata Salecl

The well known communist joke inquires: 'What is the difference between an optimist and a pessimist in the Soviet Union?' The reply is, 'A pessimist thinks that everything is so bad that it can't get worse, while an optimist thinks that it can.' Today, many Russians and other East Europeans still hold such an 'optimistic' view, since they are confronted with the economic chaos of early capitalism, which makes their lives even more difficult than under the communist regime. Some people thus feel deep despair and are daydreaming about those lost times of less freedom but more social security.[1] For such nostalgic people, the fall of the communist regime was the event that caused the disarray of their lives. Clinging to this perception, they act like the hysterics who always find a point in their symbolic economy, a particular event, that instigated their suffering. Such a hysteric usually concludes: 'If only my mother hadn't done this in my youth... if only that encounter had never occurred...if only I could turn the clock backwards and arrange things to develop differently.' The belief in such an 'if only' is a necessary fantasy that enables the hysteric to sustain the position of a suffering innocent victim. Since the clock cannot be turned back, the hysterics can do nothing to change the situation.

Those who are nostalgic about the communist past act in a similar fashion when they grumble and pine for the former times. Since these times are forever gone, they do not need to act to improve their current situation. That is why the vast majority of these people do not engage in a serious political struggle; they do not organize political parties which would, for example, fight for the return of communism. Instead, they persist in the comfortable position of the lamenting victim.[2] The paradox is that in the past they wished communism to end, but they did not truly believe that their wish could be fulfilled. Today they act in a similar fashion when they dream about returning to the safe shelter of the communist institutions, while knowing that this cannot happen. Contemporary Romania presents a model case in this regard, since it is governed by those ex-communists who now form the new capitalist elite, but whose ideology promises the re-establishment of communist welfare. However, as I will try to demonstrate, this longed-for communist past bears the marks of trauma: Ceausescu and the architectural monuments of his regime.

The effort to reinstall a former past opens a variety of theoretical questions.

How is the identity of the subject related to the symbolic order and which memory of the past does the subject invoke? Since this past never existed in the way it is now remembered, what is the logic of this memory? In the case of the communist nostalgia, questions also arise over how the new regime should deal with the visible monuments of the previous regime (communist statues, architecture), and what it means to remove them or to integrate them into the post-socialist ideological universe.

Identity and institution

Certain prisoners serving life sentences display the impossible desire: they endlessly dream about 'freedom', but when they attain it through eventual parole, they nostalgically remember the 'non-freedom' of their prison life. This impossible desire is a major theme of the movie *The Shawshank Redemption* (director Frank Darabont, 1994) based on the short story by Stephen King. In the film, the prisoner Red, serving a life sentence, narrates a story about another lifer, Andy, a young banker convicted of murdering his wife and her lover. Andy is a very special person: he radiates a certain calmness, as if the horror of prison does not touch him in his inner being. In contrast, other prisoners are, as Red says, 'institutionalized men': their identity depends on the place they have in the prison hierarchy. When released from prison they become broken individuals who either commit another crime in order to be reincarcerated or decide to end their life. Andy claims that he is innocent; however, he does not perceive himself as a suffering victim, but in a stoic way he endures the oppression of prison. His one particularity was to always have a big poster hanging in his cell: first it was Rita Hayworth, then Marilyn Monroe, and later other beauties. When, after nineteen years of prison life, Andy suddenly disappears, it becomes clear that it was this poster that hung over and hid a large hole in the wall, which he slowly dug and through which he finally escaped.

At this point Andy's story ends and the prime actor becomes Red himself, who after thirty-eight years is unexpectedly paroled. However, Red knows that he too is an 'institutionalized man' and that life outside has no meaning, but what prevents him from collapsing is the example of Andy. (Here the film version and the short story slightly differ.) In the film, the prisoner Andy once asked Red to do him a favour: if and when Red is released, he should find a field in Maine where something is hidden under a black stone. Andy, therefore, directly encourages Red to search for a secret, thus giving Red hope, an object of desire. In the original short story, the search for this object is more profound. Andy reveals to Red his own plan that, after coming out of prison, he will find a black rock under which lies a key to a bank safe. In this safe, a friend has stored bonds and documents for Andy's new identity, which will enable him to start new life in Mexico. It is essential that Andy does not directly encourage Red to find the secret under the black rock, but only reveals his (Andy's) own object of desire. Since, as Lacan says, 'desire is always desire of the Other, the notion of the secret rock quickly becomes Red's own obsession. Red, when released, starts searching for the field in Maine and when he discovers the rock, he also discovers its secret: a letter from Andy addressed to him. In this letter, Andy encourages Red: since he has come so far, he can go even farther and join him in Mexico: 'Remember, hope is a good thing.'[3] And Red starts on his journey, hoping that he will succeed.

For the convicts, the jail sentence does not simply present a frustrating hardship; they find a special enjoyment in their suffering. The point is not that they find a pleasure in grumbling over the injustice of the jail sentence. What is essential is how, in the oppressiveness of the prison situation, the prisoners organize their identities. The convicts find a special enjoyment in establishing internal rules, forming hierarchies, humiliating each other and pitting one inmate against another. The prison thus provides a ground on which each prisoners forms his identity, either as the one who knows how to play with the rules, climbs in the hierarchy and masters the others, or as the one who is endlessly victimised by the others.

How is one to understand here the notion of identity? Those theorists who conceive of identity in terms of subject positions insist that identity is primarily linked to the problem of intersubjectivity. The subject's identity thus depends on the relationship to 'the Other,' in the sense of the social symbolic structure as well as the concrete other subject. In the case of prison, the identity of the prisoner becomes determined by the place the prisoner has in relation to the symbolic organization of the prison, as well as to the other prisoners. Lacan, however, would go further: for him, identity is the way the subject deals with his or her radical lack. By taking on a symbolic identity, by identifying with a place in the social symbolic network, the subject tries to avoid the encounter with this lack, the unsymbolizable real that determines the subject in his or her inner being. The subject thus searches for places in various social hierarchies in order to escape the trauma of the real.

In the prison situation, the real in a specific way relates to the crime. In the wider social world itself, crime is the real around which the law establishes itself (or according to Hegel, out of which the law emerges as the negation of crime). However, crime is also what law tries to encompass, but what nonetheless always escapes law's grasp. The crime committed by the subject destructs the subject's former identity, since it also touches the unsymbolizable kernel, the lack around which the subject structures his or her identity. Thus, after committing the crime the subject will never be the same again; it will never form its identity in the same way as before. The new identity that the subject forms in prison thus has to do with the real of crime, or better, this identity enables the subject to escape the real of crime. That is why, as it is clear from the film, the prisoners do not talk about their crimes or boast about their murders: they all claim that they are innocent and that their conviction was a horrible mistake. This happens not because prisoners would be sorry for their past deeds, but because that which is more in the prisoner than he himself, that which makes him a convict – the crime – has to remain hidden, unspoken, in order for the prisoner to form his new symbolic identity.

The identity of the prisoner is thus primarily linked to an unspeakable crime, the real. However, it also relates to the perception of the unattainable 'freedom' outside the bars. But when this 'freedom' is attained, for many prisoners this causes total collapse, the loss of all they had: their identity breaks down when they come out of prison. In King's story, the prototype of such an broken prisoner is the old librarian Brooks, who commits suicide when in his old age the authorities release him from prison:

> He was crying when he left. Shawshank was his world. What lay beyond its walls was as terrible to Brooks as the Western Seas had been to superstitious fifteenth-century sailors. In prison, Brooksie had been a person of some importance. He was the librarian, an educated man. If he went to the Kittery library and asked for a job, they wouldn't even give him a library card.[4]

How does one become such an 'institutionalized man'? As Red contemplates: 'At first you can't stand those four walls, then you get so you can abide them, then you get so you accept them...and then, as your body and your mind and your spirit adjust to life on an HO scale, you get to love them.'[5]

However, what is the difference between Andy and other prisoners? Andy, although the only really innocent prisoner, takes seriously the prison rituals. On the surface he submits to the rules, but meanwhile he starts undermining the institution of the prison from the inside. (Andy does not 'undermine' only the wall in his prison cell, but also the illegal financial businesses of the prison authorities.) By following the rituals and accepting prison as a necessary evil, Andy nonetheless does not organize his identity around prison. He decides upon a goal, the object of his desire – opening a hotel in Mexico – around which he then organizes his life by slowly plotting his escape. It is this object of desire – in Andy's terms named 'hope' – which gives him a special freedom.[6] The other prisoners, in contrast, do not take the rituals seriously, they constantly complain about them and try in every way to escape the prison coercion. But paradoxically, the institution holds onto them precisely at that point when they think that it will lose control over them forever, the moment of their release from prison. While Andy submits to the rituals on the outside but not in his inner self, with the other prisoners it is the other way around: they rebel against the constraints of the prison, but from the inside the institution has a hold on them. And when the external coercion, against which they rebelled so much, ceases to exist, the prisoners' world collapses. As old Red recognizes, once outside of prison, he cannot even go to the toilet, since for so many years he was used to going there by order.

Andy, therefore, has the object of desire that gives him some kind of inner 'freedom' and prevents him from collapsing under the pressure of prison rituals. During the long years when Andy was digging his escape tunnel, he was not sure that he might really succeed, but by slowly progressing with his work on the hole, he organized a ritual which kept his desire in motion. The turning point for him came when he realized that the hole could actually lead to freedom: 'All at once he must have realized that, instead of just playing a game, he was playing for high stakes...in terms of his own life, and his own future, the highest....All of a sudden, instead of just being a toy, that stupid hole in the wall became his master...'[7] But Andy does not collapse at this point, he does not 'lose his head': the object of his desire does not 'swallow' him when it becomes attainable. On the contrary, since Andy obeys the ritual and his object of desire is subordinated to the symbolic order he retains his 'normality'. Once on the outside, he also organizes his ritual when he starts building a hotel and finds a new goal. Andy's freedom is thus always subordinated to some ritual, to some discipline, while for the other prisoners, freedom as such is their object of desire: what they desire is to come out, and attaining this goal will supposedly change everything for the best. However, when they obtain freedom, it destroys them, since the structure ceased to exist that kept their object of desire – freedom – at bay, that is, subordinated to the ritual of prison.

In King's story, what keeps Red alive is identification with Andy as his ego ideal. Through this identification, Red organizes for himself another ritual the search for the secret object of Andy's desire, that keeps Red's own desire in motion. The fact that desire is always desire of the Other means that desire has to be subordinated to the symbolic order, while still remaining the strive for something else, something that the symbolic order cannot encompass. Thus Red can say that: 'Andy was the part of me they could never lock up, the part of me that will rejoice when the gates finally open for me...'[8] But the identification with Andy also enabled Red to find another institution when the prison one ceased to exist.

There is a connection between this story and the experience of socialism. In socialism the 'Andys' were those people who were not traumatized because of their confinement within totalitarianism, but were slowly undermining the regime itself. Their identification with the regime was on the surface, but it did not touch their inner being. For these people, their world did not collapse when the system disintegrated and they lost the security of the oppressive institution. In contrast, the before-mentioned nostalgic people were the real 'institutional-ized men', who constantly criticized the institutions, but whose identity fully relied on them. Now, where do these two types of people differ? The answer is twofold: first in their 'crime' and second in their perception of the institution. Under socialism, everyone was in the eyes of the Party potentially guilty of some crime (disbelieving in the regime, petty stealing at the workplace, bribery and so on). But this was not the guilt that really traumatized the people; another more horrible guilt was linked to the fact that most of the people in some way or another collaborated with the regime (they denounced their colleagues in order to save their own skins, they did not oppose injustices when they should have, they were simply quiet).[9] And it was the guilt for this 'crime' that essentially determined their identification with the system. Even if people officially did not identify with the regime, they nonetheless formed their identities around the trauma of their guilt. As a result, they passively criticized the system without ever endangering its foundations. In contrast, the 'socialist Andys' were those dissidents who did not get trapped into this circle of guilt. They also did not believe that 'freedom' exists without the institution, the happy outside. Their undermining of the socialist regime did not try to achieve the ultimate freedom; instead, it aimed to produce a different kind of institution, possibly a more democratic one.

The nostalgia of memory

The subject, therefore, in order to escape the traumatic kernel in his or her inner being, endlessly searches for some point of identification with the symbolic order which would give him or her a place in the social structure which means a promise of an identity. When this attempt fails, what remains is the memory of some 'happy before' when everything was 'different.' What is the logic of this memory?

Freud with his famous concept of 'screen memories' (*Deckerinnerung*) showed how the subject usually has some quite irrelevant memory that is produced to cover up something that the subject does not want to remember. Thus, what is important remains suppressed and what is insignificant becomes retained in the subject's memory. For Freud:

> What is recorded in the memory is not the relevant experience itself – in this respect the resistance gets its way; what is recorded is another psychical element closely associated with the objectionable one – and in this respect the first principle shows its strength, the principle which endeavours to fix important impressions by establishing reproducible memory pictures. The result of the conflict is therefore that, instead of the memory which would have been justified by the original event, another memory is produced which has been by some degree associatively displaced from the former one.[10]

The subject produces this displaced memory in order to avoid the trauma of another memory, so that the story that the subject is telling to him or herself is not shattered in its coherence.

In a social context, such displacement of cultural memory goes on continuously. In Slovenia, the latest example is the Christian Democrats' attempt to extend maternity leave to up to three years, which they claim is necessary to increase the very low birth rate, solve unemployment and, above all, fulfill the psychological right of children to have a parent taking care of them during the first crucial years. In their attempt to convince the public, the Christian Democrats have invoked the image of the happy family life in the past, when people lived in rural communities in households of the extended family, where children had love and attention from their parents and where mothers who did no work could devote themselves fully to each child's upbringing. Of course, this happy family never existed. The memory that is repressed is the memory of parental indifference or even violence that actually characterized premodern family life. In the past, children in the rural areas were mostly perceived as a much needed workforce and were treated very poorly: as babies their arms and legs were wrapped up so that they could not move, they would get alcohol to calm their crying, they would eat with servants, and so on. Paradoxically, this violence tends to be completely forgotten in the rightist's nostalgia for the past.

For Lacan, memory primarily has to do with non-remembering the trauma, the real around which the subject centres his or her very being. When we tell our stories, it is the point at which we touch the real that our words fail, but fail so as to always come back to the trauma without being able to articulate it. As Lacan says:

> The subject in himself, the recalling of his biography, all this goes only to a certain limit, which is known as the real....An adequate thought, *qua* thought, at the level at which we are, always avoids – if only to find itself again later in everything – the same thing. Here the real is that which always comes back to the same place – to the place where the subject in so far as he thinks, where the *res cogitans*, does not meet it.[11]

Thus one can imagine that prisoners who do not talk about their crime and insist on their innocence occasionally bury their memory of crime: in their thoughts they would try to endlessly avoid encountering the trauma, only to find it constantly returning in the unconscious.

The subject, therefore, forms memory in order to get certainty, to fashion a story that would grant the subject a perception of wholeness, of his or her identity. But it can also be said that one remembers so that the social symbolic structure stays fully in its place. Freud's early hysterical patients were very convincing in their remembering, but as Lacan points out: 'What is at issue in this remembering could not be known at the outset – one did not know that the desire of the hysteric was the desire of the father, to be sustained in its status. It was hardly surprising that, for the benefit of him who takes the place of the father, one remembered things right down to the dregs.'[12] The main dilemma of the hysteric is, what does she represent for the big Other, what kind of an object is she for the big Other? By getting this answer, the hysteric tries to overcome the constitutive lack that bars her as a subject. This search for the 'father figure' is for the hysteric a way to find confirmation of her own identity. This search also includes a demand for the 'father figure' not to be barred. But the impossibility of this demand forces the hysteric to endlessly search for new authority, new 'father figures'.

However, the paradox of the hysteric is that the authority she searches for is also the authority that she herself wants to control. Such an attitude could be exemplified by an ex-student of mine who engaged in long debates during my lectures, but at the end of the class she said: 'Why do you allow me to talk so much in the class? You should stop me and go on with your lecture, since I prefer to listen to you and not to myself.' I can imagine that if I had imposed my authority on her and prevented her discussions, she might have reported me to the department chair, while also saying to him: 'What kind of an authority are you when you take your time and patiently listen to such a stupid complaint as mine?'

For the subject, the very process of remembering is, therefore, an attempt to get and keep the big Other firmly in its place, to secure the existence of the symbolic order so that the subject will achieve some certainty about his or her identity. Nostalgic remembrance of socialism could similarly be understood as an attempt of those living in post-socialist chaos to find some stability, a symbolic order that would grant them their identities. But in this remembrance, we encounter also a problem of how one should deal with the relics of the past: How should the new regime 'erase' the historic memory of the old regime which is materialized, for example, in communist monuments, architecture and so on.?

Here, we have to distinguish between two perceptions of the problem, that of the East Europeans themselves and that of the Western media. After the fall of the communist regimes, when the East Europeans started removing the communist monuments, some Western intellectuals openly criticized this action, since in their perception destroying the monuments was equivalent to erasing memory. Such a thesis is presented a documentary film *Disgraced Monuments* (1992) by Mark Lewis and Laura Mulvey, which deals with the removal of the communist monuments in Russia. The film compares the way the post-socialists have been demolishing the communist statues with the way the Bolsheviks tore down the monuments of the Tsar regime. In both cases the pedestal usually remained; only the statue of the hero on top was changed. This comparison of the two regimes implies that the current and former rulers do not differ in how they deal with historical memory and how raving destruction of the old monuments does not enable society to discontinue its connection with the past revolutionary ideology.

A simple answer to such a critique is that no regime comes into power after a more or less violent upheaval without tearing down the pictures and statues of the previous rulers, especially if these rulers are perceived as totalitarian dictators. In a country where the transfer of power occurs democratically, one can easily add to the statue of the previous president the statue of the new one. But in an authoritarian regime, or in a country where a new hopefully democratic regime replaced a previously totalitarian one, one should not expect this to happen. If we take the case of post-Hitler Germany, one does not expect to see the Fuhrer's pictures in public places, although they are part of the German historic memory.

The gaze of those Westerners who regard the postsocialist removal of the monuments as a barbaric blow against one's history is not a gaze from a neutral position. Here again one encounters the perception that East Europeans are so 'different' from Westerners, which means that they are not able to deal with their history in a 'civilized' way. On the one hand, it is easy to agree that demolition of monuments is an inadequate way for the public to deal with its frustrations and that the symbolic remnants of the previous regime cannot be easily swept under the carpet, but on the other hand, one cannot expect that simple preservation of the monuments would help the new regime to work through the trauma of the previous one.

An interesting idea about how to 'save' such monuments was presented by the Russian-American artists Komar and Melamid. In their view, the communist monuments should today be assigned some new 'useful' role. Thus, they made candlesticks from busts of Lenin, in order to realize Lenin's desire to enlighten the people; busts of Marx were turned up side down, since this is what he himself had done with Hegel's philosophy; and the monumental statues of euphoric revolutionaries are pushed a little over the edge of the pedestal so that their forward-marching feet hang in mid-air, which symbolizes how actual realization of the communist project itself remained up in the air. Komar and Melamid, therefore, took seriously the communist project and used its art to deal a little less seriously with the deadlocks of the historical memory.

Under socialism, some monuments arose that cannot simply be removed or 'redecorated' in the Komar–Melamid way: these are the grandiose buildings of socialist architecture. And the most astounding of such monuments is Ceausescu's 'House of the Republic', lately renamed as the 'People's House'.

The state as a work of art

In the late 1970s, Ceausescu began his project of rebuilding the centre of Bucharest so that architectural reality would properly reflect the greatness of Romanian communism. Bucharest, which used to be called the 'Little Paris' of the Balkans, suddenly became a big building site. Ceausescu demanded demolition of almost a quarter of the old town centre with its picturesque streets, old churches, monasteries, hospitals, schools and so on.[13] In its place a new socialist administrative centre began to appear, comprised of a grandiose palace and a broad avenue with neo-baroque fountains surrounded by neoclassic apartment blocks. The construction went forward very quickly: tens of thousands of labourers and hundreds of architects and engineers worked day and night on the project. This rebuilding, of course, demanded enormous financial sacrifice and significantly increased the economic hardship of the Romanian people. At the time of the collapse of Ceausescu's regime, the project has reached its final stage. The question became, what should be done with this massive architectural venture? As political debates over the project became heated, the main dispute centered on the fate of the palace. Some people insisted that the palace had to be demolished; others proposed that it become a museum of communist terror; still others suggested that it be transformed into a casino. The new regime decided to complete the project and to establish the palace as the site of the new parliament and as an international congress centre. The palace, however, remains one of the most traumatic remnants of the communist regime. It has a sublime quality; it is beautiful and horrible at the same time, provoking both admiration and disgust. However, before analyzing today's perception of the palace, let us try to explain what led Ceausescu into its creation.

It is common knowledge that Ceausescu, who used to enjoy the real support of the people, in the last years of his rule fell into some kind of a psychotic delirium, into an obsession with his own grandiosity. He became a megalomaniac: a king who

Figure 7.1 The People's House, Bucharest, elevation from the Avenue of Unity

believes that he is a king. His architectural project tried to materialize this megalomania. One explanation for Ceausescu's obsession with changing the architecture of Bucharest is that once, when traveling abroad, he came to realize that he liked neither traditional Western architectural style nor socialist architecture. He found something close to his ideal in North Korea, where his friend Kim Il Sung began constructing a new political and architectural centre in Phenian. Romanians and Koreans soon started competing to see who would build the more prestigious and grandiose city.[14] But the main difference between Romanian and Korean administrative centres is that the latter was constructed on empty ground, while Romanians had to sacrifice a large part of the old Bucharest.[15] What was the purpose of this sacrifice? Why was it necessary to demolish old historical buildings, churches, hospitals and schools?

The purpose of this demolition certainly was not only to find a space for Ceausescu's architectural exercises. Had Ceausescu simply wanted to find a place for his 'artistic' creations, he could have easily chosen some vacant land outside of the city as the site of his dream town. The demolition should be understood as the essential part of his project. It could even be said that the destruction of buildings, the erasure of the historical memory was more important than the construction of the new centre. The 'wound' Ceausescu made in the 'living flesh of the city', as Romanians tend to characterize the project, has a special symbolic meaning.[16]

Ceausescu's undertaking should be understood as a *creatio ex nihilo*, an attempt to make something out of nothing which would totally eradicate the previous symbolic order which had been realized not only in the previous political system but also in its material remnants, its architecture. Lacan has linked this *creatio ex nihilo* with the destructive nature of the death drive. The latter is for Lacan 'a creationist sublimation, and it is linked to that structural element which implies that, as soon as we have to deal with anything in the world appearing in the form of the signifying chain, there is somewhere – though certainly outside the natural world – which is the beyond of that chain, the *ex nihilo* on which it is founded and is articulated as such.'[17] The death drive is, therefore, a drive of destruction that undermines the social symbolic space; however, linked to it is a will for a new start, a start from the point of nothing. Lacan also points out that the death drive 'is to be situated in the historical domain; it is articulated at a level that can only be defined as a function of the signifying chain.'[18] History is to be understood here as something we remember, i.e. as something that is registered in the signifying chain and exists only through this chain. Here, one has to take into account the distinction Lacan makes between memory and remembering (*rememoration*). Only the latter 'pertains to the order of history', thus, for Lacan: 'One mustn't confuse the *history*, in which the unconscious subject inscribes himself, with his *memory...*'[19] History is of the order of the symbolic, while memory touches the real, the trauma that resists the symbolization.

In Ceausescu's case it could be said that his intention was to erase history, but in this effort he produced the trauma which now invokes the memory of the lost past. Thus people today recall the 'happy' past, the social security of socialism, in order to escape the memory of the trauma. This trauma includes not only Ceausescu's violence and destruction; the trauma also touches on the passivity which allowed this annihilation to happen. Here again we encounter the 'crime' of people being too afraid to oppose the regime and the unconscious feeling of guilt that accompanies this non-action.

Ceausescu's creationism tried to undo the old signifying chain in order to establish a totally new symbolic organization. By razing the historical monuments, Ceausescu aimed to wipe out Romanian national identity, the fantasy structure of the nation that is forged around the historical old buildings, churches, and then to establish his own version of this identity.

Ceausescu's architectural madness comes out most clearly in the way his urban project dealt with the river crossing the city. For Ceausescu, the river functioned as a psychotic object that had to be totally controlled, regulated, divided into a good and a bad part. Thus he decided to double the riverbed: the river was divided into two levels, the lower level being the channel for the dirty water, and the upper level the channel for 'proper' clean river. The river also intruded into Ceausescu's urban planning, since it crossed the main avenue that leads to the palace. To avoid this intrusion, construction workers covered over a portion of the river. Hence, where one would expect some bridge, the river is simply erased, covered by concrete which is enhanced with a green and ornamented by a fountain.[20]

In general, Ceausescu's architectural project constructed an ideal beautiful art work by combining elements from various architectural styles.[21] Something similar was recently undertaken by the above-mentioned artists Komar and

Melamid, who designed and conducted a survey to find out which motives and which colours people perceived as the most 'artistic' and which ones they perceived as ugly. Then, based on their findings the artists created two pictures: the first incorporates those elements chosen as the most beautiful and the second is a mixture of those elements chosen as the most unappealing. The ideally supposedly beautiful picture is in blue and green and presents a romantic landscape with trees, animals, clouds, sun and so on. The supposedly ugly picture consists of modernist triangles in black and red. The picture which is supposed to unite the most beautiful elements looks like a kitschy postcard, while the ugly picture looks like simple abstract art. For both pictures, it is essential that their 'ideality', the way they try to perfectly embody 'beauty' and 'ugliness' without a leftover, annihilates their intended aesthetic effect and produces a feeling of horror. The same goes for Ceausescu's architecture. The blocks around the great boulevard are designed in an eclectic way, combining all kinds of architectural styles. At first they look like replicas of the same kind of neoclassical houses that one finds in most of European cities; but their ornamentation (balconies, arcades, arches, etc.) combine neo-gothic, neo-baroque, modernist and old Romanian architectural elements, which together create some kind of a postmodern effect. If the traditional socialist apartment block represents all that is ugly in architecture, Ceausescu's buildings try to embody all that is supposedly beautiful. However, it is precisely the excessiveness of the 'beauty' that causes this architecture to look kitschy.[22]

Figure 7.2 The People's House, Bucharest, detail of side elevation

Figure 7.3 The People's House, Bucharest, detail of interior

How does the present Romanian regime perceive the palace? In a brochure written for visitors, the palace is first described as 'a "giant" built during the "golden age" of the dictatorial regime and born in the mind of a man for whom the nation of 'reasonable sizes' did not exist'.[23] The palace is presented as the second largest building in the world (after the Pentagon), but the most prominent because it is the most disputed one. This controversy almost resulted in its annihilation, but: 'Realizing its enormous values, in fact a Romanian inheritance in danger of being destroyed and robbed, people began to look at the building with less hostility and named it the "People's House".' The rest of the text reads as Ceausescu's promotion material, with its descriptions of the glory of the palace and what the people sacrificed for its completion. Thus, we are reminded that this is:

> not a palace from Aladdin's stories, but a real one, showing the true wealth of Romania: stone, marble and wood from the Romanian mountains and forests....Today, the monumental building stands for the most precious symbol of democracy in Romania, that is the Parliament, serving the high and noble aim we have all aspired for: equal and complete representation of the Romanian people.

By presenting the palace as a national symbol, the current political elite has specifically incorporated this traumatic palace into its political discourse. The symbolic power of the building, supposedly made only from Romanian materials, is straitened by the fact that it was produced through enormous hardship of Romanian people. However, it is essential to appreciate how the palace has become an actual realization of Ceausescu's original intention. As a parliament, the People's House is made to stand for the 'complete representation of the Romanian people'. This all-encompassing construction could be understood as a final stage of Ceausescu's vision, which has try to give form to an ideal total society. Thus, when today's regime claims for itself that it completely represents the people, Ceausescu's dream of totality is, in some way, realized. However, Ceausescu is not the only megalomaniac who tried to change reality to fit his ideal. Surprisingly, many past and present architects tried to do the same, but were limited in their endeavour by the lack of power and resources. Even in the most admired American contemporary architectural inventions – the shopping malls and Disneyland – one can find points of comparison with Ceausescu's project.

The mall of Romania

In today's world, we are witnessing the slow disappearance of the city, since the machinery of cyberspace has erased the cement of the traditional urban planning thus creating a new kind of city, 'a city without a place attached to it'.[24] However, there is yet another significant change in contemporary architecture: the construction of *a place without the city*. The prototypes of this construction are shopping malls and Disneyland. My claim is that Ceausescu's project tried to realize the same utopia of building a place without the city and that such a vision is not far from what malls or Disneyland represent in America. Let us first point out the similarities between the idea of the mall and Ceausescu's project.

For both projects, it is essential that they erase the symbolic dimension of the city. Ceausescu tried to do so by flattening the old part of Bucharest and by demolishing old villages. In a more subtle way, the malls are doing the same: they are destroying the social fabric of suburban towns by causing the collapse of small shops and by offering new supposedly public spaces in their stead.[25] For the mall developers, it is essential that, on one hand, the mall appears as the new public space in American suburbia, but on the other hand, this place is legally defined as a private one, which limits the rights of visitors to engage in activities that do not meet with the approval of the mall's management. In the mall people are not allowed to hold demonstrations, distribute leaflets, sign petitions and so on without the permission of the owners. The freedom of speech is, therefore, limited in the mall.

What Ceausescu's project and the mall also have in common is surveillance. American malls are the Panopticons of the twentieth century: hidden cameras control every corner of the mall, numerous guards observe the movements of the people, and the architecture itself (the way the mall is structured, how the entrances are placed, etc.) helps to make surveillance possible. In comparison to the mall, Ceausescu's Panopticon adopts a more traditional surveillance strategy. From the palace, which sits on an artificial hill (under which lie three floors of hidden tunnels), one has a view over a large part of city. It is significant that the palace, observed from the avenue, appears to have no entrance; there are only numerous windows, which give the impression of an all-present gaze. The palace thus functions like the surveillance tower in Bentham's Panopticon where the observer remains hidden but his all-penetrating gaze is nonetheless always present.

What is the logic of this kind of surveillance? In the Panopticon, to create the impression of the inspector's omnipresence, it is essential that he remain invisible, hidden in the tower, so that the prisoners never know when they are actually being observed. To obtain this effect, it is not necessary for the inspector to be actually present; it is enough that the prisoners presume his existence. For the inspector, it is only necessary to occasionally expose some prisoner and to reveal him the facts which show that he had been closely monitored; then the fear of being unknowingly observed will spread among the other inmates.[26]

Surveillance under communism functioned in a similar way. Hence for the regime to create the impression of omnipresence, it was not necessary to control each individual, it was enough to strike only occasionally randomly controlling a small number of people in order to inspire fear among the population as a whole. On a parallel, cameras in the malls or theft protection devices in the shops, also do not need to be on all the time; it is enough to use them occasionally and to publicly expose suspected thieves in order to create the impression of total surveillance.

Although Ceausescu's project appears to be functionally very different from the mall, its economic purpose is actually the same. Both the mall and Ceausescu's project combine commercial and administrative spaces. American malls nowadays are no longer purely places to shop, but closed 'cities' with offices, hotels, cinemas, entertainment centres and so on.[27] Lacking the entertainment part, Ceausescu's project nonetheless looks like an open mall; at the main crossroad of Avenue Uniri, one finds the largest department store in Bucharest, while the whole avenue is lined with the small boutiques of world famous designers, antique and jewellery shops, souvenir shops and so on. Plaza Uniri thus offers something for every one: cheap department store goods for the lower classes, souvenirs for the tourists and elegant clothing for the *nouveau riche*.[28]

Of course, one cannot claim that Ceausescu's original idea was to build a socialist version of the shopping mall. However, both projects have the same goal of trying to realize some utopia. Already, decades ago, the American writer Bradford Peck, who was also the owner of a department store, developed in his novel *The World a Department Store* an ideal social vision in which the state would resemble a department store that dutifully supplies its obedient citizens with all the goods they need, from food to housing. Other well-known American utopias imagine a new world where the production process will be reorganized so that people will no longer need to work but will instead simply indulge in their consumerist desires.[29] Such an American utopia is, of course, not so different from the communist one.

The ideology of the American shopping malls is nicely supplemented with its other great consumerist-entertainment invention, Disneyland. As Margaret Crawford says: 'While enclosed shopping malls suspended space, time and weather, Disneyland went one step further and suspended reality. Any geographic, cultural or mythic location…could be reconfigured as a setting for entertainment.'[30] In Disneyland, national pavilions became 'stand-ins for the act of travel itself, ersatz souvenirs. A trip to Disneyland substitutes for a trip to Norway or Japan.'[31] But significantly, Disneyland does not try to reproduce reality the same way as, for example, wax museums try to do: Disneyland 'presents its reconstructions as masterpieces of falsification.'[32] Disneyland, therefore, produces a 'reality' that is admittedly a fantasy. As Umberto Eco points out: 'Disneyland not only produces illusion, but – in confessing it – stimulates desire for it: A real crocodile can be found in the zoo…but Disneyland tells us that faked nature corresponds much more to our daydream demands.'[33] Hence, technology is perceived as something that can produce more reality than nature itself.

What is repressed in this acknowledging of the fantasy is the reality of the capital: Disneyland can easily admit to being a fake, but can never openly acknowledge that all its fantasy houses lead to another shopping experience. But to gain the freedom to shop, the visitors freely submit themselves to the constraints of the place: the surveillance of the guards, long waiting lines, impersonal voices over the loudspeakers telling them what and what not to do, etc. The Romanian Securitate would have been thrilled to have had such power over people. But my idea here is not to make a Foucauldian analysis of surveillance in contemporary society, pointing out how no significant differences exist between socialism and Western democracies. My concern is rather to ask what is the logic of the fantasies produced in architectural settings like Ceausescu's project or Disneyland, and for whom are these fantasies staged.

The similarity between Disneyland and Ceausescu's project concerns primarily their designers' perception of reality and fantasy. Ceausescu had incorporated into his fantasy construction all the 'best' architectural forms from Athens to Paris and Rome. Here again the fiction is more real than the reality itself. No longer does one need to go to Paris or Rome to admire the real stuff, when Bucharest offers the best replicas of all these places. Now there is one crucial feature specific only to Ceausescu's project: for his fantasy project to attain the status of reality, the original, the 'real' reality has to be destroyed or at least prohibited. Ceausescu, of course, could not annihilate the boulevards of Paris, but he could forbid his people to visit them. While Disneyland convinces you in a 'democratic' way that there is no point to going to see the original, since the faked thing is much more enjoyable, Ceausescu has to prohibit the original.

This is also obvious from the way his second architectural project was conducted, the construction a new type of socialist village. In the last decade of his rule, Ceausescu decided to transform the countryside, ruin the old villages and build model socialist rural centres. With his program of so-called systematization, Ceausescu wanted to realize the ideal of a harmonious distribution of productive forces all over Romania. To achieve this goal, villages were supposed to be 'transformed into industrial *agricultural or agro-industrial* towns…becoming polyfunctional communities with all the economic, socio-demographic, urban and cultural features of socialist civilization.'[34] This project caused enormous suffering for those people who were displaced from their old homes and forced to live in the new soulless 'villages', which were composed of poorly constructed apartment blocks, sometimes without running water.

Today Bucharest has a "Ceausescu-land' – officially called the Museum of Romanian Villages – where at the outskirts of Bucharest one finds a compound of actual remnants of the old Romanian rural village houses and, of course, souvenir shops. If in Disneyland, one no longer needs to go to Japan because the pavilion of ersatz 'Japan' replaces the real thing, in 'Ceausescu-land' one can enjoy old villages only when the real thing has been destroyed.

For whom is such an architectural fantasy like Ceausescu's project or Disneyland staged? The answer is for the big Other, or better, for that point in the social symbolic structure known as the Ego Ideal, with which the subject identifies and from where the subject sees itself in the way it wants to be seen. To understand this notion, let us take another architectural example. In the early twenties, it was Le Corbusier who wanted to built an ideal city. His idea was to tear down part of Paris and build a new centre composed of skyscrapers with skywalks and gardens underneath. This new city would provide the environment that Le Corbusier saw as 'inherent in an advanced industrial society'.[35] For Le Corbusier, his project was thus a fulfilment of the demands coming from some greater order, the principles of industrial society. These principles were for Le Corbusier the big Other for whom his fantasy was staged; or, more precisely, Le Corbusier had posited this principle in the place of his Ego Ideal from where he then observed himself in the way he wanted to be seen, as a dutiful creator who would make reality accord with the ideal. Similarly, for Disney the big Other was the world of technology realized most perfectly in the movies. Disney's 'cartoon utopia'[36] was just the first stage in reproducing the perfect world of technology, since Disney intended to build an actual city which would represent the proper urbanism of the electronic age. Only the author's death prevented him from realizing this dream. But Ceausescu succeeded in realizing his. For him, the big Other was the ideal communist society. Ceausescu simply perceived himself as the executor of this higher will: it was the ideal of the future classless society that demanded changes in urbanism. Ceausescu identified with the point in the social symbolic structure from where he then saw himself as the creator who would refashion reality so that it corresponded to the ideal.

The difference between the two projects concerns the contrast between socialism and capitalism. Under socialism a belief in reality still existed; that is why Ceausescu had to actually tear down the city. Under capitalism, however, one does not need to destroy an existing reality in order to achieve a desired goal; builders of new shopping malls have no need to demolish the old village's shops, since these businesses will sooner or later close down on their own. Capitalism can thus build new fantasy places and the virtual reality of the capital will cause all the destruction necessary to increase profits.

Under socialism, ordinary people, like prisoners serving life terms, believed that pure freedom can exist without the big Other. But when the big Other of communist ideology collapsed, such people either started to search in vain for new ideologies and new institutions that would grant them stability, or they brought back memories of the 'happy' past. In the end, those people with nostalgic need for the big Other are not so different from their fallen leader. Both organized their identities in regard to the communist ideal. The difference is only that Ceausescu believed in the big Other's existence and presented himself as a tool in its hands, while the people did not believe in the big Other even though their entire identity was wrapped up in it. The paradox of the big Other is that it does not exist, but it nonetheless functions. The tragic aspect of the Romanian story is that Ceausescu did not realize that the big Other is just a symbolic fiction, while at the same time, the people did not recognize that this fiction has more power over them than they ever imagined.

Notes

1 New political elites play hard on this nostalgia by creating populist ideologies which promise to re-establish the security of the good old days without communist totalitarianism. For example, General Alexandr I. Lebed, a rising star in Russian politics and a nationalist, appeals to the disenchanted masses by promising them the end of corruption and the establishment of order, claiming that 'life under the new democratic regime is far worse than in Soviet times. "There was stability", he [Lebed] said.

"A 120-rouble pension was enough for a more or less decent life. You could study for free. You could get free medical assistance, not the best but decent. You could get a cheap holiday. Eighty percent of the population relied on these natural privileges" ' (*The New York Times*, 13 October 1995).

2   The paradox is that these people usually do not come from the ranks of the previous Party establishment (since the majority of the latter quickly became new capitalists), but from the working classes. These ordinary people were in the past usually privately critical of the regime and made jokes about it, but publicly they meekly obeyed the communist rituals.

3   Stephen King, 'Rita Hayworth and Shawshank Redemption', in *Different Seasons*, New York, Penguin, 1982, p. 105.

4   King, p. 49.

5   King, p. 97.

6   Red detects this 'freedom' when Andy tells him about his plan of establishing a hotel and encourages him to join him in business: ' "You think it over", he [Andy] said casually....And he strolled off, as if he were a free man who had just made another free man a proposition. And for a while just that was enough to make me *feel* free. Andy could do that. He could make me forget for a time that we were both lifers, at the mercy of a hard-ass parole board...' King, p. 79.

7   King, p. 96.

8   King, p. 99.

9   This feeling of guilt is further elaborated in Chapter 3 of my *The Spoils of Freedom: Psychoanalysis and Feminism After the Fall of Socialism*, London: Routledge, 1994.

10   Sigmund Freud, 'Screen Memories', SE III, p. 307.

11   Jacques Lacan, *The Four Fundamental Concepts of Psycho-Analysis*, trans. by A. Sheridan, Harmondsworth: Penguin Books, 1979, p. 49.

12   Lacan, p. 50, translation modified.

13   Among demolished buildings were twenty-six churches and two monasteries, while 40,000 inhabitants were displaced from their old homes.

14   During his many friendly visits to North Korea, Ceausescu and his architects quickly copied some of the Korean's architectural inventions and then realized them in Bucharest, making them even more splashy. Gheorghe Leahu, *Bucurestiul disparut*, Bucharest, Editura Arta Grafica, 1995, s. 119; see also Pierre v. Meiss, 'Fragmentiertes Bucharest', *Werk, Bauen+Wohnen* 3 (1993) and Catherine Durandin in Despina Tomescu, *La Roumanie de Ceausescu*, Paris: Editions Guy Epaud, 1988.

15   The earthquake that struck Bucharest in 1977 greatly 'helped' Ceausescu, since some of the buildings were thus destroyed. A rumour also holds that Ceausescu was so afraid of death that he ordered studies showing which part of the city was less likely to be struck by a future earthquake and then decided to build his palace at this place.

16   People today perceive the Palace in a paradoxical way, since the disgust is mixed with secret admiration. Along with the new ruling elite, the most victimized people – the Gypsies – are also enchanted by the 'beauty' of the Palace. Rich Gypsies, for example, require the architects who design their houses to use some architectural elements from the Palace. The Gypsies never identified with Ceausescu in the past, since they were treated in the most racist way by his regime. Their admiration for his architecture, therefore, reveals a strange identification with their persecutor.

17   Jacques Lacan, *The Ethics of Psychoanalysis*, London: Routledge, 1992, p. 212.

18   Lacan, p. 211.

19   Jacques Lacan, Seminar 2, p. 185.

20   Ceausescu was obviously interested in regulating water, since in the early 1980s he also built a Danube–Black Sea Canal, again spending enormous sums of money. But when the Canal was open, 'the volume of shipping traffic passing along it was only 10 per cent of that previously predicted. Domestic traffic even had to be re-routed to

make the waterway appear busy.' Martyn Rady, *Romania in Turmoil: A Contemporary History*, London: IB Tauris, 1992, p. 66.

21 At the end of the nineteenth century, American architects similarly promoted the so-called 'city beautiful' project, which tried to modify the chaos of American city planning by designing boulevards and plazas which are replicas of European architectural styles.

22 The palace is also made out of a mixture of architectural styles. It thus looks like a combination of a castle and Moscow's Lomonosov University. Added to this design are Greek columns and Roman arches. But the real excess is the inner decoration: the marble, wooden embroideries, kitschy neo-baroque furniture and carpets. Significantly, the most luxurious room which was constructed for the meetings of the Party's Central Committee, is now called the 'The Human Rights Room'.

23 The leaflet for visitors of the palace, entitled 'International Conference Centre', Bucharest: Artmedia Group.

24 Michael Sorkin (ed.), *Variations on the Theme Park: The New American City and the End of Public Space*, New York: Hill and Wang, 1992, p. 12.

25 One finds another type of the reversal between private and public in Orange County, where homes are 'technically "privately owned", because their ownership is in the hands of individuals, not corporations, freedoms traditionally associated with private ownership no longer exist. One finds, for example, restrictive rules binding home owners *vis-à-vis* such matters as the species of shrubberies which can be planted in the yard, the types of dogs they can own, as well as the…colour restrictions on house exteriors.…The rules constraining home owners in Irvine read much like those which occupants of military housing must sign before moving in, and for good reason.' Dean MacCannell, *Empty Meeting Grounds: The Tourist Papers*, Routledge: New York, 1992, pp. 82, 83.

26 Bentham's Inspector has the attributes of a God-like being, a being whose power comes from a fictional presupposition of its existence. Here the fiction of the God has more power that any real God could have, since the omnipresence of God relies precisely on his ability to observe us without ever being observed himself. Lacan pointed out that people love God precisely for the fact that he does not exist. This notion has to be read together with Lacan's claim that love aims at the lack in the other, thus we love in a person what is more than he or she in him or herself – the point of impossibility in the other. In regard to God this lack in the other concerns the very nonexistence of God, the fact that he is a non-entity.

27 The similarity between the mall and Plaza Uniri is also in the decoration of the place. It is significant how both in the mall and in Ceausescu's project one finds lots of fountains, flower gardens with benches, etc.

28 Paradoxically, the 'realization' of Ceausescu's project is today a new mall that was built at the outskirts of Bucharest, where one can find the best hotel in Bucharest, a congress centre, World Trade Centre and a mall of luxurious shops. Today this hermetically closed place is the upperclass haven for the Romanians, but with its tight security and luxurious goods, it also presents the ideal of a post-Ceausescu era.

29 Edward Bellamy, *Looking Backward*, New York: Penguin Books, 1960. See also Margaret Crawford, 'The World in a Shopping Mall', in Sorkin (ed.), *Variations on the Theme Park*, p. 19.

30 Crawford, p. 16.

31 Michael Sorkin, 'See You in Disneyland', in Sorkin (ed.), *Variations on the Theme Park*, p. 216.

32 Umberto Eco, *Travels in Hyperreality*, New York: Harcourt Brace & Co., 1990, p. 43.

33 Eco, p. 44.

34 Ion Iordachel, 'Dynamic of Social Structure in the Present Stage of Development in Romania,' in John W. Cole (ed.), *Economy, Society and Culture in Contemporary Romania*, Research Report Number 24, Department of Anthropology, University of

Massachusetts, Amherst, 1984, pp. 19, 20. Iordacel explains Ceausescu's program of systematization, saying: 'Through a rigorous, scientific analysis of socio-economic, political, and cultural realities, comrade Nicolae Ceausescu, in a valuable, creative and original synthesis, has shown a deep understanding of the qualitative and quantitative transformations in our country, the dynamic of Romanian society in the future...' when, as Ceausescu predicted, 'our socialist society will reach a superior level of civilization, the material and spiritual level of the people will increase, and the human personality will multilaterally flourish' (Report on achieving the decisions of the XIth Congress of the Romanian Communist Party, 1978.) (Iordachel, p. 16).

35 Robert Fishman, 'Utopia in Three Dimensions', in Peter Alexander and Roger Gill (eds) *Utopias*, La Salle, IL: Open Court Publishing Company, 1984, p. 104.

36 Sorkin, *Variations the Theme Park*, p. 232.

8   Architecture or revolution?[1]

Neil Leach

'Architecture ou Révolution?', wrote Le Corbusier in 1922. 'It is the question of building which lies at the root of the social unrest of today; architecture or revolution.'[2]

Le Corbusier, in common with many architects of the Modern Movement, was convinced of the social role of architecture. In an era of great social and political change, Le Corbusier perceived architecture as a crucial instrument in addressing the ills of contemporary society. An appropriate architecture would combat social unrest. Architecture could prevent revolution.

While Le Corbusier saw architecture as a way of avoiding revolution, the architects of post-revolutionary Russia saw architecture as a way of supporting the aims and ideals of a Marxist revolution. Architectural theorists, such as Alexei Gan and Moisei Ginzburg, looked to architecture for a means of resolving the particular problems of post-revolutionary Marxist society. Buildings should not simply reflect passively changing social conditions; they should be active instruments of change. Thus for Gan and Ginzberg, buildings themselves were to be 'revolutionary', and were to operate as active social condensers.[3]

On the face of it, Le Corbusier's position seems diametrically opposed to that of Gan and Ginzburg. Yet an alternative reading is possible, and it could be argued that Le Corbusier spoke of avoiding political 'revolution' not because he was opposed to the concept of revolution as such, but rather because he recognised in architecture the possibility of a 'revolution' that would go beyond the political. As Fredric Jameson has observed, 'he saw the construction and the constitution of new spaces as the most revolutionary act, and one that could "replace" the narrowly political revolution of the mere seizure of power.'[4] Thus, far from being against revolution, Le Corbusier could be seen as a supporter of reform in its most radical and far-reaching sense. It is clear that both Le Corbusier and the architects of the new Russia recognised in architecture the same potential, the possibility of alleviating social problems and of creating a new and better world. Architecture for the pioneers of the Modern Movement had a role as a democratic force within a democratic society. Architecture was to be a force of liberation, overtly political and emancipatory in its outlook.

At the other end of the twentieth century, in the light of the recent 'revolutions' in Central and Eastern Europe, the relationship between architecture and revolution deserves further consideration. Clearly, this relationship needs to be interrogated beyond the naive utopianism of the Modern Movement, and the term 'revolution' should not be taken lightly, nor treated uncritically. Too easily, such a term may be appropriated to dress up shifts in political power which, far from overturning a previous regime, simply replicate the *status quo* in an alternative formal variant. Too easily also, such a term may be smuggled into empty slogans and adopted by the artistic avant-garde to refer to merely ephemeral changes in fashion.

Architecture and revolution: these terms need to reconsidered and their relationship rethought. What influence can architecture claim to have on the social and the political? What is the status of architecture as a force of social change? What is the link between aesthetics and politics? What relationship may there be between architecture and revolution? Can there be a 'revolutionary' architecture?

Aesthetics and revolution

The argument for a link between aesthetics and revolution has been made most forcefully by Herbert Marcuse. For Marcuse, the revolutionary may exist within the aesthetic. Although he addresses literature, the same situation, he claims, would apply to the visual arts.[5] Marcuse goes beyond traditional Marxist aesthetics which views art as an expression of social relations, to perceive art as a potential critique of social relations. It is precisely the aesthetic form of art which allows it to be autonomous from the given social relations. 'In its autonomy,' Marcuse claims, 'art both protests these relations, and at the same time transcends them. Art therefore subverts the dominant consciousness, the ordinary experience.'[6] From this, he concludes that art can be revolutionary in the stylistic changes that it brings about, which disrupt accepted aesthetic conventions and reflect broader social changes. But beyond the domain of the technical, art can also be revolutionary in a more direct fashion. Art can represent the 'prevailing unfreedom', and can therefore break through 'the mystified (and petrified) social reality'. Thus art can be liberational by opening up 'the horizon of change': 'In this sense, every authentic work of art would be revolutionary, i.e. subversive of perception and understanding, an indictment of the established reality, the appearance of the image of liberation.'[7]

For Marcuse, art was necessarily abstracted from the given social reality by a process of sublimation. The material was thereby reshaped according to the rules of aesthetic form. Art therefore came both to represent reality and to challenge it, by shattering the 'reified objectivity of established social relations'.[8] Art was for Marcuse a re-interpretation of reality transported to the realm of the aesthetic. It is precisely in its aesthetic form that art can function as a critical force in the struggle for liberation, not through some empty notion of pure form, but by virtue of its content having become form.

Marcuse is quite categorical, then, in his support for a revolutionary aesthetics. Yet his position amounts to a deeply utopian one, and can be challenged on several accounts. In contrast to mainstream Marxist aesthetics, art for Marcuse was not proletarian. Marcuse remained deeply suspicious of the mass media which he would see as the 'principal agent of an engineered social consensus that denied real human interests'.[9] In common with Theodor Adorno, he could be accused of promoting an elitist notion of art, or a 'high' art. Adorno himself presents a more recondite elaboration of the question of the role of art, and draws a distinction between the unifying and pacifying nature of the 'culture industry' and art proper. Although a distinction could be made between Adorno's more pessimistic 'negative dialectics' – his 'romanticism of despair' – and Marcuse's optimistic utopian 'romanticism of revolt', there are clear parallels between the two positions. As with Marcuse, so too with Adorno art establishes an autonomy from the concrete world of social relations, and it is through this critical distance that it can maintain its critique of that world. Thus an apparent distinction is drawn between art proper as 'high' and the culture industry as 'low' art. Postmodern thinkers would argue that Adorno's treatment of the 'culture industry' is overly simplistic and monolithic, and that it does not allow for resistance within popular culture itself.[10] This criticism of Adorno could equally be levelled at Marcuse, whose celebration of an autonomous art fails to recognise the critical capacity of more popular forms of cultural expression.

Marcuse's position is also questionable on other accounts. Even accepting a view of art as autonomous, it could be argued that any attempt to politicise art must be compromised in its very nature. It is as though an effective opposition can be detected between politics and art. Walter Benjamin exposed the problem in his essay, 'The Work of Art in the Age of Mechanical Reproduction'.[11] Benjamin explored the problem of how fascism used aesthetics to celebrate war. The aestheticisation of war by the futurists, in particular, succeeded in redressing the ethics of war by transporting them into the realm of aesthetics. In effect it could be extrapolated from Benjamin's argument that aesthetics brings about an anaesthetisation of the political, and this applied not only to fascism but to any form of politics.[12] Yet, almost paradoxically, Benjamin concludes the article with the comment, 'This is the situation in politics which Fascism is rendering aesthetic. Communism responds by politicizing art.'[13] As Susan Buck-Morss has pointed out, according to Benjamin's own argument, the term 'aesthetic' must completely change its orientation if it is to retain some political content. If the aesthetic might be employed to disguise the political and to render it acceptable by transporting it into an aestheticized realm, a realm where ethics have been eclipsed and artistic 'licence' prevails, then clearly the aesthetic might be seen in opposition to the political.[14] The aesthetic might be perceived – somewhat paradoxically – as inducing an anaesthetizing effect, in that the overstimulation of sensory perception induced by the aesthetic moment has the effect of numbing the senses, creating a form of aesthetic cocoon, thereby isolating the individual from the harsh reality of politics. According to such an argument, the aesthetic reduces and subsumes political content. It counters and absorbs the political, rendering it impotent. But does this mean that the aesthetic is apolitical? Precisely not. Aesthetics, according to this argument, must be seen along the same axis as politics. Yet its role is assiduously negative. Its masking of the political remains an intensely political act.

Alternatively, it could also be argued that even a so-called 'critical aesthetics' does indeed remain political (although perhaps not in the manner which might have been intended) by subscribing, albeit unwittingly, to a 'politics of acquiescence'. In its 'claims' to political agency – 'claims' that prove inevitably to be exaggerated – 'critical aesthetics' is diverting attention away from the primary *locus* of politics which must be seen as *praxis* itself, in that significant political gestures are less likely to take place in art galleries than in the streets outside. Through this diversionary strategy, a 'critical aesthetics', it could be argued, *acquiesces in* – rather than *resists* – the dominant political condition.

Beyond this, there are further problems over the question of political content in a work of art. Where art is not being used in a directly communicative manner – as slogans, advertising and so on – the nature of its engagement with its audience is mediated by the very abstraction of its aesthetic form, and its capacity to communicate 'political content' is therefore compromised. Nor should it be assumed that the reception of that content on the part of the reader is unproblematic, unless one is to resort to a hermeneutics of reading. Yet the shortcomings of hermeneutics – and indeed the whole project of phenomenology – have been all too often exposed. Hermeneutics is based on the premise of collapsing of the subject into the object, so that the agency of the reader is somehow overlooked and the reader is therefore deemed to have direct and unmediated access to the work of art. Furthermore, this approach does not entertain any sense of 'difference', such as cultural or gender difference. The reader in this context is treated as an essentialised, universal, ahistorical *persona*. Phenomenology presupposes the existence of a pre-given human body – an essentialised human body – which, in the context of architecture, acts as the standard unit by which to 'experience' space. Phenomenology, in this sense, may prove as universalising as any structuralist account of the world. In short, the reading of any work of art is problematic, and although there have been attempts by Habermas and others to overcome 'death of the author' arguments by introducing a notion of intersubjective communication, the bare fact remains that there can be no one privileged reading of a work of art.

At best we might account for readings of a work of art through some form of 'symbolic meaning', thereby bringing the whole debate down to a 'politics of the individual'. Symbolic meaning – like beauty – lies in the eye of the beholder, although it is no less real for that. Yet symbolic meaning, as Fredric Jameson has observed, is 'as volatile as the arbitrariness of the sign'.[15] It is as though one reading may too easily invert into its opposite. Noah's nakedness might mean respect or disrespect.[16] The Holocaust may be taken as the logical consequence of rationality or the inevitable result of irrationality. This is not to sanction relativism, so much as to highlight the need to acknowledge the agency of the interpreter and the perspective within which an interpretation is made.

Within the context of the whole aesthetics and politics debate, the relationship between an ideology of the aesthetic and a more general ideology needs to be considered. What underpinned much Modernist art was the attempt to challenge existing conventions. In this sense, Modernist art was 'revolutionary'. Yet there is a danger in conflating the aesthetic with the social. An aesthetic 'revolution' which challenges the values and norms of the world of art should be distinguished from a social revolution which challenges the existing power structures within a broader political context. The confusion which seems to have beset much Modernist art in its claims to be 'revolutionary' beyond the realm of the aesthetic has been to equate the aesthetic with the social. In effect, there has been an elision – a sleight of hand – which attempts to legitimatise a connection which ought to be seen as no more than allegorical. Yet this is not to deny that the two realms – the aesthetic and the social – may intersect on occasion, so that the aesthetic revolution may engage directly with the social revolution under a specific constellation of circumstances. The possibility of such an event is perhaps greater in the context of architecture, where the involvement with the social is more direct than in other forms of aesthetic expression.

Architecture and politics

Architecture poses a special question. Architecture is deeply embedded within economic and other structures of power, and its capacity to operate as a critical force of change is therefore compromised. The architect, furthermore, is no free agent and can act only vicariously on behalf of the client. If any authorial position is sought, we should perhaps look to the client rather than to the architect. At the same time, architecture has its own special siginificance as the most public of all the arts, and the one which may most acutely influences the social. This distinguishes architecture from other arts, in that its capacity to act autonomously – in Marcuse's terms – as a critical commentary on the realm of the real, is compromised by its instantiation within the realm of the real. The very presence of architecture gives it a social impact, so that any 'negativity', any critical capacity within architecture, is all but cancelled by the 'positivity' of its presence. (See Fredric Jameson, pp. 73–4.) The very physicality of architecture always threatens to install a new *status quo*, and undermines its capacity to be 'subversive'.

Yet the problem of a revolutionary architecture has to be addressed ultimately within the context of the more general question of architecture and its influence on the social. Within the popular imagination there has been little doubt about architecture's capacity to condition a response within the user. Indeed the common view seems to be encapsulated in Georges Bataille's 'definition' of architecture. For Bataille, architecture – especially monumental architecture – not only reflects the politics of an epoch, but also has a marked influence on the social:

> Architecture is the expression of the true nature of society, as physiognomy is the expression of the nature of the individuals. However, this comparison is

applicable, above all, to the physiognomy of officials (prelates, magistrates, admirals). In fact, only society's ideal nature – that of authoritative command and prohibition – expresses itself in actual architectural constructions. Thus great monuments rise up like dams, opposing a logic of majesty and authority on all unquiet elements; it is in the form of cathedrals and palaces that the church and state speak to and impose silence upon the crowds.[17]

Such a view, however, must not go unchallenged. The interaction between architecture and the political deserves to be interrogated further. This is not to deny, of course, the status of architecture as a political act. Certainly, if we are to believe Stanley Fish, every act – and this includes the architectural – is inscribed within some ideological position.[18] There is no platform, according to Fish, which is not constrained by some ideological imperative. Indeed, there needs to be an ideological content in that this is precisely what gives an act its force. This may not be obvious because ideology remains largely invisible, yet it is through its very invisibility that ideology derives its potential. Ideology constitutes a form of background level of consciousness which influences all our actions.

A distinction must be made, however, between the act of building itself and subsequent semantic 'readings' of that building. The political content of the act of building is perhaps the more obvious, but it is likewise the more often over-looked and forgotten. In the case of the Stalinallee in Berlin, for example, the act of building was deeply political and was marked by considerable social unrest. Demonstrations over the low level of pay for building workers on the project erupted on 16 June 1953, and spread the following day to other parts of the city.[19] As could be expected the demonstrations were brutally suppressed, and about a dozen demonstrators were killed. Yet what dominates discussion of the Stalinallee is not this all but forgotten moment in its construction, but the question of whether the project can be read semantically as 'totalitarian'.[20]

It is precisely in the these semantic readings of architecture that the fragility of associations between architecture and the political become most apparent. In their discussion of 'democratic' architecture, Charles Jencks and Maggie Valentine recognise the subject as problematic. They observe that neither Frank Lloyd Wright nor Vincent Scully, both of whom had written on the subject of architecture and democracy, had managed to relate the politics to any typology or style of building.[21] Yet while they also note that Aldo Rossi and others had claimed that there was no direct link between style and politics, they themselves persist in an attempt to define an 'architecture of democracy'. Their approach relies on semantic readings. For Jencks and Valentine, as it transpires, the problem rests ultimately in the complex 'codes' which 'democratic architecture' adopts. It must avoid excessive uniformity ('An architecture of democracy that is uniform is as absurd as a democracy of identical citizens') yet equally it should avoid excessive variety ('an architecture where every building is in a different style is as privatised as a megalopolis of consumers'). 'Thus a democratic style', they conclude, '...is at once shared, abstract, individualised and disharmonious.'[22] Jencks and Valentine emphasise the aesthetic dimension as though this has some direct bearing on the political. Yet their argument is undone by its own internal inconsistencies. How can classical architecture symbolise both Greek democracy and Italian fascism? Can there be any essential politics to a style of architecture? Can there ever be a 'democratic architecture'?

Here we must recognise that political content in architecture must be seen as associative. Architecture can only be imbued with political content through a process of 'mapping'. Architecture achieves its political – and hence equally its gendered – status through semantic associations, which exist within a temporal framework and are inherently unstable. These semantic associations depend on an historical memory within the collective imagination. Once this memory fades the semantic associations will be lost, and the building may be reappropriated according to new ideological imperatives. Thus the main Berlin Olympic Stadium, an emblem in 1936 for the Nazi Olympics, has now lost those associations in the eyes of those who visit it regularly to watch everyday football matches. A similar process inevitably occurs when a building changes its use, from Victorian villa to academic department, from police station to brothel, from dictator's palace to casino. Unless the memory of its previous social use is retained, all earlier associations are erased. While a building through its associations might appear as deeply political, it must be understood that these politics are not an attribute of the architectural form itself. Political content does not reside in architectural form; it is merely grafted on to it by a process that is strictly allegorical. To perceive the political meaning, one has to understand the allegorical system in which it is encoded. Yet this is not the allegorical system that one might identify, for example, with Renaissance painting, where allegory relies on a narrative of fixed symbols with which the painter works. The allegory to which I refer is an allegory of association. A closer comparison, therefore, might be the way in which abstract painting has been read as political, and promoted by the CIA – so the story goes – as a tool of postwar propaganda.

Fredric Jameson highlights the problem of the allegorical nature of this 'mapping' of the political onto the architectural. Whatever political content might seem to be invested in architectural form may subsequently be erased or rewritten:

> I have come to think that no work of art or culture can set out to be polit-
> ical once and for all, no matter how ostentatiously it labels itself as such, for
> there can never be any guarantee that it will be used the way it demands.
> A great political art (Brecht) can be taken as a pure and apolitical art; art
> that seems to want to be merely aesthetic and decorative can be rewritten as
> political with energetic interpretation. The political rewriting or appropria-
> tion, then, the political use, must be allegorical; you have to know that this
> is what it is supposed to be or mean – in itself it is inert.[23]

He further elaborates this in his incisive critique of Kenneth Frampton's essay on critical regionalism. What is crucial is the 'social ground' of architecture. When removed from its contextual situation, architectural form would be exposed for what it is. Architectural form, as Jameson notes, 'would lack all political and allegorical efficacy' once taken out of the social and cultural movements which lend it this force. This is not to deny that architecture may indeed have 'political and allegorical efficacy', but rather to recognise that it merely serves as a vehicle for this within a given 'social ground'. Thus, to return to our earlier quotations from Bataille, it is 'in the *form* of' – through the *medium* of – 'cathedrals and palaces that the church and state speak to and impose silence upon the crowds'. Remove the memory of the church and state, and the buildings would become empty vessels to be appropriated towards some other political end. Yet the point to be made here is that architecture is *always* contextualised within some social ground. It is therefore always appropriated towards some political end. But that political content is *not* a property of the architectural form itself. To view architectural form as inherently 'politicised' is, for Jameson, a misguided project:

> It was one of the signal errors of the artistic activism of the 1960s to suppose that there existed, in advance, forms that were in and of themselves endowed with a political, and even revolutionary, potential by virtue of their own intrinsic properties.[24]

Architecture, then, may be seen to be the product of political and social forces, yet, once built, any political reading of it must be allegorical. As such, we should take care to distinguish an aesthetic reading of form from a political reading of content, even though the aesthetic terminology – 'reactionary', 'totalitarian' and so on – may ape the political. Failure to recognise this distinction would allow the difference between the two to be elided, and the aesthetic to be read as necessarily political.

Indeed the shortcomings of any attempt to 'read' a politics into architectural form are brought out by the contradictions that may exist between such 'readings' and the practices that actually take place within the building. The importance of the consideration of practice over semantic concerns has been highlighted by Adrian Rifkin in the context of Jean Nouvel's Institut du Monde Arabe.[25] This is a building which purports to celebrate Arabness through the arabesque patterning of the facade. Yet if we focus less on semantic readings of the facade and more on to a politics of use of the building itself, we may discover that – far from celebrating Arabness – the building replicates the cultural imperialism that is at play elsewhere in Paris. While the elegant Parisians eat their couscous in the restaurants, the Arabs may be seen working in the kitchens. In short, the building is supporting, rather than resisting, the dominant 'orientalizing' cultural impulse. All this begins to call into question not only the process of reading a politics into architectural form, but also the effect that any such political reading might have on the user.

The use of space can therefore be political, even if the aesthetic cannot be. Yet one might still argue that architecture – in its very physical form – must indeed be political, through the influence that it exerts on the users of a building. In other words, there is an association to be made between the form of a space and the political *praxis* within that space. This prompts the further question as to whether architecture in its physical form may somehow influence the politics of use.

Space, knowledge and power

One of the central preoccupations for Michel Foucault is the relationship between power and space, and he throws some light on this issue in his discussion of Bentham's panopticon. In this now famous piece, Foucault explores the question of how architectural form may influence social behaviour. The panopticon is a plan for a prison. It has a central tower in which the guard sits, and the cells are arranged radially, so that from the tower the guard is afforded a view all around – as the name 'panopticon' implies – into each of the cells. Meanwhile, the openings in the tower itself, through blinds and other devices, prevent the inmates in the cells from knowing whether or not the guard is looking at them. Thus the inmates remain under the perpetual control of the gaze of the guard.[26] The principle which Foucault is trying to illustrate is that the architecture may become an apparatus for 'for creating and sustaining a power relationship independent of the person who operates it.'[27] In other words, it is the architectural form of the panopticon which helps to engender a form of social control. Such an example would seem to suggest the possibility of architecture determining social behaviour.

Foucault revisits this question in a subsequent interview with Paul Rabinow, where he acknowledges that architects are not necessarily 'the masters of space' that they once were, or believed themselves to be.[28] Thus he appears to qualify this position on the capacity for architecture to determine social behaviour. On the question of whether there could be an architecture which would act as a force of either liberation or oppression, Foucault concludes that 'liberation' and 'oppression' are not mutually exclusive, and that even in that most oppressive of structures, some form of 'resistance' may be in operation. Liberty, for Foucault, is a practice that cannot be 'established by the project itself'. 'The liberty of men is never assured by the institutions and laws that are intended to guarantee them.'[29]

Architecture, therefore, cannot in itself be liberative or repressive. As Foucault comments, 'I think that it can never be inherent in the structure of things to guarantee the exercise of freedom. The guarantee of freedom is freedom.'[30] Architectural form, Foucault concludes, cannot in itself resolve social problems. It is only politics that can address them, although architecture can contribute in some way, provided it is in league with the political. Thus Foucault concludes: 'I think that [architecture] can and does produce positive effects when the liberating intentions of the architect coincide with the real practice of people in the exercise of their freedom.'[31] Foucault is therefore not contradicting but merely qualifying his earlier comments on the panopticon. It is not the form of the panopticon which controls the behaviour of the inmates. Rather, it is the politics of use – the fact that the building is operating as a prison – which is ultimately determinant of behaviour, and the architecture is merely supporting that politics of use through its efficient layout.

The position of Michel Foucault on this matter is clear. In opposition to the utopian visions of Marcuse and others, Foucault would emphasise the politics of everyday life over architectural form as the principal determinant of social behaviour. 'The architect', he comments, 'has no power over me.'[32] According to such an approach, there could be no 'revolutionary' architecture in the Marcusian sense of an architecture that might constitute some critical force of change. Yet this is not to deny the capacity for architecture to 'produce positive effects' when it is in league with the practice of politics. Such an approach, of course, introduces an important temporal dimension into consideration. As political practice changes, so the efficacy of the architectural form to support that practice may itself be compromised.

After the revolution

Architecture is traditionally seen as built politics, yet the problem is considerably more complex than might first appear. Extrapolating from Foucault's argument, we might conclude that there is nothing inherently political about any building or any style of architecture. It is a question rather of what political associations a building may have. Buildings, according to the logic of Foucault's argument, would have no inherent politics, if by 'politics' we infer a capacity to influence the social. Rather, a building may facilitate – to a greater or lesser extent – the practice of those politics through its very physical form. We may recognise, for example, the naivety of the Jeffersonian 'grid-iron' plan which was carpeted across the United States in an effort to promote democracy. The supposed democracy of an anti-hierarchical, uniform layout such as the grid was of course challenged by the use of that form in the layout of that most anti-democratic of spaces, the concentration camp.

What then are we to make of Nicolai Ceausescu's Palace, the People's House, in Bucharest? Towards the end of Ceausescu's dictatorship and immediately after his execution the building was almost universally decried. It was denounced as totalitarian architecture, a symbol of Ceausescu's own regime, to be compared to the architecture of other totalitarian regimes. After the revolution, it would appear that much of the population was in favour of destroying this monument to Ceausescu's dictatorship. Some years later we find a shift in attitudes. While most architects continue to dismiss the building, the majority of the population would seem to approve of it. The building has emerged as an important parliament building and a popular conference centre, whilst the monumental Avenue of Unity leading up to the palace has become the most expensive real estate in Bucharest. For many the palace represents the centre of the city.[33]

What, then, is the political content of this building? One could argue that only the construction of the building – which itself entailed the destruction of some precious remnants of old Bucharest – could be construed as political in itself. Any subsequent political reading of the constructed edifice, however, must be merely allegorical. The building may only be *associated* with a political position, but even that will depend upon the collective memory of the population. As that memory fades, so the building may take on new political associations. Thus the palace may shift in its political 'content' from monument to communist dictatorship to symbol of a new democratic Romania, in a mechanism not dissimilar to the 'floating signs' of the fashion system. We might therefore conclude that if we are looking for a link between architecture and revolution, such links may exist only in the realm of shifting semantic associations.

It is only perhaps if we are to understand architecture, along with the other visual arts, as offering a form of backdrop against which to forge some new political identity, that we might recognise a political role for architecture, albeit indirect. For this backdrop, although neutral in itself, will always have some political 'content' projected on to it. And it is as a 'political backdrop' – politicised, that is, in the eyes of the population – that the People's House will act as a form of screen 'reflecting' certain political values. As it is recoded as the symbol of a new democratic Romania, the building will be seen to embody that new national identity, for national identity is always a fantasy structure articulated through various 'myths of the homeland', and made manifest in the built environment. And it is precisely through the population reading itself into such a building that a new sense of Romanian identity might be forged.

Notes

1 An early version of this paper appeared in Maggie Toy (ed.), *Beyond the Revolution*, London: Academy Editions, 1996.
2 Le Corbusier, *Towards a New Architecture*, Frederick Etchells (trans.), London: Butterworth Architecture, 1989, p. 269. 'Architecture ou Révolution' was to be the original title of *Vers Une Architecture*.
3 On this see Catherine Cooke, *Russian Avant-Garde: Theories of Art, Architecture and the City*, London: Academy Editions, 1995, p. 118.
4 Fredric Jameson, 'Architecture and the Critique of Ideology', in Joan Ockman (ed.), *Architecture, Criticism, Ideology*, Princeton, NJ: Princeton Architectural Press, 1985, p. 71.
5 Herbert Marcuse, *The Aesthetic Dimension: Towards a Critique of Marxist Aesthetics*, London: Macmillan Press, 1978, p. x.
6 Marcuse, *The Aesthetic Dimension*, p. ix.
7 Marcuse, *The Aesthetic Dimension*, p. xi
8 Marcuse, *The Aesthetic Dimension*, p.7.
9 For Marcuse on mass culture see C.A. Rootes, 'Mass Culture' in William Outhwaite and Tom Bottomore (eds), *The Blackwell Dictionary of Twentieth-Century Social Thought*, London: Blackwell, 1993, pp. 369–70.
10 See, for example, the comments of J.A. Bernstein in Theodor Adorno, *The Culture Industry*, J M Bernstein (ed.), London: Routledge, 1991.
11 Walter Benjamin, 'The Work of Art in the Age of Mechanical Reproduction', *Illuminations*, Harry Zohn (trans.), London: Fontana Press, 1973, pp. 211–35.
12 The link between aesthetics and anaesthetics has been explored by Susan Buck-Morss, 'Aesthetics and Anaesthetics: Walter Benjamin's Artwork Essay Reconsidered', *October* 62, Fall 1992, pp. 3–41.

13 Benjamin, *Illuminations*, p. 235.

14 One is reminded here of the deeply aestheticised Nazi Nuremburg rallies, and of crimes committed in the name of art, such as the infamous murder of a bourgeois doctor by Italian futurists.

15 Fredric Jameson, 'Is Space Political?', in Neil Leach (ed.), *Rethinking Architecture*, London: Routledge, 1997, p. 258.

16 Jameson, 'Is Space Political?', in Neil Leach (ed.), *Rethinking Architecture*, p. 258.

17 Georges Bataille, 'Architecture', in Neil Leach (ed.), *Rethinking Architecture*, p. 21.

18 Stanley Fish, *There's No Such Thing as Free Speech – And It's a Good Thing Too*, Oxford: Oxford University Press, 1994.

19 Bernard Newman, *Behind the Berlin Wall*, London: Robert Hale, 1964, pp.31–42.

20 Tafuri, in contrast to other commentators, reads the project not from a political perspective, but strictly in terms of urban planning 'aesthetic' objectives. Manfredo Tafuri and Francesco Dal Co, *Modern Architecture*, New York: Abrams, 1979, pp. 322, 326.

21 Charles Jencks and Maggie Valentine, 'The Architecture of Democracy: The Hidden Tradition,' *Architectural Design*, Profile 69, London: Academy Editions, 1987, pp. 8–25. For Vincent Scully on architecture and democracy, see Vincent Scully, *Modern Architecture: The Architecture of Democracy*, New York: George Braziller, 1974; for Frank Lloyd Wright on the subject, see Frank Lloyd Wright, *An Organic Architecture: The Architecture of Democracy*, London: Lund Humphries, 1939; *When Democracy Builds*, Chicago: University of Chicago Press, 1945.

22 Jencks and Valentine, 'The Architecture of Democracy: The Hidden Tradition', p. 25.

23 Fredric Jameson, 'Is Space Political?', in Neil Leach (ed.), *Rethinking Architecture*, pp. 258–9.

24 Jameson, 'The Constraints of Postmodernism', in Neil Leach (ed.), *Rethinking Architecture*, p. 254.

25 Lecture given to the MA in Architecture and Critical Theory, University of Nottingham, May 1995.

26 Although Bentham's panopticon was never built, the principle of the layout can be seen in numerous buildings, such as James Stirling's Seeley History Library, Cambridge. Here the control desk is positioned centrally, with all the desks and shelves laid out radially around it, affording an unobstructed view and allowing the librarian to monitor the entire space. A more sophisticated form of panopticism operates with close circuit surveillance cameras.

27 Michel Foucault, *Discipline and Punish*, Alan Sheridan (trans.), London: Penguin, 1979, p. 201.

28 Paul Rabinow (ed.), *The Foucault Reader*, London: Penguin, 1991, p. 244.

29 Rabinow (ed.), *The Foucault Reader*, p. 245.

30 Rabinow (ed.), *The Foucault Reader*, p. 245.

31 Rabinow (ed.), *The Foucault Reader*, p. 246.

32 Rabinow (ed.), *The Foucault Reader*, p. 247.

33 The popularity of the building among the general public was endorsed when in July 1995 Hagi, the international footballer – and possibly the most popular public icon in Romania – held his wedding reception there.

III

Strategies for a new Europe

9   Traces of the unborn

Daniel Libeskind

For some time now I have been working on a project I have termed the 'Traces of the Unborn', a term describing the need to resist the erasure of history, the need to respond to history, the need to open the future: that is, to delineate the invisible on the basis of the visible. Out of this meditation I have developed certain planning and architectural concepts which reflect my interest and commitment to the memory of the city, to the time in which it dwells, and to the freedom it represents.

> *Even if anywhere-becoming-somewhere arrives, the age of the closure of sites might yet bid farewell to 'genius loci', that idol of politics, the ultimate onto-theological component of Architecture Appropriated.*

The consideration of these issues with respect to the future development of the contemporary city raises fundamental questions concerning damage to urban fabrics past, present and future, whether this damage is caused by war, economic conditions or political ideology. Faced with these conditions, contemporary urbanism must leave aside conventional forms of contextualism and utopianism in favour of strategies enabling the transformation and metamorphosis of existing realities which take the discontinuity of the city as a positive point of departure for the construction of new urban perspectives.

> *The 'genius loci' is but a realm invested with twenty centuries of metaphysical oppression masking the impotence of ecumenic empires to control places and the human addition to the orientation of space.*

There is an important need in every society for icons which constitute a particular area, the structures which form the texture of living memory. In refuting the past and the future alike, the eternal present of transformation and metamorphosis must be incorporated in an urban framework which encourages the creation of unpredictable, flexible and hybrid architectures. At the same time the given should not be treated as an obstacle or as a form of pathology, but rather as an opportunity pregnant with new relations and urban experiences.

Figure 9.1 Daniel Liebeskind, Landsberger Allee, Berlin, competition development model, 1994

The implication for the city and Architecture which follow from the de-theo-retization of somewhere are constructively exhilarating.

It is necessary for contemporary architects and planners to challenge the whole notion of the Masterplan with its implied finality, its misguided ambition of eternal recurrence of the same through replication. Rather, they must develop open and ever changeable methodologies which reinforce the processes of transformation and articulate the dynamic of change in a diverse and plural-istic architecture. They must both trace and steer through time and space the course of the city; the city as both a memory and a dream, as the House of Being and the Matrix of Hope.

The line of incision cutting the mind is straight and long – slice manipulating death.

Following Paul Valéry's axiom that 'humanity is permanently threatened by two dangers: order and disorder', my own search for a new and responsive urbanism navigates between the Scylla of nostalgic historicism and the Charybdis of totalitarian *tabula rasa*. In doing so, it rejects both simulation in the service of respectful modesty, and destruction in the service of ideological purity. It is the search for a process which seeks to define the often invisible meanings embodied in the misunderstood discarded, transient or forgotten typologies and situations which make up the specific energy of the city. It addresses the city's complex history as a heterogeneous spatial and temporal network, whose connections and contradictions form the basis for critical modes for intervention.

Is there a site somewhere which does not commemorate the 'turn' of history toward its own presence, while anticipating someone else's absence?

The resulting structures suggest a new connection or knot between urban areas and their surroundings, between buildings and their sites, interacting with existing conditions by both supplementing and subverting networks of traffic, street pattern, building and open space. They are open, flexible matrices, out of which can emerge forms of architecture and urban space whose expression and representation are indistinguishable from the political space they occupy. This matrix represents a histogram of invisible realities and their relations, a graph in time and space describing the equation of a city's soul.

Is there a place anywhere – even somewhere out of this world – which does not claim to be the focal point for the transport of Being, a Being always disappearing in a post-mortem of the future?

The city is the greatest spiritual creation of humanity; a collective work which develops the expression of culture, society and the individual in time and space. Its structure is intrinsically mysterious, developing more like a dream than a piece of equipment. Given this, alternatives are required to traditional urban planning ideas, which imply continuity based on projection. My own project in search of the contemporary city represents one possible alternative, an approach which understands and celebrates the city as an evolving, poetic and unpredictable event.

10 Resisting the erasure of history

Daniel Libeskind interviewed by Anne Wagner

WAGNER: In your piece 'Traces of the Unborn', you call for, 'the need in every society to identify icons which constitute a particular area, the structures which form the texture of living memory'. Do you recognise there to be a problem in architecture having some fixed political and symbolic meaning when, as Fredric Jameson comments, meaning is grafted onto architecture by a process of association, thereby being extremely arbitrary and constantly shifting?

LIBESKIND: I think that Fredric Jameson's analysis of architecture is based on linguistics and on the idea that language is a predominant prison-house of the mind. I think architecture plays a completely different role. The icons of architecture are not connected to language in any causal or linear way. Therefore I would say that the notion of an icon in architecture should not be confused with the notion of an icon in literature or as a figurative linguistic trope. Therefore icons in architecture have a very different function from the shifting function of words in language or numbers in a mathematical system.

WAGNER: So would you say that symbolism in a building is more permanent?

LIBESKIND: I would not say symbolism, but just the nature of space, the nature of the fact that you have material in a place, to which you can point, that is here. This 'here' to which you can point with your finger is not some abstract 'here', it is not interchangeable with any other 'here'. It is kind of absolute *vis-à-vis* the relativistic ideas which language might develop, about a 'here'. When you point to somewhere, like the window, the place, the door, the passage, you are in a place. That is why one should really think about the word 'icon'. It is not something very obvious, what it would be in architecture. But certainly I mean it in a spatial sense, not in some sort of abstract sense of a concept.

WAGNER: So thinking about the GDR housing at the Alexander Platz, would you identify this as an icon?

LIBESKIND: Sure, because the spatial organisation of the city into large slivers of linear cuts constituted by the walls of the blocks, is a lived experience. It is not an abstraction, it is not something that you can change by renaming it for example, give it another name. Say it is not the GDR. It does not matter whether it is GDR or not, you have that space. That is why I think that in order to see architecture in continuity, not as something which is disruptive or transversal towards people's lives, but is a betterment, one has to deal with these conditions. It is a very good example. You can call it now no longer the GDR, it is now the western, it is Germany. But this has not changed the nature of that space or its experience and you have to work with that space. No one can afford to ideologically just wipe it out of their minds and say, we don't like it, we like the old streets of the medieval Berlin, because this is just wishful thinking. One has to deal with that space which of course is also historical space where people have grown up there. That is their home and one should not be contemptuous, as I have said to many Berlin critics, and not underrate its potency – that it is home, and that it is here, and that it is even appreciated. It was very much appreciated if people were able to get their housing there, they were lucky to live near the Alexander Platz in such a block.

WAGNER: The condition of Eastern Europe and post-Communist society plays a major role in the particular considerations of Germany today. Do you see this condition of Germany as one which is particularly susceptible to simulation of memory? Freud talks about the idea that following a painful experience, memory is forcibly repressed. Would you attribute the unconditional acceptance of western values as a symptom of this repressed memory?

LIBESKIND: That is a difficult question. Of course Germany has a history of the erasure of memory, of the need to radically transform society with each political or global change. We have witnessed this in German history, especially in Berlin. If one looks for example at the rapidity with which the Wall disappeared, almost overnight, without any public discussion, it was just a political decision to take it away. It was obvious that a new era had started by the removal of the Wall. Now people ask, wasn't the Wall a part of the history of Berlin? That is true. But I would say that other Eastern European countries have the same problem, because it actually all goes back in some sense to the destruction unleashed by the Second World War and particularly by the Holocaust. The fact that there has been a rebirth or a renaissance of European space, cities and economies is based on a certain legacy of a repressed history for all those countries. We know very well that Poland, the Czech Republic, the Ukraine and Western Germany were rebuilt by the Allied powers of the war, but the money of the Allied powers which rebuilt these countries was the money of the Third Reich, which was money in a large measure, from expropriated, stolen properties of people who had lived here. Even the very rebuilding of Europe, in the post-war Europe, by the Allies, and it is only now coming to public view, has an attached ethical question. We will wonder I think in the next century, what the reconstruction really meant. After the war and it continues, because as you know, so many Jews were citizens in the millions of Poland, Germany, of these countries, who are no longer here to claim any stake in the life of these societies, because they are no longer there. So it is a larger issue about Europe. It is the same issue as in America. Building in America raises, and will continue to raise in the next generation, big questions about what was land, how was property built? Most of it was illegitimately stolen from the Indians. Public human rights issues will become a part of architecture in the next century.

WAGNER: Do you see this as having something to do with the culture of simulation?

LIBESKIND: Absolutely. Yes, it does have very much to do with what you call simulation.

WAGNER: How do you deal with the dilemma of wishing to build, yet wishing to retain memory intact?

LIBESKIND: Memory is built. Memory is not something which is just there. It is also constructed. It is an interesting issue, what is memory? What is remembrance? Every remembrance is always in a 'now'. When we remember we are not in the past. We are always remembering now. The nature of memory also changes with the present and with the future. I think there is no difference in architecture than in life in general, in literature or in any other remembered experience. It is partly based on an ecological structure. Let's say imagination, the vivid reincarnation of the experience in order to retrieve those things which one did not know were there. Very often and most likely it is material objects in their opacity which evoke that memory. The unconscious knowledge or imagination of what was there. So you have to stumble across a stone and fall down to remember what was on the ground.

Figure 10.1 Construction site, Potsdamer Platz, Berlin, 1997

WAGNER: So what you remember as you stumble is almost irrelevant...

LIBESKIND: Exactly, it is an act which opens – lets you react. I think that is the function of architecture. If it is good, if it is not a simulation, if it is not completely buried in its own ideology, then it is open to different experiences...

WAGNER: Berlin is a city where the relationship of the building with the city has been overtly exemplary of the political era within which it was built. Speaking to former GDR architects, they consider an advantage which they developed to be their ability to see the city as a whole, not restricted by boundaries and building law. Their view of a building within the city is far different from the western view. When identifying icons for retention of memory, what role does this relationship play?

LIBESKIND: Obviously a very big one, because the city is always the horizon of working and of building in the city. But that relationship is not always a symbiotic one. It is not always that the building represents this relationship, or that the building is based on a certain obvious relationship. What one has to open up is, what is the relationship between the city and a built work, because often it would be in conflict with, for example, the horizon which a city has established in ideology. In the GDR you could say there was a certain utopian element of a city which is based on the pure relationships of social relationships. But no more so than the kind of utopia of a capitalist city in which the relationships are guided by profit motive. It just shows the limits of both utopian systems. In my understanding what is important is to analyse, in a more pragmatic way, what is the relationship with the icon. Icon is something irrational, it is not something which is a product of a causal system of linearities. It is something which is there like an angel, like a complete breakdown of all logic in which images have grown up around a city. That is where icons, if they are the right ones, continue to exert power, seemingly without any relationship to history. One could not even believe in the Madonna, but yet the Madonna appears in a similar form of entertainment. So the words, the icons, the images and the buildings do have a kind of critical role.

WAGNER: More on a general theme now in an attempt to place you: according to some commentators the complex factors of phenomenology and Husserl have in the past informed your work. How does this now still influence your design and your thinking?

LIBESKIND: It is true that I read a lot and I thought a lot, that I was interested in philosophy. But I think the difference is in architecture, that architecture is not a translation of any philosophy. It cannot be. It cannot actually be a projection of any philosophy. One can of course talk about it in philosophical terms, but what it is, is something actually alien, it has a problematic and anxiety producing relationship to language because what is built is a translation. But like all translations it is something else. So one would have to ask, what is a translation? If you translate a poem from one language to another, you can say it is a mathematical problem, because you have to get a result which captures a certain experience. But how to get that result? We know of no system which can translate a poem by Goethe from German to English. Although it is a mathematical problem because you are set to equalise in another language, the content, sound, feeling of a poem. So, sure, there is the problem of translation but that only shows that no system including a philosophical one can actually capture that relationship. I would say in all honesty, that one has to think of architecture itself as some trans-philosophical or counter-philosophical movement which because of what it deals with, is in many ways a philosophy in itself. It is not a philosophy like language, because it does not have a system of that sort, but it is something, it might even be ahead of the Husserls and the Derridas, without, of course, diminishing their work, they are great at what they do, but they are always acting from within a site that has already been structured for them, in the space of their thinking. So even the critique of sight or the revelation of any linguistic structure is already pre-produced in an architectural setting, which did not come from any philosophy of that sort. It had nothing to do with thinking. Recognising that in architecture, that it is oblivious to any philosophical movements. Look at how much language has changed and how little architecture has changed. So what is the relationship between philosophy and architecture? I think it is a very different one.

WAGNER: A relationship due to the position of the viewer?

LIBESKIND: The viewer might have it, but even when the viewer thinks about it, he can't change the architecture. That is the main point. You can change the interpretation of a text, this is what Derrida actually told me, you can always read the text differently, you can also interpret it differently, but it would not make any difference, because it would be there, just as you encountered it at first, with the same stairs, the same windows, the same roof, the same walls, the same flowers. So you can interpret it in a hundred different ways, yet it would remain.

WAGNER: Do you see this to have something to do with the positivity of architecture hindering it from being critical. In your piece 'Fragments of Utopia' you talk about needing a distance, you call for the mad in the world to come forward, where it is actually the distance from the system which you find yourself in which you are calling for, which gives you the opportunity to be critical, subversive. Does architecture play a role in this context?

LIBESKIND: It does because architecture is to a larger degree the movement of materials. It is not about movement of concepts, or of ideas, it is of stones, of earth. Of course one can look at a building the way one can look at an electrical plant, or some technical installation. You do not need to know anything about electricity, about electrical plant, or about wiring. You can just look at it, how does it look? Without knowing anything about it, like a Martian, and of course you would not see an electricity plant or an industrial infrastructure of any sort. Architecture has that component in it, because whatever one looks at it as, it has that other side, which is that it is doing something other than the claims that are made for it, very often.

WAGNER: So would you say that the construction process is the only point where philosophies can be imposed with political intent and then after this the pattern is all that may be read?

LIBESKIND: After that interpretations take over, but architecture is oblivious to any interpretations. You can see how buildings in different times have a different role, and yet their actual structure continues to be oblivious. Like the ruins of Greek temples, we have no gods, no one believes in Delphi, but the very remnants of that space continues to be there, without the gods, without the political. They continue to show themselves in some way in their total uselessness as being architectural. So I think that is the role of architecture. It is the use of its own uselessness. That is not just the transparency that Fredric Jameson talks about, about shifting signifiers. It is a space that calls itself even when the materials continually decline and are hardly there.

WAGNER: What concerns do you have about the development of a new national identity for Germany? To what extent do you feel that national identity is the role of architecture?

LIBESKIND: I have always called for the non-identity of Germany. I would say why would you want an identity. You should develop the non-identity of Germany. In other words its blurred structure which is here as well. I have never thought that nations and national architecture is of relevance any more.

WAGNER: But they are in the process of seeking this stability image...

LIBESKIND: Of course, and I have been one of the few critics of it. I don't think it is important any longer. It never was actually. It was deadly to cities and to human beings in general. Instead of identity I would look for the opposite, the non-identifiable in a city and in the political, in the sense of nation, peoples and races, blood and earth. Anyway I think that is the general desire of the larger public to see the disappearance. Of course with the disappearance of these structures one also has the cold forces of revenge, of all these things to resurrect themselves. But they are different problems. There are right-wing architects, fascist architects who really believe that you should impose an order on the people, call them to order by making a background in which they are fixed, killed and dead; and those who believe that architecture has the dynamic role in transforming what people thought they were and who they thought they were.

WAGNER: In effect brainwashing...

LIBESKIND: Yes, exactly.

WAGNER: You are speaking against the masterplan as such. Because of the fact that icons are selected in a particular period, again this selection adheres to a certain vision of what is important in a place. So in a way it has qualities of another form of masterplan. How do you deal with this dilemma?

LIBESKIND: I think it is still different to the masterplan. Of course one cannot relinquish one's responsibility. Buildings do not just get built and evaporate, the way texts do. You can file a text in a library and not read it any more. Buildings continue to be there on the streets and if they are good they continue to function in a totally different context, as different kinds of buildings, a different kind of icons even. Yet there is a relationship to their non-original or original core. It is not that one does things which are mediocre, senseless and shifting, what is called today 'light architecture', or simple architecture or architecture that is virtual. In the sense that it really has no being, because its being is just changed by light and by technology. I think that the icon, the emblem, memory do have a place and they are not interchangeable and it is not desirable to make memory virtual and to make identity shift its boundaries without any reason for it. But there is a difference between masterplanning and that concept, because masterplanning is based on a totality, on a totalisation of all the data. If you evoke the word emblem, it is not something like that. It is not based on any totality. In fact it is based on kind of a nothing, because where does an icon come from? It does not come from any agreement of political sort, of what it is. If it is there and it becomes something institutionalised it has a different setting. But that is why angels are so interesting! Nobody believes in angels. No one has seen an angel for a long time and yet an angel is not discredited, it is not a completely discredited entity the way steam engines are because of the pollutants.

WAGNER: Turning to the masterplan which is being proposed for the centre of Berlin, you write in your piece 'Fragments of Utopia' about the suppression of the critique which is very overtly discussed in literature, yet in architecture this critique is silenced. It is almost accepted as a part of nature that these masterplans are to be implemented...

LIBESKIND: But whether it will happen we do not know...

WAGNER: What sort of mechanisms are there which might stop the process?

LIBESKIND: It could be the economic mechanisms which might stop it. The economy is a very flexible entity. It is very radical the shift of capital into the city and out of the city. The world economy might have a much bigger impact than the traditional planners and the traditionally authoritarian types who are controlling the city appreciate. It might well be that all the discourse on what is to be built will evaporate and none of the plans which are supposed to happen will actually happen. I am just speaking hypothetically, but I think we should not be too quick to say that just because people have said and claimed and authorised things to happen, that those things will actually happen. And if they happen they may actually happen in a deformed way. They may be deformed and distorted beyond visibility of what their original aims were. Nothing has happened on the Potsdamer Platz in all these years. The only thing that has happened is what I predicted would happen: people are renovating those buildings, to make them better to live in and use them. It is obvious! You do not have to be smart to see that.

WAGNER: One more question particularly to do with Fredric Jameson. You are in a way what he calls for in a paradigmatic architect. Do you have any problems with his viewpoint generally?

LIBESKIND: I know Fredric very well. He is a very intelligent critic. I think one has to delve into the architectural dimension. What is it that architects actually do? What do planners really do? In a way it is possible from a philosophical point of view to distance oneself from the world of architecture. To see it as a field. But in a way the subversion of architecture is that it does not really exist in any one point of space, in that sense. It is disseminated and transformed in its practical application and in its use. I would say that we are yet to see a truly dramatic analysis of architecture, in philosophical terms, in the form of what Derrida or Jameson have done to political theory or to the ideology of language. There seems to be a fundamental problem in architecture, because architecture is both the same as what we say it is, it comes out of this agreement and is negotiable within a framework. But it is also something completely other, totally oblivious to the control which all systems of logic and dissemination. That is the interesting thing about architecture. Its trajectory seems to move in a very different direction from the trajectory of culture itself. It is a kind of mystery tour, that one has to follow what that is, how does it develop itself or not develop itself? What determines its forms, this also has a lot to do with the public.

WAGNER: The impression I got from speaking to formed GDR architects, was that the buildings which represent the GDR now deny the initial ideology which they were based on, because the reality of architecture is so closely linked to the political and economical considerations. Retaining those buildings retains memories of a specific reality, rather than the ideology...

LIBESKIND: Not only that, but it introduces another important issue. When you have to get 1,000 people living in a certain place, in a certain 'here' and a certain 'now' and you have a certain amount of money, you have a mechanistic problem. It is not by coincidence that we have housing blocks, whether in East Germany or in Rotterdam, or in London, or in a totalitarian society like China today, or in a free society like Western Germany – it really makes no difference, because we are talking about this material fact, that you are to get people up and living in a certain place. There is a limitation on the means in which you can economically organise, the iconic representation of what living together or not living together might be architecturally. These housing blocks are no different from the housing blocks in Rotterdam. They are no more ugly or no more nice than what you see in London. But we see them differently because we are seeing them with all the interests and all the blindness. But if we were to see them, as I said, as Martians would see them, we would see a very different city developing, a very different space developing. The Martians would not know anything about the GDR. They would see that all the claims having been made, it would not really matter much. There was such a limitation to what architecture was able to do and of course also the social condition.

WAGNER: So social conditions and the reality almost suffocate the ideology in the end...

LIBESKIND: This is true, and the realities of architecture particularly. Look at how similar buildings within any particular social complex, industrial society are *vis-à-vis* the relative rural society. It is a bigger picture. I guess I got away a little from Fredric Jameson, but I would like to say, that someone is yet to write this analysis of architecture – the Martian history of architecture, the natural history of architecture. It is a paradoxical thing but it would be interesting. It would need to be an architect too, because not being an architect one would never understand that architects actually don't do anything. They don't carry material, they don't make drawings, don't plan things. Those are just large categories and one would have to apply the dramatical analysis: what do people do when they do architecture, can we call it under one term. Is it a singular? I would say not, I would add a 's' to it, 'architectures'. What would be the common area between the Greek temple and the housing block in the GDR?

11 The humanity of architecture

Dalibor Vesely

The wall which for a period of time separated Eastern and Western Europe was partly real and partly imaginary. It was certainly imaginary in view of the more fundamental developments, values and identities which cannot be changed in a few decades.

In the attempt to understand the nature and the implications of the artificial division of Europe, too much importance is very often given to the difference of political regimes and very little to the universality of primary developments or continuity of traditions and their identities. To those who lived in the Eastern European regimes, the link between politics and culture was only too obvious. It was also quite obvious that there is more than one level of culture, and that politics cannot change or influence all of them. It did not take long to discover that behind the official politics of the day are deeper issues and problems common to countries in both the east and west. The technical transformation of reality, politics and everyday life, the cult of efficiency and the determinism of technological and economic thinking tend to transcend political systems. It is not difficult to see retrospectively that in certain areas such as politics or everyday life, for instance, the process of technical transformation was probably more radical and advanced in the East, despite the general tendency of all industrial societies to develop a more effective form of an appropriation and monopolization of power, collecting and control of informations and steady promotion of surveillance.

That there is a common ground shared by societies on both sides of the wall has been revealed already in the international character of the prewar avant-gardes where even the most doctrinaire utopian projects of the Russian constructivists, motivated to a great extent by totalitarian political thinking, were received by the intellectuals and artists in the west as congenial with their own efforts. The unity of interest behind different political orientations cannot be explained politically. This became eventually clear to many of us living on the east side of the wall. It became clear that what was at stake was not politics itself but its foundations, the humanity of institutions, of everyday life and in our own field, the humanity of architecture.

The notion of humanity is very often used as an argument and criterion for the suitability of buildings and created spaces. The argument itself is usually reduced to a talk about 'human scale', a term which means by implication much more than it can possibly express. The question of what is or what is not human preoccupied mankind for years, and the answers represent today a formidable body of knowledge known better as anthropology.

In the first encounter with the concept or discipline of anthropology, it is not necessarily clear what is its meaning, value or relevance for architecture. It is true of course that there is already a vast literature which claims to be an important contribution to the anthropology of architecture, but the term 'anthropology' remains mostly unclear and very often confused. In the Anglo-Saxon countries, for instance, anthropology is seen almost exclusively as a discipline concerned either with the human evolution (physical anthropology) or with the study of so-called 'primitive' societies or cultures. In the first case, the nature of human beings is too closely linked with the physical, mostly skeletal remains, while in the second case it is rather lost in the broader field of culture which includes religion, history, politics, ethics, art and so on. The architectural relevance of physical anthropology is rather minimal. It is only due to its close links with archaeology that it can be occasionally of some importance. Studies of primitive cultures, on the other hand, represent an inexhaustible source of experience and architecturally relevant knowledge, but it is doubtful if such studies should be described as anthropological. It is in the end the nature of a particular culture rather than human nature which is the goal of these studies.

The goal of anthropology is the study of man which touches on some of the most important questions: the nature of our humanity and the humanity of our inhabited world. Attempts to understand what is truly human in our being and in our world are as old as the available written records. We know them as a search for immortality, salvation, heroism, freedom, emancipation and creativity, but also as attempts to understand our fallibility, finitude, vulnerability to evil, the conditional nature of artificial existence and the limits of an emancipated creativity. What is characteristic for the premodern history of these attempts is their dialectical nature. The essential nature of human existence was not seen in absolute terms or in isolation from the broader context of reality (world) in which human beings are always situated. As a result, the stability of human nature appeared always as relative to history and change, but in that relativity would be discovered important moments of identity and historical continuity.

It was the loss of the dialectical understanding of human nature that created the conditions for the formation of modern anthropology with an exalted view of man and with the ambition to become the foundation of all knowledge. In a sense anthropology, has taken the place of traditional theology.[1] We have already seen some of the consequences of this development in the reduction of human nature into an object of physical investigation and into a subject dissolved and very often lost in cultural relativism. This level of reduction is clearly reflected in one of the major dilemmas of this century, the dilemma between the confidence and rigour of scientific knowledge and the deep confusion of our cultural values. In architecture, we can see the dilemma in the discrepancy between the impressive possibilities and achievements of contemporary technology and the poverty of most design. In other areas of culture, the same discrepancy is very often identified as a discrepancy or discontinuity between the modern sense of objectivity and the given subjectivity of man, as a discontinuity of history and nature, reflected in the tension between natural sciences and humanities.

This situation was addressed by a new anthropology which came into existence during the 1920s with the aim of restoring the concreteness of human phenomena and developing a new dialectical understanding of human nature.[2] The renewed interest in anthropology was only a part of a broader tendency to create new and more solid foundations for modern thinking in a situation dominated by highly specialized and very often alienated knowledge.[3] The new discipline, referred to most often as philosophical anthropology, represents a synthesis, a coherent philosophical interpretation of all anthropologically relevant knowledge. The result is a new understanding of human nature situated beyond the false dichotomy of body and soul, or nature and history, taking into account that human beings are corporeal and situated in the world. It is due to these conditions that human beings are what they always only can be.

The understanding of our situatedness and what makes us essentially human are probably the two most important contributions made by philosophical anthropology. However, because our main interest is architecture I shall speak about anthropology in that context.

We probably would agree that one of the most pressing questions which we face almost every day is the adequacy of our design to the given requirements and expectations, not only to those established by the brief or the client, but also by the culture in which we live. In the complexity and ambiguity of our contemporary culture it is not always easy to see what are, or what may be, the criteria of a desired adequacy. However, there is a link between adequacy and the fulfilment of a particular purpose which is always articulated in a concrete human situation such as reading, conversation, work and so on. In contrast to the apparent ambiguity, uncertainty and fast-changing nature of our everyday life, primary human situations show a surprisingly high level of stability and permanence. It is enough to look closely at the way we organize our dwellings or other places we inhabit, how we dine, listen to music, engage in conversation and so on to see how little most of the primary human situations change their basic character. A very good illustration of how stable certain situations can be is the experience of the American team in their last space laboratory mission. In the dining area which could have been organized in many different ways because of zero gravity, they insisted on eating around an ordinary table, facing each other. This cannot be explained by reference to habits, convention or social reasons. The meaning of this apparently simple situation is much deeper. It is embedded not only in the structure of a particular situation but also in its long history. It is through situations that we can understand the reciprocity of our experience and of the surrounding world, and as a result the human qualities of the world itself. Situations endow experience with durable dimensions in relation to which the whole sequence of other experiences can acquire meaning, form intelligible series and, eventually, a history. The stability and meaning of situations depend on the reverberations of meanings through the depth of their history. History in this case should be seen rather like a memory which extends into the anonymity of our evolutionary development about which René Dubos, the specialist in environmental medicine, has this to say:

> The evolutionary development of all living organisms, including man, took place under the influence of cosmic forces that have not changed appreciably for very long periods of time. As a result, most physiological processes are still geared to these forces; they exhibit cycles that have daily, seasonal, and other periodicities clearly linked to the periodicities of the cosmos. As far as can be judged at the present time, the major biological periodicities derive from the daily rotation of the earth, its annual rotation around the sun, and the monthly rotation of the moon around the earth.[4]

This is obviously only a small illustration of some of the conditions under which the regularity of the events of our life were constituted and became eventually the source of other regularities and movements structuring the rest of our life. It is only in reference to the ultimate source of regularities, which is also the source or possible identities, that we can raise questions about human nature and its identity in time, about the constancy of the human situation and eventually about the adequacy of design.

So far we have discussed mainly the human 'conditions' of adequate design, saying relatively very little about human 'possibilities'. In order to answer our questions, we must consider both human conditions and possibilities simultaneously. But what are the human possibilities of adequate design? Is there a limit to human possibilities? I do not think that there is a direct answer to such questions. And yet in design the limit of our possibilities coincides with the limits of our imagination, which is essentially a mode of representation. In recent decades representational possibilities reached a level where imagination meets the imaginary. In certain cases the representation of reality appears, at least to some people, more interesting than reality itself. This state of affairs can be perhaps best described as experimental. The belief that design can be oriented entirely towards experimental goals and results became a historical possibility, but not without its own limits and dilemmas. The current development of experimental design has already reached the possibility to produce 'intelligent' buildings, and has found in this domain its ideal fulfilment. The knowledge required for the design of such buildings is mostly derived from the theories of information, simulation and artificial intelligence. However in recent years development in the field of artificial intelligence has encountered serious difficulties, particularly in areas related to the successful creation of simulated environments. The main reason for the difficulty is the impossibility to simulate and programme the situational nature of the embodied human intelligence.

> The stagnation of each of the specific efforts in artificial intelligence suggests that there can be no piecemeal breakthrough to fully formed adult

intelligent behaviour for any isolated kind of human performance. Game playing, language translation, problem solving and pattern recognition each depend upon specific forms of 'information processing', which are in turn based on the human way of being in the world. And this way of being-in-a-situation turns out to be unprogrammable in principle using presently conceivable techniques.[5]

For those who see architecture in terms of autonomous structures, efficient systems or simulated environments, this state of affairs represents a real dilemma. The future of the discipline, as it now appears, depends on the conditions and circumstances of situational embodiment which have been left behind or ignored. The dilemma becomes a paradox when we realise that to create a space in which human activities could be embodied and situated was always the main task of architecture.

The belief that the main purpose of architecture can be fulfilled through experimental design or simulation may therefore be illusory. This possibility is reinforced by the most recent development in environmental simulations, known better as virtual reality, which the protagonists themselves describe as 'simulated hallucinations'. If this represents the trend of the future development of design, what could be more illusory than hallucination?

This brings us back to anthropology, which tells us how hallucination is related to imagination and perception. Under normal conditions, imagination and perception are closely linked in a relation of reciprocity in which perception is more open to the conditions of our experience while imagination moves towards the open possibilities of experience. The limits of imagination are determined by the given conditions and by a process of mutual communication and continuity. Hallucination, on the other hand, transcends the conditions of communication. 'Hallucination causes the real to disintegrate before our eyes and puts a quasi-reality in its place.'[6] In such a situation, 'the hallucinatory phenomenon is not part of the world, that is to say it is not accessible; there is no definite path leading from it to all the remaining experiences of the deluded subject or to the experience of the sane.'[7]

There is an obvious link between hallucinatory experience and the product of hallucination, between man and the world he/she creates. 'Sickness seen from a higher aspect has to be considered as a disturbance of the relation between man and world, a disorder involving both.'[8] The nature of life in a hallucinatory world is, I believe, a sufficient indication of the limits of human possibilities and indirectly of human nature. At the same time it is also a reminder of our finitude and of the conditions of our sanity. 'What protects us against insanity or hallucinations are not our particular powers but the structure of our space.'[9]

If we accept the actual lived space as a criterion of sanity and concreteness, it is quite obvious that there is no appropriate representation which would exhaust its richness. We cannot represent space as it is, as a continuum in its totality, and yet we can experience it in its wholeness, understand it, share it and create it. What makes meaningful representation possible is the communicative context of culture in which we are always situated and which would perhaps be more appropriate to describe as communicative space.

The authenticity of representation, its meaning and adequacy ultimately depend on its ability to represent, i.e. to communicate with the given conditions of a concrete human situation. It is due to the continuity of the meaningful communication that architectural space acquires an order and meaning. The historical development in which architecture became a separate discipline, relatively isolated from other areas of culture and even from the concrete situations of everyday life, makes communication (dialogue) increasingly more difficult and at the same time more vulnerable to replacement by the monologue of experimental thinking.

We may not yet fully understand the consequences of that shift, but we can certainly anticipate them from the consistency of symptoms such as loss of meaning, a confused sense of reality, emptiness of buildings and spaces, the growing room for hallucinatory experiences and growing cultural fragmentation. The difference between communicative and experimental design reflects in many ways the difference between creativity and production. To create is to bring to existence what was not here before, but in such a way that the result is fully reconciled with everything that is already here. Production, on the other hand, tends to ignore the restrictions of the given reality and moves towards the limits of what can be done, crossing very often and quite deliberately the boundary of the imaginary and hallucinatory level of reality. In the productive attitude, the hallucinatory quality of products is not seen as problematic or negative but very often as desirable.

The deep understanding of creativity is probably the most valuable contribution of modern philosophical anthropology. Lack of space prevents me from elaborating further and I will use instead a quotation which illustrates very well the enigma of creativity:

> 'Nature is on the inside', says Cézanne. Quality, light, colour, depth, which are there before us, are there only because they awaken an echo in our body and because the body welcomes them. Things have an internal equivalent in us; they arouse in us a carnal formula of their presence. Why shouldn't these in their turn give rise to some visible shape in which anyone else would recognize those motifs which support his own inspection of the world?[10]

The reciprocity of experience and the surrounding world is a key to a situational understanding of architecture as we have discussed so far.

It is not difficult to see that the problems of architectural design as well as the questions of representation, continuity of meaning, the limits of experimental thinking and the distinction between creation and production applies also to other areas of life including politics. The political and social institutions of European societies were mostly created in accordance with their specific traditions. However, institutions can also be produced, and under certain conditions, as we have seen, the production can cross the boundary of the imaginary and hallucinatory level of reality. The fact that this has taken place mostly in the totalitarian regimes does not mean that the same can happen also in other societies.

Historical experience and critical understanding together with the insight of disciplines not restricted by the narrow political or ideological reasoning can help us to see the deeper foundations of modern politics and the important tendencies in the development of modern culture.

Notes

1 The development of modern anthropology can be traced back to the sixteenth century to Pompanazzi, *Oration on the Dignity of Man* (the term anthropology appears for the first time in a work under the same title by O. Casman, 1596). The development culminated in the works of L. Feurbach and A. Comte in the middle of the nineteenth century.

2 The pioneering work is M. Scheler, *Die Stellung des Menschen im Kosmos*, first published in Berlin in 1928 and H. Plessner, *Die Stufen des Organischen und der Mensch*, Einleitung in der philosophischen Anthropologie, Berlin, 1928.

3 The first steps in that direction can be traced in the works of Nietzsche, Dilthey, Freud and to some extent in the Anglo-Saxon pragmatism. The foundational work was done by Husserl, Scheler and eventually by Heidegger.

4 René Dubos, *Man Adapting*, New Haven, CN: Yale University Press, 1965, p. 42.

5 H. Dreyfus, *What Computers Can't Do*, New York: Harper and Rowe, 1979, p. 302.

6 M. Merleau-Ponty, *The Phenomenology of Perception*, London: Routledge, 1974, p. 334.

7 Merleau-Ponty, *The Phenomenology of Perception* p. 339.

8 T. Kisiel, 'Aphasiology, Phenomenology, Structuralism' in *Language and Language Disturbances*, ed. E. Strauss, 1974, p. 202.

9 Merleau-Ponty, *The Phenomenology of Perception*, p. 291.

10 M. Merleau-Ponty, 'Eye and Mind', in *The Primacy of Perception and Other Essays*, ed. James Edie, Evanston, IL: Northwestern University Press, 1964, p. 164.

12 Disjunctions

Bernard Tschumi

Following the collapse of communism in Central and Eastern Europe, and the establishment of a new society, architects should look to new forms of architecture. It is not sufficient to accept uncritically the traditions of the past. The new Europe needs a radically new architecture, an architecture of disruptions and disjunctions, which reflects the fragmentation and dissociation within culture at large.

Disjunction and culture[1]

The paradigm of the architect passed down to us through the modern period is that of the form-giver, the creator of hierarchical and symbolic structures characterized, on the one hand, by their unity of parts and, on the other, by the transparency of form to meaning. (The modern, rather than modernist, subject of architecture is referred to here so as to indicate that this unified perspective far exceeds our recent past). A number of well-known correlatives elaborate these terms: the fusion of form and function, program and context, structure and meaning. Underlying these is a belief in the unified, centred, and self-generated subject, whose own autonomy is reflected in the formal autonomy of the work. Yet, at a certain point, this long-standing practice, which accentuates synthesis, harmony, the composition of elements and the seamless coincidence of potentially disparate parts, becomes estranged from its external culture, from temporary cultural conditions.

Dis-structuring

In its disruptions and disjunctions, its characteristic fragmentation and dissociation, today's cultural circumstances suggest the need to discard established categories of meaning and contextual historics. It might be worthwhile, therefore, to abandon any notion of a postmodern architecture in favour of a 'posthumanist' architecture, one that would stress not only the dispersion of the subject and the force of social regulation, but also the effect of such decentering on the entire notion of unified, coherent architectural form. It also seems important to think, not in terms of principles of formal composition, but rather of questioning structures; that is, the order, techniques and procedures that are entailed by any architectural work.

Such a project is far removed from formalism in that it stresses the historical motivation of the sign, emphasizing its contingency and its cultural fragility, rather than a historical essence. It is one that, in current times, can only confront the radical rift between signifier and signified or, in architectural terms, space and action, form and function. That today we are witnessing a striking dislocation of these terms calls attention not only to the disappearance of functionalist theories but perhaps also to the normative function of architecture itself.

Order

Any theoretical work, when 'displaced' into the built realm, still remains its role within a general system or open system of thought. As in the theoretical project *The Manhattan Transcripts* (1981), and the built Parc de la Villette, what is questioned is the notion of unity. As they are conceived, both works have no beginnings and no ends. They are operations composed of repetitions, distortions, superpositions and so forth. Although they have their own internal logic – they are not aimlessly pluralistic – their operations cannot be described purely in terms of internal or sequential transformations. The idea of order is constantly questioned, challenged, pushed to the edge.

Strategies of disjunction

Although the notion of disjunction is not to be seen as an architectural concept, it has effects that are impressed upon the site, the building, even the programme, according to the dissociative logic governing the work. If one were to define disjunction, moving beyond its dictionary meaning, one would insist on the idea of limit, of interruption. Both the *Transcripts* and La Ville employ different elements of a strategy of disjunction. This strategy takes the form of a systematic exploration of one or more themes: for example, frames and sequences in the case of the *Transcripts*, and superposition and repetition in La Villette. Such explorations can never be conducted in the abstract, *ex nihilo*: one works within the discipline of architecture, though with an awareness of other fields such as literature, philosophy or even film theory.

Limits

The notion of the limit is evident in the practice of Joyce, and Bataille and Artaud, who all worked at the edge of philosophy and non-philosophy, of literature and non-literature. The attention paid today to Jacques Derrida's deconstructive approach also represents an interest in the work at the limit: the analysis of concepts in the most rigorous and internalized manner, but also their analysis from without, so as to question what these concepts and their history hide, as repression or dissimulation. Such examples suggest that there is a need to consider the question of limits in architecture. They act as reminders (to me) that my own pleasure has never surfaced in looking at buildings, at the great works of the history or the present of architecture but, rather, in dismantling them. To paraphrase Orson Welles: 'I don't like architecture, I like making architecture.'

Notation

The work on notation undertaken in *The Manhattan Transcripts* was an attempt to deconstruct the components of architecture. The different modes of notation employed were aimed at grasping domains that, though normally excluded from most architectural theory, are indispensable to work at the margins, or limits, of architecture. Although no mode of notation, whether mathematical or logical, can transcribe the full complexity of the architectural phenomenon, the progress of architectural notation is linked to the renewal of both architecture and its accompanying concepts of culture. Once the traditional components have been dismantled, reassembly is an extended process; above all, what is ultimately a transgression of classical and modern canons should not be permitted to regress toward formal empiricism. Hence the disjunctive strategy used both in the *Transcripts* and at La Villette, in which facts never quite connect, and relations of conflict are carefully maintained, rejecting synthesis or totality. The project is never achieved, not are the boundaries ever definite.

Disjunction and the avant-garde

As Derrida points out, architectural and philosophical concepts do not disappear overnight. The once fashionable 'epistemological break' notwithstanding, ruptures always occur within an old fabric that is constantly dismantled and dislocated in such a way that its ruptures lead to new concepts or structures. In architecture such disjunction implies that at no moment can any part become a synthesis or self-sufficient totality; each part leads to another, and every construction is off-balance, constituted by the traces of another construction. It could also be constituted by the traces of an event, a program. It can lead to new concepts, as one objective here is to understand a new concept of the city, of architecture.

If we were to qualify an architecture or an architectural method as 'disjunctive', its common denominators might be the following:

- Rejection of the notion of 'synthesis' in favour of the idea of dissociation, of disjunctive analysis.
- Rejection of the traditional opposition between use and architectural form in favour of a superposition or juxtaposition of two terms that can be independently and similarly subjected to identical methods of architectural analysis.
- Emphasis placed, as a method, on dissociation, superposition and combination, which trigger dynamic forces that expand into the whole architectural system, exploding its limits while suggesting a new definition.

The concept of disjunction is incompatible with a static, autonomous, structural view of architecture. But it is not anti-autonomy or anti-structure; it simply implies constant, mechanical operations that systematically produce dissociation in space and time, where an architectural element only functions by colliding with a programmatic element, with the movement of bodies, or whatever. In this manner, disjunction becomes a systematic and theoretical tool for the making of architecture.

Notes

1 This section is reproduced with permission from Bernard Tschumi, *Architecture and Disjunction*, Cambridge, MA: MIT Press, 1994.

13 The dark side of the *domus*

The redomestication of Central and Eastern Europe

Neil Leach

Within recent architectural theory architecture as 'dwelling' has become something of a dominant paradigm amid calls for a regionalist architecture and celebration of the concept of *genius loci*.[1] This is an approach which emanates from the work of the German philosopher, Martin Heidegger, and which has been pursued by those who have developed his thought – architectural theorists such as Christian Norberg-Schulz and philosophers such as Gianni Vattimo.[2] Many have looked to an architecture of 'dwelling' as a means of combatting the alienation of contemporary society and of resisting the homogenising placelessness of International Style architecture.

In the context of Central and Eastern Europe, in particular, architects have looked to such an approach as an antidote to the bland uniformity of state architecture of the communist years. It is an approach which reflects the sudden upsurge of interest in the philosophy of Heidegger within culture in general following the collapse of communism. What I wish to argue, however, is that taken to an extreme 'dwelling' itself – the logic of the *domus* – can have negative consequences. There is, I would maintain, a negative side to 'dwelling', a dark side to the *domus*, which makes this approach somewhat inappropriate for a new Europe which has already come under the shadow of the dark side of nationalism.

Heidegger and the question of dwelling

According to Heidegger, one's capacity to live on this earth – to 'dwell' in the phenomenological sense – is an essentially architectural experience. The very Being of being is linked to one's situatedness in the world. This is the thesis that comes out most clearly in his essay, 'Building, Dwelling, Thinking'. As the title of this essay infers, for Heidegger there is a clear link between 'dwelling' and architecture. The whole concept of 'dwelling' is grounded in the architectural. For Heidegger, a building should be on and *of* the soil, *of* the location on which it is built. He illustrates this with the example of a Greek temple, which sits so naturally within its setting it is as though it has been 'brought forth' by its setting. Throughout Heidegger's thinking there is an emphasis on the soil, on the earth, and this applies especially to the question of architecture. Buildings are not buildings in the abstract, but they gain their very sense of presence through being situated where they are, through their *Dasein*. 'Does not the flourishing of any work of art', he asks, 'depend upon its roots in a native soil?'[3] This evocation of the soil, this call for a 'situated' architecture, can be read as an evocation for the *heimat*, for the homeland. For Heidegger, it is not in the cities but in the countryside – where one is most in touch with nature and tradition – that the sense of homeland may flourish:

> Homeland is most possible and effective where the powers of nature around us and the remnants of historical tradition remain together, where an origin and an ancient, nourished style of human existence hold sway. Today for this decisive task perhaps only the rural counties and small towns are competent – if they recognise anew their unusual qualities, if they know how to draw the boundaries between themselves and life in the large cities and gigantic areas of modern industrial complexes.[4]

This appeal to the homeland would appear to be part of a consistent nationalistic outlook in his thought, which is echoed in a series of forced etymological strategies in his writings which attempt to lend authority to the German language by tracing the origins of certain German words to ancient Greek. All this would seem to infer that there is a potential nationalism that permeates the whole of his thought, a nationalism which, in the context of prewar Germany, shared something in common with fascism.

It would be wrong to associate Heidegger's thought too closely with the excesses of fascist ideology. There is much to be praised in his work, and one could argue that his philosophy need not necessarily lead to a nationalistic outlook, and that to judge his thought solely at the level of the political would be to do him an injustice. Indeed his work is open to a variety of interpretations, and the complexity of his thought defies any neat categorisation. But equally, the point should be made that his work *lends* itself to a nationalistic outlook, and that his own life was *inscribed within* a nationalistic outlook. Thus it hardly seems inconsistent that a philosopher such as Heidegger should have belonged at one stage to the National Socialist party, a stand for which he has been highly criticised.

It is in 'The Self-Assertion of the German University', his rectoral address of 1933, that Heidegger most closely associates his thoughts with the aspirations of National Socialism. He unequivocally links the question of Being to the '*soil and blood* of a *Volk*':

> spirit is the determined resolve to the essence of Being, a resolve that is attuned to origins and knowing. And the *spiritual world* of a Volk is not its cultural superstructure, just as little as it is its arsenal of useful knowledge and values; rather, it is the power that comes from preserving at the most profound level the forces that are rooted in the *soil and blood* of a Volk, the power to arouse most inwardly and to shake most extensively the Volk's existence.[5]

Similar themes are echoed in Heidegger's speech in honour of the German nationalist hero, Albert Leo Schlageter, who had been executed in 1923 for acts of sabotage against the French army of occupation. Here the 'soil' is specifically identified with the Black Forest:

> Student of Freiburg! German student! When on your hikes and outings you set foot in the mountains, forests and valleys of this Black Forest, the home of this hero, experience this and know: the mountains among which the young farmer's son grew up are of primitive stone, of granite. They have long been at work hardening the will. The autumn sun of the Black Forest bathes the mountain ranges and forests in the most glorious clear light. It has long nourished clarity of heart. As he [Schlageter] stood defenceless facing the rifles, the hero's inner gaze soared above the muzzles to the daylight and mountains of his home that he might die for the German people and its Reich with the Alemannic countryside before his eyes.[6]

And it was precisely in the soil of this Alemannic countryside that Heidegger declared his own thought to be rooted: 'The inner relationship of my own work to the Black Forest and its people comes from a centuries-long and irreplaceable rootedness in the Alemannian-Swabian soil.'[7]

The very evocation of the soil in Heidegger echoes a consistent trope within fascist ideology. As Klaus Theweleit has argued in the context of prewar German fascism, this evocation can be understood in psychoanalytic terms as a need to reinforce and protect the ego by identifying with a larger body.[8] This larger identity would be constituted in a social order, and would be embodied in a figurehead and a physical location: *ein Volk, ein Reich, ein Führer*. Identity therefore becomes territorialised and mapped on to a geographic terrain. The individual becomes one with the land in a process of identification which is itself mythic, and this process is often supported by other myths of identification. In this dissolving into nature, difference is suppressed and a new identity is forged with mother earth. Thus we find constant references to natural phenomena – storms, blood and soil – in fascist ideology. As Ernst Jünger, a figure who exerted a great influence on Heidegger, wrote of prewar German fascism:

> What is being born is the essence of nationalism, a new relation to the elemental, to Mother earth, whose soil has been blasted away in the rekindled fires of material battles and fertilised by streams of blood.[9]

It can be seen that it is precisely in the context of an identity rooted to the soil that those groups not rooted to the soil become excluded. Traditionally, Jews and gypsies are both 'wanderers', although each for different reasons: the gypsies largely by choice, the Jews mainly by necessity. Neither are rooted to the soil. The 'wanderer' does not fit within a concept of situatedness or rootedness to the soil, and therefore does not fit within the philosophy of the *heimat*. The 'wanderer' is the element that cannot be controlled, cannot be domesticated, cannot be contained within the logic of the *domus*. The 'wanderer' is therefore treated as the 'other', the excluded one, and is perceived as a threat to the nation. Just as nationalism forms a symbolic identification with the soil, so it also generates an antagonism towards all that cannot be identified with the soil. For it is precisely the fear of flows and movements which cannot be stemmed, as Klaus Theweleit has observed, that characterises the fascist obsession with control.[10]

The *domus* and the megalopolis

Heidegger's involvement with the National Socialists has been known to German intellectuals for some time, but it was not until the publication in 1987 of Victor Farias's *Heidegger et le nazisme* that the full extent of his involvement with the organisation and his anti-semitism became known to French intellectuals. This event fanned the flames of what was to become known as the 'Heidegger controversy'. Those who have attempted to defend him for his political indiscretions have claimed that he was either politically naive or that his own philosophy is essentially apolitical.[11] Others, such as Jean-François Lyotard, have been less charitable towards him. In his book, *Heidegger and 'the jews'*,[12] Lyotard uses 'jew' with a lower case 'j' to signify not just Jews themselves, but all minority groups who might be perceived as the 'other': outsiders, non-conformists, artists, anarchists, blacks, homeless, Arabs and anyone else who might be perceived as alien and potentially threatening. For Lyotard, the crime in Heidegger, and so too in all thought, lies in the forgetting, and the forgetting of the forgetting. It is in what is left out, what is excluded, what is in effect 'repressed', that his thinking is at fault. This more general forgetting also includes the more specific forgetting: the failure on the part of Heidegger to acknowledge and apologise fully for his support of National Socialism.[13]

Lyotard picks up the problem of Heidegger's thought in the context of architecture in his piece, '*Domus* and the Megalopolis'.[14] Lyotard contrasts the traditional *domus* with our present condition, that of the megalopolis. In other words he is contrasting two models of existence, two ideals of living. Although the one, the *domus*, is associated with the simple homestead and the other, the megalopolis, with the city, he is not contrasting the homestead with the city so much as the condition of the homestead with the condition of the city. He is contrasting the myth of the *domus* – the phenomenon of 'home' – with the more alienated model of 'city life' within the age of the megalopolis.

The traditional *domus* has been presented as a bucolic idyll, where all you do is serve the *phusis* – the natural order – and place yourself at the service of its urge. The traditional *domus* has its natural rhythm which contains and controls everything. The domestic hierarchy of the *domus* likewise has its natural order, with the master and mistress, the *dominus* and the *domina*, and the *ancilla*, the female servant. Yet this image of the bucolic idyll, for Lyotard, remains but an image. Since the time of Virgil, the *domus* has no longer been possible. 'Domesticity', Lyotard comments, 'is over, and probably it never existed, except as a dream of the old child awakening and destroying it on awakening.'[15] The current *domus* is but a myth, a product of the megalopolis, the nostalgic yearning for what can now only be a mirage. For Lyotard there can be no more *domus*; the megalopolis has now stifled the *domus*, and has 'gnawed away' at the *domus* and its community. With the advent of the megalopolis the traditional values of the *domus* have been transformed, and the hegemony of the natural order has been supplanted by the artificial.[16] But the crucial point for Lyotard is that the *domus* constitutes a form of myth. It is not that myths – 'the myths we live by' – are in themselves bad, but rather that there is something potentially deceptive about myth, because its own identity *as* myth is often concealed. And it is precisely in its reliance on the mythic that Heidegger's own thought is most suspect.

In such a context, the values of the *domus* likewise become facades. They can never be invoked but only mimicked, as in the case of the Nazis. Thus, for Lyotard, the 'service' of nature in the original *domus* leads inexorably to the 'service' – *dienst* – of Heidegger's rectorship address, a hollow and ironic sense of 'service', where 'knowledge service' is treated at the same level as 'labour service' and 'military service'.[17] The *domus* here has a different 'take'. For in the age of the megalopolis – in an age when the god-nature has been doubled as an anti-god – when there is no 'nature' to serve, service is incorporated within a generalised system of exchange – business – whose aim is profit, and whose governing principle is performativity. Under this new condition the violence of the *domus* is exposed. Everything that was ordered and contained within an hierarchised structure, which served to replicate and repeat the cycle of domesticity, all that was once tamed and controlled, 'domesticated' within the *domus*, is revealed for what it is in the figure of modern man, *homo re-domesticus* (redomesticated man). To quote from Lyotard:

> The undominated, the untamed, in earlier times concealed in the *domus*, is unleashed in the *homo politicus* and *homo economicus* but under the ancient aegis of service, *Dienst...Homo re-domesticus* in power kills in the street shouting 'You are not one of ours'...The ruin of the *domus* makes possible this fury which it contained and which it exercised in its name.[18]

What masquerades as the *domus* in fact constitutes 'domestication without the *domus*'. It contains a violence repressed within it. 'The untameable was tragic', for Lyotard, 'because it was lodged in the heart of the *domus*.'[19] And here we might recognise a Freudian moment within Lyotard. Indeed the house itself, as Freud suggested, can be taken as a model for repression. The terms which Freud uses in this context – *heimlich* (homely) and *unheimlich* (uncanny) – are terms with clear architectural resonances.

For Freud, the *heimlich* contained the *unheimlich* repressed within it: 'For this uncanny is in reality nothing new or alien, but something which is familiar and old-fashioned in the mind and which has become alienated from it through a process of repression.'[20] It is as though the very foundations of the house and of all that is homely are built on the repression of its opposite, the *unheimlich*

be unleashed. If, after the events of 1989, freedom itself was a 'shock', there was a greater shock in the unexpected neo-Nazi violence that accompanied the rise of nationalism in the East. But it was a shock that might perhaps have been anticipated. Within the *heimlich* of the homeland there lurks the *unheimlich* of nationalism, and the very 'phenomenon of home' contains a potential violence.

In envisaging a new Europe beyond the Wall we should be open to an alternative model of architectural theory more congenial to the complexities of modern society, a model which likewise avoids the domination and exclusion implicit in the *domus*, and which can accommodate the more flexible modes of existence that characterise our contemporary condition. Perhaps, then, rather than continuing to champion the *domus*, the architecture of 'dwelling' – which, it has been argued, is the mythical product of a postmodern age – we might look instead to more appropriate models suggested by the megalopolis, the city itself. And it is to the specific model of the city as cosmopolis that I wish to turn. For, just as there is a dark side to the *domus*, the cosmopolis provides an acceptable face to the megalopolis. The cosmopolis as a form of 'city life' offers an ideal that deserves to be reappraised.

The city constitutes the condition of the present, and urbanity, as Iris Marion Young has observed, remains 'the horizon of the modern, not to mention the postmodern condition'.[32] If, furthermore, we are to understand our current condition as largely that of a transitory, fleeting society, the predominant – if not universal – mode of existence, it could be argued, is often precisely that of the 'wanderer'. The Jew, the gypsy, the 'other' of society provide in some senses the model for the contemporary moment; rootless, international, mobile, deterritorialised.[33] This is in opposition to the rooted, the nationalistic and the static. If the *dominus*, the stable and controlling master of the *domus*, is the creature of the traditional community, the 'wanderer' represents the freedom and flux of the city. As such, the 'wanderer' is the archetypal creature of our contemporary condition, a creature whose existence reflects the very transiency of the city.

Often commentators of modernity criticised the city as alienating, fragmentary, violent and disordered. Georg Simmel, for example, observed how the metropolis spawned the modern *blasé* individual whose disinterested existence within the city evokes the circulation of capital itself. The modern city dweller has developed a form of anonymity, itself a defensive cocoon against the overstimulation of life in the metropolis. Yet this very anonymity breeds a certain tolerance. The city, for example, tends to accept difference, and to accommodate the 'other'. Traditionally, the city has provided a refuge for minorities: it is the city where the Jew, the outsider, the 'wanderer' has often found a haven. 'City life' is the ideal where 'difference' is acceptable and on occasions even celebrated, to the point where minority interest groups have often been spawned by the city.

By comparison, the 'community' – the figure of the *domus* – can be seen to be an homogenising, universalising model, which absorbs and therefore denies 'difference'. The notion of 'community' is based on a myth of unmediated social relations. It assumes that all subjects are transparent to one another, and that somehow each can fully understand the 'other'. 'Difference' is therefore collapsed into a single totalising vision, which itself breeds a certain intolerance to whatever does not conform to that vision. It is only when the city mimics the village, when it fragments back into 'neighbourhoods' which constitute autonomous individual units that this model begins to break down. Within 'neighbourhood watch schemes' and other exclusionary mechanisms the principle of the city – the heterogeneous, open cosmopolis – is supplanted by the principle of the village – the homogeneous, closed *domus*. As the extreme of this condition, we might cite past examples of sectarian and political divides within cities such as Belfast, Beirut or indeed Berlin.

This is not to say that 'city life' is always perfect. Clearly the city, no less than the *domus*, has its negative aspects. The city can equally be seen as the site of crime, destitution and inequality. Not everyone can enjoy the 'freedom' of the city. Nor indeed can every city be perceived as similar, and in evaluating each individual city many specific social and economic considerations need to be taken into account, Nonetheless 'city life' – the life of the cosmopolis – offers an alternative to the model of the *domus*. The cosmopolis retains the germ of an ideal more in tune with our contemporary cultural conditions. It suggests a possible model for living together in a form of interdependency, a model which can allow for the fluidity and flux, the complexities and multi-faceted solidarities of contemporary society, and which is characterised by a non-oppositional, non-hierarchical openness to the 'other'. Writ large, the *cosmopolis* suggests a model for a pluralistic, open Europe, free from the exclusions of nationalism.

And if the new Europe is to be an open, cosmopolitan Europe, then surely we require an architecture whose language and forms match such an ideal: an architecture which transcends the rigid constraints of the *genius loci* – that 'ultimate onto-theological component of Architecture Appropriated' as Daniel Libeskind has described it – and which resists the nihilistic unfolding of tradition: an 'open' architecture. Perhaps then we should be envisaging not 'architecture' so much as 'architectures', unpredictable, flexible and hybrid 'architectures', as Libeskind calls for in the context of Berlin;[34] architectures which match the fluidity, flux and complexity of contemporary existence, an existence that is epitomised by the cosmopolis; architectures that might therefore be described as 'cosmopolitan architectures'; architectures born of the spirit of the cosmopolis, but not limited to the cosmopolis: cosmopolitan architectures for a cosmopolitan Europe.

Notes

1 An earlier version of this paper appeared in *The Journal of Architecture*, vol. 3, Spring 1998, pp. 1–12.
2 Christian Norberg-Schulz, *Genius Loci: Towards a Phenomenology of Architecture*, London: Academy Editions, 1980; Gianni Vattimo, 'The End of Modernity, The End of The Project?', trans. David Webb, *Journal of Philosophy and the Visual Arts*, Academy Editions, pp. 74–7.

3 Martin Heidegger, *Discourse on Thinking*, trans. J.M. Anderson and E.H. Freund, New York: Harper & Row, 1966, p. 47.

4 Martin Heidegger, 'Homeland', trans. Thomas Franklin O'Meara, *Listening*, vol. 6, no. 3 (autumn, 1971), pp. 231–8, cited in Michael Zimmerman, *Heidegger's Confrontation with Modernity*, Bloomington and Indianapolis: Indiana University Press, 1990, p. 71.

5 Martin Heidegger, 'The Self-Assertion of the German University' in Richard Wolin (ed.), *The Heidegger Controversy*, Cambridge, MA: MIT Press, 1993, pp. 29–39. Other examples of pro-Nazi rhetoric on the part of Heidegger are to be found in this volume.

6 Martin Heidegger, 'Schlageter' in Richard Wolin (ed.), *The Heidegger Controversy*, Cambridge, MA: MIT Press, 1993, p. 41.

7 Martin Heidegger, 'Schneeberger', p. 216, trans. Thomas Sheehan, cited in Sheehan, *Heidegger: The Man and the Thinker*, Chicago: Precedent Publishing, 1981, p. 213.

8 Klaus Theweleit argues in the case of German Freikorp soldiers that it is often precisely the underdeveloped and 'not-fully-born' egos of young males within a particular constellation of social and political circumstances where this 'need' is most acute. Klaus Theweleit, *Male Fantasies*, vol. 1, trans. Stephen Conway, Cambridge: Polity Press, 1987; vol. 2, trans. Chris Turner and Erica Carter, Cambridge: Polity Press, 1989.

9 Cited by Theweleit, vol. 2, p. 88. For the influence of Jünger on Heidegger, see Michael Zimmerman, *Heidegger's Confrontation with Modernity*, Bloomington and Indianapolis: Indiana University Press, 1990, pp. 66–93.

10 Theweleit, vol. 1, pp. 229–435.

11 See, for example, Fred Dallmayr, *The Other Heidegger*, Ithaca, NY and London: Cornell University Press, 1993; Philippe Lacoue-Labarthe, *Heidegger, Art and Politics*, trans. Chris Turner, Oxford: Blackwell, 1990.

12 Victor Fairas's work was translated into English in 1989, as *Heidegger and Nazism*, trans. Paul Barrell *et al.*, Philadelphia: Temple University Press. Jean-François Lyotard, *Heidegger and 'the jews'*, trans. Andreas Michel and Mark Roberts, Minneapolis: University of Minnesota Press, 1990.

13 These questions are discussed at length in Richard Wolin (ed.), *The Heidegger Controversy*, Cambridge, MA: MIT Press, 1993. See especially the exchange of letters between Herbert Marcuse and Martin Heidegger. Other books on this subject include Hans Sluga, *Heidegger's Crisis*, Cambridge, MA: Harvard University Press, 1993.

14 Jean-François Lyotard, *The Inhuman*, trans. Geoffrey Bennington and Rachel Bowlby, Cambridge: Polity Press, 1991, pp. 191–204.

15 Lyotard, p. 201.

16 For Lyotard what takes over from the 'control' of the *domus* in the megalopolis is a form of techno-science which offers a new form of control, one that is no longer territorialised and historicised, but computerized.

17 Lyotard, p. 195. See Martin Heidegger, 'The Self-Assertion of the German University' in Richard Wolin (ed.), *The Heidegger Controversy*, Cambridge, MA: MIT Press, 1993, p. 35.

18 Lyotard, p. 197.

19 Lyotard, p. 202.

20 Sigmund Freud, *Art and Literature*, Penguin Freud Library, volume 14, trans. James Strachey, London: Penguin, 1985.

21 Freud, p. 347.

22 See Fredric Jameson, *The Seeds of Time*, New York: Columbia University Press, 1994, pp. 189–205.

23 Lyotard, p. 198.

24 On this see Paul Virilio, *The Lost Dimension*, trans. Daniel Mosheberg, New York: Semiotext(e), 1991.

25 Theodor Adorno, *The Jargon of Authenticity*, trans. Knut Tarnowski and Frederic Will, London: Routledge, 1973. For Adorno, Heidegger's thought hides behind contentless jargon. It represents a self-referential system which, by failing to address the real political and economic framework of society, serves only as an ideological mystification of the actual processes of human domination.

26 Fredric Jameson, 'History Lessons', pp. 79–80.

27 Jean Baudrillard, *Simulacra and Simulations*, trans. Sheila Faria Glaser, Ann Arbor, MI: Michigan University Press, 1994, p. 12.

28 Walter Benjamin, *Reflections*, trans. Edmund Jephcott, New York: Schocken Books, 1978, p. 248.

29 On this see Geoffrey Harris, *The Dark Side of Europe: The Extreme Right Today*, Edinburgh University Press, 1994.

30 Vaclav Havel, *Summer Meditations*, trans. Paul Wilson, London: Faber & Faber, 1992, p.104.

31 Renata Salecl, 'The Ideology of the Mother Nation in the Yugoslav Conflict', in Michael Kennedy (ed.), *Envisioning Eastern Europe*, Ann Arbor, MI: University of Michigan Press, 1994, pp. 87–101.

32 Iris Marion Young, *Justice and the Politics of Difference*, Princeton, NJ: Princeton University Press, 1990, p. 237.

33 Manchehr Sanadjian explores the concept of 'deterritorialisation' in 'Iranians in Germany' in *New German Critique*, 64, Winter 95, 3–36; see also Caren Kaplan, 'Deterritorialisations: The Rewriting of Home and Exile in Western Feminist Discourse', *Cultural Critique*, 6, Spring 87, p. 191.

34 Daniel Libeskind, 'Traces of the Unborn', p. 127.

14 Architecture in a post-totalitarian society

Round-table discussion conducted by
Bart Goldhoorn

Architecture and society

Do architects in contemporary Russia still serve some kind of public interest or are they only fulfilling the demands of the private client? What role could urban design, the most public aspect of the architectural discipline play in the development of the Russian city? How will the Russian city change over the next twenty years?

SELIM KHAN-MAGOMEDOV: In the twentieth century architects have been concerned with the problems of the general population's living conditions. In our country this was especially evident in the 1920s and 1930s, and, to some extent remains so to this day. Today, everything in the past is being criticized. The denial of that which preceded is characteristic for the Russian mentality – this was the case in the time of Prince Vladimir Krasnoe Solnyshko, and in the time of Peter the Great and later, in the classical epoch, when the majority of traditional boyars' palaces were disfigured in attempts to mimic European styles. Nevertheless, architecture is basically a positive form of art always reacting in a positive way to any assignment, even if it is an imperial one. We must realize that in architecture, unlike literature or painting, there can be no such thing as 'critical realism'.

    It is difficult to discuss the contemporary role of urban design in the development of the Russian city. We have rejected the old rigid regulations, and yet there is still no real new legislation on urban planning, just as there is no real land market. All this is only in the making, and it is hardly possible to say in advance how the results of this process will be reflected in future architecture.

    Discussing what the image of the Russian city will be in 20 years is more meaningful from a structural than from an aesthetic point of view. From the 1930s onward we have undergone a process of urbanization that has no European precedent, in which urban populations increased to four or, perhaps, five times their previous levels. As a result the ratio of population density between cities and domesticated non-urban territories has changed sharply. This is a terrible situation.

In reaction, a strange trend is developing, in which city-dwellers flood the abandoned suburbs with datchas. For example, on a map of the Moscow area we see huge settlements that are popping up like mushrooms, whose populations in the summer months exceed the population of nearby villages by 100 times. This is a very interesting situation, undeservedly neglected by architects. The concept of the 'second home' does not exist in America or in other developed countries.

Another interesting change in the urban situation can be connected with changes in the price of land within city limits. These changes could result in the removal of restrictions on building heights and the development of the Russian city along the American model.

ANDREI BOKOV: It is too early to speak about a complete reorientation of the architect towards the demands of private clients, not least because private clients these days still represent a rather insignificant segment of the market which itself has not fully developed. Nevertheless, this segment already plays a significant role in the way architects understand their task.

The question, however, is not what kind of commission the architect is executing – a state or a private one – but whether in fulfilling the assignment the architect feels within himself the presence of some kind of 'higher' task, not necessarily directly connected to the realization of anyone's objectives. Architecture is born just then, when the architect is confronted with this other distinct task and when the client appreciates it in the same way.

Urban planning, traditionally understood in our country as a phenomenon belonging more to the repertoire of the last century, with its ideas of super-order and hyper-order, was born in the midst of large empires. Such an urban planning can't exist any longer. In place of it the concept of 'the urban component' has arisen, to be considered when solving every concrete architectural problem.

The coming twenty years for the Russian city will, it appears, be a period of restoration of normal 'blood circulation'. The Russian city will make up for the lost opportunities of seventy years of artificial restraint and stagnation. The direction of the forthcoming 'normal' development is difficult to predict as yet. The inflow of investments in the centre of Moscow, for example, could give rise to intensive underground urbanization, thus avoiding the construction of skyscrapers within the limits of the Garden Ring, and Moscow's La Defence can be situated way out in Lubertsy [a Moscow suburb].

A polarisation between slums and the centre will doubtlessly appear. It is not difficult to imagine what the areas of 16 and 22 storey apartment blocks will be transformed into within the near future. On the other hand, the rich areas – sumptuous houses, restaurants, clubs etc. – will certainly continue to develop. Perhaps, after a while, the propertyless working classes will burn these houses down, move into them, marry the widowed housewives and learn to speak French.

VYACHESLAV GLAZYCHEV: Behind the term 'public task' I see a dangerous myth: the ideological abstraction found in the word 'the people'. In a civilized society, when dealing with the city, architects enter into relations not simply with 'the people' but with a specific community. Assuming the role of clients, our present bureaucrats frequently act in the name of a community of citizens that does not yet exist. As a result, the assignment is still not private in character, as far as it remains anonymous.

The more precisely the architect fulfils a private assignment – that is, not individually or bureaucratically private, but treated as private, having lost its anonymity – the more he can introduce additional value to his work. Even if a commission is formally bureaucratic, when it willy-nilly attains a certain individual character, it creates opportunities for the architect to become personally involved, regardless of the type of property. Therefore I don't see a contradiction between the terms 'private customer' and 'public task'.

As already noted by my colleagues, urban planning in the former sense will cease to exist. The advocates of this idea and the establishment connected with it are dying out. Right now I am translating a book by the American non-conformist Roberta Gratz with the title, *Living City*, where she introduces a term I like very much, namely, 'urban husbandry'. It designates a new type of attitude towards the urban environment in which local corrective alterations and improvements are continuously introduced. This attitude is comparable to working with clay: some patching up here, adding something there, changing this or that, *et cetera*.

Some positive movements in this direction are already occurring, for example, the discovery of a smaller scale and the subsequent increase in the density of activity in urban areas.

Paradoxically enough, the middle-sized Russian cities, with which I have worked over the last three years, have advanced much further towards this new ideology than Moscow, and because of this, the processes occurring at present in these cities may be of even more interest in relation to the future of the Russian city.

The active privatization of urban land in small and middle-size cities along with the occurrence of certain legislative measures (such as the rigid zoning codes already operating in Vladimir) instantly changes the situation, promoting in particular the revival of old urban centres with small-scale buildings of wood and stone. These buildings immediately acquire a valued status and become places in which potential and real investors are interested.

EVGENY ASSE: First of all it is necessary to say that when a Western liberal intellectual like Bart Goldhoorn speaks about the 'public task' of the architect, he means, of course, not an abstract construct from the arsenal of Soviet ideological clichés, but the quite real problem of professional responsibility, which for a long time has been condition *sine qua non* for architects in the West. In the end, responsibility for the quality of life of the users of architecture is not only a responsibility towards one client but towards a significant group of people. Conscientious architects in countries like Holland or Switzerland try to build in a system according to some civil norm, which in Russia, unfortunately, does not and probably cannot exist.

And at the city level: all architects now feed themselves on commissions (that violate all norms!) for the renovation of apartments for new Russians, and refuse to see that this results in freezing out the centre's original inhabitants, who are leaving for the city outskirts in huge numbers. Certainly, the centre requires reconstruction, but many countries – not without the influence of socially responsible architects, by the way – have for a long time had municipal legislation, blocking the creation of districts of people with a single level of income, thus preventing the emergence of slums.

Speaking of norms, I have in mind not only norms in a cultural sense, but also regulative parameters that determine the 'normal' (i.e. 'natural') development of the city. The absence of such norms (zoning, simple regulations) is a characteristic feature of the current period in the life of the Russian city. Everything used to be decided in an autocratic way by urban design councils – 'this way, that way; lower, higher.'

The same general absence of norms, of the conception of some kind of normal decent way of life, makes me sceptical about whether we can expect any fundamental positive changes in the Russian city in the next twenty years. At the best, alcoholics, who are presently accustomed to crowding around liquor booths, will get a café or pub where they can drink comfortably – and this will already be quite an improvement.

Architecture as a profession

The professional position of the architect seems to have changed dramatically in recent years. To what extent can we speak about a change in the relations between architect and authorities, architect and client, architect and builder, and architects and their colleagues?

SELIM KHAN-MAGOMEDOV: It is possible to describe the first fifteen years of the development of Soviet architecture as a 'period of anarchy' – the authorities were engaged in other business and architects happily avoided their supervision. The second period was already strongly marked by governmental taste, though the architectural standards remained relatively high. As for today's situation, I do not know how it is in the provinces, but in Moscow the authorities scandalize architects with their behaviour. We have two academies and God knows what else, and everybody watches silently as the mayor of Moscow dictates the style of new buildings, just like it was under Lazar Koganovich.

In the relations between architect and client a lot of new and interesting aspects have appeared. The architect will not receive dictatorial power over construction in the near future (although this would be ideal). Instead, a period of eclecticism and disintegration of stylistic unity will inevitably appear, accompanied by a certain reduction of aesthetic quality.

Basically, in a normal situation the architect should dictate to the builder. In general radical projects stimulate the development of engineering and building technology. In our country this was the case in the 1920s, when, for example, the public service union forced Mosstroi to make a six-month search for an engineer who could calculate the cantilever for Melnikov's Rusakov club. In general, challenging projects stimulate the development of engineering and construction technology. But since the time of Khrushchev the situation for the architect has crucially changed. He has ended up in the role of the horse, on which the builder sits. As a result, everybody now sees how far we have lagged behind in building technology.

Internal relationships within the profession are confused these days by the lack of a real creative hierarchy. The Union of Architects has not taken up the task of establishing one. For example, in the 1920s we had the Moscow Architectural Society, which organized competitions for all large buildings. Competitions were going on constantly, and as a result of this the hierarchy changed radically, since the same architects received first and second prizes in a dozen or so competitions. Unfortunately, nothing like this is happening now.

ANDREI BOKOV: It seems that I am much more involved than my colleagues in the fundamentally new system of relations in and around the architectural sphere that is currently emerging in Moscow. For instance, I witnessed a most interesting change in the behaviour of Yury Mikhailovich [Luzhkov, the Mayor of Moscow]. Two years ago he would come to the Union of Architects or to the Municipal Building Department saying: 'Guys, this is architecture, this is your business, so please, decide for yourselves.' But in the course of two years he was successfully reeducated, taught to specify, to design and to make decisions in our field. And at the same time the whole system of perspective planning, financing and all client services (receipts, etc.) is now handed to the Department of Construction. In short there has never before been such a concentration of authority and money in the hands of a small group of people – and this at a time when the total amount of construction in Moscow is growing significantly. The main problem is that there is no mechanism to combat this situation. As a result we have the unprecedented, complete bureaucratization and centralization of the architectural process, rigid aesthetic control, complete absence of both innovation and insurance against large-scale error.

Now about the client. Here he comes: uncultivated, uneducated, does not pay or tries not to pay. When we can expect new Medici among such clients is not clear to me.

With the builder it is even more interesting. He simply says: 'Who are you? What do we need you here for? Whadda you doin', drawing? Well I got this...."Hey, Nicky, show'm whatcha got".' – and his hungry brother somewhere from hungry Moldavia brings out something that has been slapped together that night. Or even better: a contractor from the Northern

Caucasus is invited to Moscow, since this is now very fashionable. He installs his machinery here, buys a client under the name of Moskapstroi – and no questions asked. What use is an architect to him? He buys the permits. 'Whadda you mean, "architecture"? Here I got "Moskompriroda" [The 'Moscow Ecological Committee'] – they take ten thousand for the permit, and here the historians – they cost five thousand, here I got it all written down.' And the investor brings his own foreign architect in on a leash. As a rule, he doesn't appear to be one of the best.

What can the relations between colleagues be like when there is no stable norm for basic business relations anyway? In Soviet times the architect occupied a certain position, which did not satisfy all of us, certainly, but nevertheless had a number of fixed characteristics. This position was granted by the highly cynical authorities, but even these authorities understood that a niche was needed for the architects, so they said, 'Oh well let them live.' Now there is a very real danger that we, together with the new power structures, with the clients and the builders, will liquidate this niche and with it the profession as a part of our culture.

VYACHESLAV GLAZYCHEV: I am just as much a Muscovite as my dear colleagues, but for the last three years I've been working outside of Moscow. In Moscow I limit myself to teaching and criticism, regarding this city as a dead zone, where it is not possible to do anything real. Therefore, all that I'm going to say will seem to be about life on another planet though a neighbouring one.

The authorities with which I normally work are the municipalities of regional cities, who appear to be quite different from the powerful Moscow bureaucracy. First, they maintain respectful relations with local architects, and the opinions of such architects on professional questions are appreciated. With me, as an external expert, the new authorities are also quite polite and gentle.

The reason they are so democratic and civilized is certainly not related to their conscientiousness, but lies in the fact that the bureaucrats in the regions are incomparably poorer than the Moscow ones, and are compelled to play a much softer game with the emerging capital owners (the industrial and proprietary elite) and potential investors. Here I play the role of intermediary, while creating a profession that is new for Russia: development consultant. This is gradually beginning to work as people realize that this way everyone benefits. It is beneficial for the urban authorities, who discover that they control great economic potential – namely, the potential of the environment. it is beneficial for the investors, who discover that their investments can be more effective than they themselves ever imagined. It is beneficial for the inhabitants, because I constantly work with public participation, and represent their interests at all levels in professional terms.

It is marvellous, that the complete independence from Moscow has increased the level of consciousness of regional authorities, and now work with these authorities takes the form of a genuine creative dialogue that you could not have dreamed of before.

The builders, whom I have encountered on a regional level, also behave quite differently. First of all, they are hustling in search of work. They buy their supplies in Krasnoyarsk and their sanitary equipment in Italy, because it is cheaper than in Moscow or in the Vladimir region. In general, they have become more interesting and dynamic people. And our relations are not very complex, at least at the present stage of preparation and determination of future opportunities.

It is difficult to imagine relations more harmonious than those I enjoy with my colleagues in the provinces. First I create work for them, rather than take it away, and they understand this quickly. Second, I am in a way their advocate, and through me they are ensured of decent working conditions.

EVGENY ASSE: In an ideal situation, relations between the architect and the authorities should be reduced to governmental regulations on building actions: allocation of a territory and then approval of the project plan. The authorities should take the form of democratic municipal representative structures, and their powers should be clearly defined. In many countries this is the way it works. Here, I return to my favourite theme: the theme of 'norms'. Contemporary Russia is characterized by the fact that norms on relations in all areas of society are non-existent or only developing.

In a normal situation the relations between architect and client are determined by a contract. If the client is a cad, you obviously cannot change that – rudeness is part of his character, but as soon as a contract is signed, the relations are immediately cast in another light, since all actions take place on a legal basis. With the question about relations between architect and builder, we are entering the realm of architectural ideology. I can not agree with S. Khan-Magomedov, when he says that the architect should be a dictator. In my view, the present situation in architecture has been inspired in many respects by the growing involvement of the architect in the building process, by his involvement in the development of building technology. In our country, due to some deliberately arrogant attitude, no architect (at least, after Burov) has really cared about construction technology and new materials. This situation is predetermined by a particular type of school – such as the Ecole des Beaux-Arts, where the compositional aspects of a project noticeably take precedence over utilitarian and technological ones. But there is another conception that implies that the architect is first and foremost trained to construct a comfortable and durable house – artistic qualities are considered secondary. There is a certain acceptable norm, and against this background some excel and some disappoint. Thus architecture is conceived as the highest form of construction. Using this model our categorical rejection of the builder as a kind of *kultur-trager* does not appear very nice.

Relations within the architectural community are no less burdened by the consequences of the absurd, Soviet way of life than are relations between architects and the outside world. For instance, architects participating in the power structures seems to be an extremely delicate problem, because it generally results in either protectionism or the blocking of colleagues' projects.

Architecture as an institution

To what degree is it necessary to regulate architecture in Russia, for example with licensing and building codes, with professional ethics, or with improved education?

SELIM KHAN-MAGOMEDOV: It is interesting to note that once again licenses for architectural design are being given to large building firms and engineers without any architectural qualifications. Until 1903 only graduated architects could receive the right to design and build structures. Then for some reason the state began to give such rights first to building engineers, then to railroad engineers, then to public service engineers, etc. Eventually, architects raised their voices, because the cities were being overrun with buildings that were unprofessional in terms of aesthetics.

The ethical question is also quite problematic. A system of securing authorship, for example, is lacking. An architect can win a competition for a theatre somewhere in Saratov, but if, for instance, he is a teacher at MArchI, the best he can expect is to be taken along with the commission to a large collective and made architect number ten. This has happened before. For example, Shchusev was always mentioned first regardless of who worked with him. The entire architectural portion of the Kievski railway station in Moscow was done by diploma students from the Institute of Painting, Sculpture and Architecture under the name of Rerberg, who was only a drainage and foundation engineer.

As an acceptable model I recall a small civil-engineering firm, existing in the 1920s, headed by the well-known building engineer Prokhorov. They used to work with sketch designs by Ilia Golosov among others, and they had an architect with the surname Mittelman (himself a former student of Golosov), who did not design so much as work up the sketches to working drawings. And he signed the drawings as a co-author.

Education, it seems to me, should continue to be universal with partial specialization. Especially now, as we change to a system of private firms, the architect can no longer expect to get commissions only for kindergartens or schools.

ANDREI BOKOV: In my view, it is necessary to correct the present situation, but not with licensing and building norms. In Russia unwritten laws have always been followed better than written ones. These unwritten laws have always existed in normal society, as well as in the criminal world. But now there are none. We need a professional union to establish written and unwritten laws There should be a court of honour in the Union of

Architects, the Union itself should be renovated, and new staff hired. What is unfolding now is nothing but a professional drama, and the only way to overcome it to find protection from clients, from authorities and from colleagues, is to establish a professional union of a new type.

VYACHESLAV GLAZYCHEV: Licensing is, in theory, a good thing, but practice up until now has been based upon the arbitrary logic of the Council under the local chief architect: graduated architect A decides whether graduated architect B has the right to work. This is an awful practice, and I am opposed to licensing in this sense. But of course, there are other ways.

At present you have as many building norms as you could want but most of them are utterly obsolete. Urban norms as an element of urban legislation are only now beginning to develop, and here is an extremely important role for the 'socially responsible architect'; in the end, I can't help using this improper expression.

How can we speak of any culture of authorship, when 80 percent of construction outside of Moscow is being done without architects, using old, stolen, adapted projects – the former work of institutes like 'Grazhdanselstroi'. These works are anonymous. This is the Wild West, and it will be for a long time. I am therefore rather sceptical about the usefulness and the feasibility of creating a new high-grade architectural union. Although it sounds sad, a whole generation, including myself, will have to die out for this to happen.

Speaking about the problem of education, I would like to return to my experiences in the provinces. Gradually I have come to the conclusion that we need an architectural school outside of Moscow and St Petersburg. The problem lies in the type of education that now exists in the capitals, with its subconscious cultural-psychological orientation does not cover the problems of middle and small sized cities, settlements, former villages, *et cetera*. In response to this situation, a small new architectural school is emerging at the Vladimir Polytechnic Institute based on a tiny group of students, with my participation. Here students are inspired not by the ambition to win a competition in Tokyo, but by the desire to work at the level of environmental organization in a decent way.

EVGENY ASSE: I categorically reject licensing in its current form. We know of many countries where there is no licensing at all, and where professionalism itself serves as a license. And if professionalism exists – the architect's life itself reinforces his right to build. Licensing as it is accepted in the USA is actually an examination of the knowledge of laws and norms, acting on the territory of a certain state. But here in Russia 'beauty' gets licensed: one brings one's watercolours to the licensing commission, so that they can testify something about the 'special intensity' of one's 'creative endeavour'. As far as licensing someone like Rerberg: I would have nothing against it if it brought us more Rerbergs, who would gather scholars around themselves and build Kievski railway stations.

For me, the problem of ethics cannot be limited merely to protecting authorship. I have already mentioned, for example, the issue of protectionism and the blocking of others' projects. But I can't share the pathos of Andrei Bokov, who assumes that all problems would be solved if we had another professional union. In our country, we have entered an epoch of atomization, not of association. All normal professional organizations are founded as instruments to protect and regulate professional activity, prevent fee dumping and adjust relations within the profession. It will be sometime before these relations will develop to the degree that it will be possible to regulate them. Then the new union will appear out of necessity.

Architectural education is now in a complex position, as it has totally distanced itself from the urgent problems of the profession. The slight injection of the VkhuteMas in our school was resolved a long time ago. Problems related to the city, to modern culture, problems of philosophy, social responsibility, ecology – all this is now outside the scope of education. Therefore in the Architectural Institute we see meaningless facades in 1:50 scale, projects in which real life is totally absent, misconceptions of constructions, materials and details. Generally speaking, the Moscow Architectural Institute is doomed, at least in its present form. This is understood by its rector, A.P. Kudriavtsev, who can only wait for the institute to die a natural death, as it is impossible to change anything anyway, given the way higher education is currently financed. That is why there is very little chance that we will soon see a new generation of architects, brought up according to modern cultural standards – a generation we need so much.

Architecture as an artistic endeavour

Does contemporary Russian architecture have any particular characteristics? Do these characteristics grow exclusively from social-economic factors, or do they have cultural roots?

SELIM KHAN-MAGOMEDOV: These days lots of national patriots have been raising their voices, not realizing that our tradition also includes post-Peter-the-Great architecture, the nineteenth century, Melnikov and Zholtovsky. Both our avant-garde, which surprised the West with its functionalism, and artistic merit and the 'Stalinist empire' style, grown from neoclassicism, are richly endowed artistically. We strongly criticized neoclassicism, but its aesthetic level was in fact very high. The whole idea of Russian 'artistry' came to life when, in the beginning of the century, we found a marvellous, stylistically-focused way out of eclecticism in neoclassicism. In general, Russian architecture, down to the recent work of 'paper architects', is distinguished by this type of advanced artistry. From an historical perspective it can be considered accumulative architecture.

I say this because a new stage of general eclecticism is arising due to our present difficulties, and this seems to be leading to a reduction in aesthetic standards. However, an attempt to artificially orient architecture on national traditions is not a solution, and theory should moderate its claims in this respect.

ANDREI BOKOV: As my colleagues have demonstrated, the notion of the profession of the architect is presently fragmenting, and alongside traditional architectural design, project management is developing. This is of course a wonderful practice, but I am not very happy with the fact that in Europe and America it has already began to dominate the architectural profession. I consider architecture to have quite a different nature, and I strive to secure the distinction between the trades. For me the significance of this is obvious – personally, publicly, culturally and practically. In project management there is no need for the deep personal feeling of freedom that is now appearing in Russian architecture, and which, I would say, forms its main feature today. I am not inclined to condemn eclecticism. Eclecticism represents to me the natural state of an architecture of a free people, an architecture beyond state dictated styles.

EVGENY ASSE: Listening to Andrei Bokov I begin to understand that in speaking about 'architecture' we all mean quite different things. What he has in mind goes back to the classical tradition of the creation of unique masterpieces, when the heroic element of the artist, his charismatic sacrificial nature is realized in some kind of architectural marvel. But architecture as a functional societal institution is not concerned with this. Certainly, it is possible to address as architects those MArchI graduates who, even with their mediocre grades, are sure that what they have to say will excite mankind. But the problem is not even that the majority of them actually have nothing to say. I try to explain to my students that architecture in general is not a tool of self-expression. The architect should rather be conceived of as a lens to be focused on a set of data from the surrounding world and generate a more or less accurate projection of this world. It is this understanding of architecture that our country lacks. Architectural discourse is also absent despite the existence of two academies, an architectural institute, a union of architects, *et cetera*. Our architecture is not only monstrous, it is monstrously unreflective. This despite the fact that intellectual agitation in the architectural world today is extremely high, maybe even higher then in the 1920s, since the situation now is much more dramatic. To expect that any architecture worthy of note could emerge cut of this mess, and that the Russian soul, in an immense artistic upsurge, will give birth to a quality that will amaze the world – this is not just vain, but even harmful.

VYACHESLAV GLAZYCHEV: Although it may seem strange, I agree with Evgeny Asse on this point. There are subjects that are allowable in theories and inadmissible in the normative consciousness, as Mr Khan-Magomedov also seems to think. To me, creativity is a wonderful subject for cultural theory and history, but in daily practice I try to avoid using the word. The German notion of *gute arbeit* is to me much more valuable, and whether my work is creative or not will be determined *post factum*. It is certainty very harmful that our education is characterized by a self-expressionistic imperative, when there is as yet nothing to express and an appreciation of culture has not yet been acquired.

SELIM KHAN-MAGOMEDOV: But if we only provide the student with social abilities, thus forgetting to make him an architect, then we are placing methodology above professional skills. This will make him or her a perfect methodologist – and that is all.

EVGENY ASSE: I was not speaking simply about methodology, but about the ability to translate the external world through one's self into architecture. Translation – this is a subject most lacking in our architectural education.

ANDREI BOKOV: I would like to make my position clear in one phrase. In my view, architecture is not simply the answer to an external challenge, i.e. it cannot come from outside like a demand. All of our activities values and preferences are motivated by completely different circumstances, and it is impossible to teach architecture as a reaction to an external irritant.

VYACHESLAV GLAZYCHEV: To convince my colleagues of the necessity of an internal challenge is, of course, superfluous. If we were not psychos with internal challenges, we simply would not have come to this round table.

IV
The Romanian question

15 Totalitarian city

Bucharest 1980–9, semio-clinical files

Constantin Petcu

> In the 2060th year from the formation of the centralized and independent Dacic state, in the 44th year from the victory of the social and national liberation revolution of the Romanian people and in the 23rd year from the 9th Congress of the Romanian Communist Party, we have inaugurated the construction of The Centre for National Councils of the Workers' Revolutionary Democracy.
>
> N. Ceausescu and E. Ceausescu, 'Foundation Text', 1988

The city centre of Bucharest is in disarray; its layout is dysfunctional and borders on the absurd. This situation is due to a series of planning violations to which the city was subjected during the 1980s, at a time when the power of the totalitarian regime came close to being absolute. The principal elements of these violent operations, 'Ceausescu's Palace' and the 'Great Boulevard to the Palace', are by now legendary. Still, the scope of the project reaches even beyond these (in)famous instances, physically and psychologically. For, behind the appearance of these elements there are a series of complicated mechanisms that have created, or made possible, this very 'appearance'. It is the purpose of this paper to study some of these mechanisms, their underlying causes and the appearances they produce.

For simplification, the main emphasis will be on three of the urban operations effected in the eighties: the modification of the National Theatre; the construction of the People's House ('Ceausescu's Palace'); and the construction of the 'The Victory of Socialism Avenue'. These operations are significant and revealing for the successive stages in the changing relations that Authority/Power kept up with the Social and the City.

Nevertheless, for elucidation, I have extended the study to cover a series of phenomena, without obvious ties among them. These include the monopolization of the Romanian mass media by the totalitarian government, the huge propaganda stadium-spectacles, certain articles on architecture that appeared in a specialized Romanian review, the surveillance and censoring of personal communication and correspondence, and the limitations imposed on printing, copying and reproduction of printed material.[1]

It should be quite obvious that the underlying causes for these various phenomena in all cases stem from blind political will. The mechanisms, partly semiotic in nature, by which these different phenomena condition each other, seem to have gone undetected, as if forgotten, hidden, in the memory of those who lived them.[2] For this reason, I have chosen to use the subtitle 'semio-clinical files' for the paper. Implied in the term is the possibility of 'treatment', the success of which depends on a correct and accurate diagnosis, that in turn depends on the recuperation of signification and meaning of the multiple signs in question. It is my intention to locate and explain, albeit partially, these socio-semiotic mechanisms, so specific for the functioning of a totalitarian system. It should be kept in mind that certain of these mechanisms function in a subtle, unseen way, and/or appear in other forms of social guises.[3]

Subliminal semiotics and politics

In 1988 an advertisement on page 9 in *Arhitectura*, the only review on architecture in Romania at the time, promptly announced the commencement of construction work for The Centre for National Councils of the Workers' Revolutionary Democracy. There was nothing unusual in this: readers of *Arhitectura* were accustomed to the convention, which had been in practice for a number of years. Dating from 1982, almost every issue of the review had similar announcements on page 9, and following pages (headed in bold characters: 'The Epoch of Nicolae Ceausescu') were dedicated to the latest political issues and the commemoration of the 'glorious achievements' of the said 'Epoch'. It should be noted, that few readers of the review – and this was true of readers of the media in general, inundated with articles of the same ilk – bothered to read them; in fact, readers tried 'not to see' the messages, in order to discover the few bits and pieces of interesting information actually on offer.

Whether the readers succeeded in evading the ever insistent messages in this way is a moot point. Perhaps, or in all likelihood, the articles managed to convey *inframessages* by the means of certain parameters, such as their omnipresence, frequency, the way they monopolised the media and so on. The significations and effects of these conjectural subliminal messages, that accompany 'Official Architecture', need further explication.

The *Arhitectura* article (and others like it), pronouncing the construction of an important edifice, immediately begs a number of questions. What does the planned edifice look like? What is its location? Who are the authors of the project? And even, who is the author of the article?

Strangely enough, the article itself does not provide answers to any of these questions. The two accompanying photographs are not helpful: the first one is a shot from the inauguration ceremony, the second is a close-up of the 'foundation text', just incorporated into the corner stone of the edifice. The text of the article sheds no further light. It consists of only three phrases: one pronounces the event, the second is a short description of the event, and the third is a reproduction of the 'foundation text'. Perusal of similar articles makes it clear that this is not an anomaly but indeed the norm of representation, or rather, the norm of non-representation, of Official Architecture.

But what exactly do these norms consist of? I shall attempt to identify some of the principal rules discerned by examination of 'page nine articles':

1 The projects of Official Architecture are not to be represented publicly. This constitutes the *absence of the signifier*. This absence precludes criticism, other than that expressed orally in an improvised commentary (that does not leave traces).

2 The building of said edifices is announced by other means than that of a visual signal (notably through the agency of speech(es)); in spite of *not being anticipated* (not signified), the constructions are *announced* (signalled) in as *abstract* a manner as possible.

3 Romanian *grands projets* were initiated in 1982. For the following six or seven years, this massive construction work was carried out in the total absence of public representation. By the end of this period, the perpetuation of non-representation had implicitly been transformed into an *interdiction of representation*.[4] This interdiction highlights the *sacred* character of the constructions.[5]

4 Any reference to these buildings is totally void of architectural signification. This constitutes the rule of a *zero degree of architectural semantics*, duly replaced by another semantics of an economical kind, one that is principally quantitative.[6] This rule is still being employed, as an effective means of discouraging architectural, urban and aesthetic critique.

5 Lacking an anticipatory signifier (one that would be open to criticism), Official Architecture presented itself as *apparition*, and inscribes itself in the same type of 'oracular orality' that defined the political discourse (or 'Official Discourse'). The unexpected demolition of certain architectural monuments, as well as some of the historical *quartiers* of Bucharest, suspended the qualities and fundamental ontological implications of the architectural object and of the city (the city as history and cultural memory). Similarly, the ontological condition of the city dwellers has been altered (they are cornered, awaiting 'decisions' that could completely change their existence and way of life).[7]

6 As Official Architecture is both *non-signified* and *non-signifying* (the same is true of Official Discourse, as we see shall see later), it signifies itself through itself, thus reinforcing its *symbolic nature*.[8]

7 The anonymity of the authors of the project confers on them the 'status' of *non-subject*. Being a non-subject, the anonymous architects, are unconsciously identified with the leader (Ceausescu) and thus become a *meta-subject*.[9] It is just this anonymity of the architect that makes possible the 'transference of paternity' unto another anonymous 'architect' of the non-subject type; i.e. the national genius (the ingeniousness of the people). On the basis of the ambiguity between client, architect and constructor, there is a tendency today among the political class to free the first two subjects mentioned from responsibility by implicating the third.[10] Indeed, the political and architectural problems raised by the building are pushed aside by placing all importance on technical and economical merits.

8   As a final comment on the norm of non-representation of Official Architecture, it should be stressed that all these rules were introduced by a technique of *sub-liminal representation* which, in combination with other procedures, has led to the preclusion of professional commentary and criticism.

From the above, we can conclude that the totalitarian regime willingly and consciously propagated the absence of the signifier of Official Architecture. Implicitly, this entails an absence of a real process of signification, a process which is, necessarily, extensive and uncontrollable. Still, the political power in question construed, around this architecture, an entire system of manipulating signals that to a great extent have their effects through unconscious semiotic channels.

Discourse as splitting of reality

The extremely totalitarian rule in the 1980s engendered an even more serious phenomenon than mentioned above. This phenomenon could be called a *generalized semiotic rupture*, by which is meant, the irreversible rupture between political discourse and social reality. Ideally, these two levels, that constitute the very life of/in the city, should interact in the form of the semiotic binary, signified/signifier, to facilitate a more or less coherent functioning. But, the growing ambiguity of the relationship between the social and, what should have been its principal signifier, political discourse, soon produced a functional alteration of the binome.

Having established itself as the 'sole signifier' of social reality – a reality that does not always correspond to 'plans' and is indeed an imperfect reality – political discourse starts to structure itself, in a second phase, in the guise of an autonomous reality, or a 'pseudo-reality'. Constructed from statistics and ideology, Official Discourse became 'perfect reality', but one that no longer represented social reality.[11] As a consequence, this 'reality', belonging to the domain of language, irrevocably loses its fundamental functions; representation, communication and instrumentation. As the social is no longer represented, anywhere, social reality increasingly finds itself reduced to silence and limited to clandestine remarks in the private domain.

The process in question unfolds in two stages. First, we have a sabotage of the 'sign of reality', leading to internal dysfunction or increasing ambiguity in the signifying relation of social representation and social reality. The second stage sees the splitting of reality, as its two semiotic components are progressively established as two independent, often contradictory, realities: a silenced social reality and a blind Official Discourse.

On the existential level, these two realities each correspond to two different modalities of behaviour, of communication and of thinking (a veritable 'double-think'). Parallel to the splitting of reality there is a splitting of each individual into two personalities, a public and a private one. A virtual division of the individual, by definition indivisible.

Furthermore, the splitting of reality paved the way for a series of paradoxal situations which brought about inversions of the semiotic functions between the two levels of reality. Examples of this, were 'visits' paid by representatives of Official Discourse to the work place (and other *loci* of social life) that demanded that social reality correspond 'at all costs' to political discourse. This meant an evermore frequent and evermore farcical staging of the expediency of an empty and false discourse that required, at all costs, a false social reality:[12] the emperor's (unmentionable) new clothes.

With the ever-increasing hollowness of Official Discourse, another representation of the social took place; and this time in an unofficial manner. This particular representation, this Unofficial Discourse, is extremely precise but its form is that of a secret expression – the reports and files of the political (secret) police – and its function is a penalizing one.

This subterranean representation (entailing detailed surveillance, microscopic and omniscopic) contributes, in a decisive manner, to the institution of two taboos of social representation, each corresponding to one of the two realities that, from that moment on, will be lived as contradictions: political discourse, being 'unique', public and publicized, and self-referential, is totally exempt from criticism; social reality being concrete, private, anonymous, clandestine, imperfect and polymorphous, is excluded from public representation (in the media).

The absurd climate of the prison-asylum introduced by the semiotic rupture of reality – and its consequence; the two semiotic taboos of representation – bears a close resemblance to the climate that characterizes the work of Kafka. Indeed, the two models for the 'architectural states', suggested by Deleuze and Guattari to represent Kafkaesque space (the two, a spatial radio-concentric model, and a spatial model of corridors, correspond to what which I call, respectively, a 'bureaucracy of Representation', and a 'bureaucracy of manipulation') works equally well to represent totalitarian space (Official and Unofficial space).[13]

Having doubled and blotted out social reality during the 1980s, Official Discourse reached an apex of 'monumental reality' by adopting and taking over the discourse of architecture; and by choosing to express, as is characteristic of supreme powers, its message in stone.[14] Thus, Official Architecture ascends to the state of Official Discourse, absorbing its falsity in the bargain, and its grandiose constructions become Political Discourse.

The pyramid and the (homogenous) city as a desert

In the three cases already mentioned – the modification of the National Theatre, the People's House and the Victory of Socialism Avenue – it is hard not to notice a powerful will, to establish a particular architectural style. Below, I will try to trace this style in outline for each of the three instances, as it was developed and improvised from one construction to another.

First, the modification of the National Theatre marks the beginning of this 'architectural epoch'. This event is all the more significant because it concerns

Figure 15.1 The National Theatre with modified facade

an alteration of a building highly representative of an (important) architectural style dating from the seventies. The operation is symbolic for the aggressive and peremptory attitude that Official Architecture affected, from this point on, in regards to all other architectural contexts.

The main transformation of the interior was based on a rejection of the mono-function of the theatre (belonging to the 'intellectual culture'), opting instead for a poly-function better suited for the promotion of 'mass culture'; a culture, at the time, limited to gross propaganda and populist manipulation. The principal elements expressing the function of the theatre – the scene, the foyer, etc. – were partially camouflaged, screened off, by a facade. After the operation the building retained an unexpressed amorphous heterogeneity and a decorative 'signifier' that fails to represent the building properly, but remains a 'simple' exercise in style.

Second, the construction of the People's House was a continuation of the experimentation and stylistic revolution which began with the modification of the National Theatre, and constituted the generating element of urban planning on a pharaonic scale. The treatment of the interior space of the building is repetitive and monotone. On a small scale, the interior space – monotone and without architectural virtue – only gains quality via a 'layer' of decorative elements; this results in a series of disparate rooms, exhibiting an eclectic amalgam of neo-styles. On a larger scale, contextually, the placement and sheer size of the construction represents a massive effort to ensure total visual domination of the city. The massive and symmetrical presence of the People's House, virtually omnipresent, visible from nearly all points in Bucharest, creates a relational space of a panoptic kind.[15] It should be noted that this edifice, the most conspicuous one in Bucharest, is the one that 'generated' the enormous operations of demolition in the centre of the city: a situation which calls forth a strong panoptical symbolism.

In contrast to the 'omnipresence' of the building throughout the city, the older urban context is carefully screened off from the central view dictated by the People's House. This blotting out is brought off by symmetrical buildings that curtain off the central edifice. In a manner of speaking, this constitutes a spatial attitude which tries to see nothing other than its own architectural style, nothing other than the space-time which it generates and controls, an attitude which could be said to be 'phoboptical'.[16]

In this way, a new city centre is created *ex nihilo*, an inaccessible centre of Power. The distinct axial layout of the planning that belongs to the building accentuates the sentiment of interdiction engendered by the inaccessibility of the edifice.

The sheer 'pyramidal' volume of the People's House explicitly signifies a perfectly coordinated hierarchical order, and a symbolical attempt to arrest time. Indeed, Ceausescu's 'foundation text', cited at the beginning of this paper, has three chronological references which all come to a halt at the very same I-here-now (introduced as a referential meta-deixis with transcendental qualities and which express the stopping of time and the stopping of history with the introduction of an 'epoch'[17]).

Third, the construction of Victory of Socialism Avenue and the Civic Centre marks the ultimate moment of delirium which finalizes the coming into being

Figure 15.2 The 4 km 'Victory of Socialism Avenue', now known as the 'Avenue of Unity'

of 'order as a style', as perpetrated on the entire city. This moment constitutes a victory of space over place,[18] a madness of reason and an excess of rationalization. Existing plans and drawings of the city conserve traces of this intervention which is a perfect example of an erasure of the history, of a period, of a city by the constitution of an epoch.

This stage of architectural exercise as Official Discourse manifests itself by a ruthless demolition of the city of Bucharest and the replacement of it by a 'new city', perfectly ordered and monolithic. The real city, its past, its history and its monuments are erased, demolished or displaced and hidden behind the new buildings. The elements of the old city are not included in the project and are subject to destruction, at any time.

As is true for the relation between political discourse and social reality, the connection between the two architectural realities – Official Architecture and existing architecture – are reduced to a minimum and become more and more contradictory. By disregarding the unity and continuity of urban planning, and by not respecting contextual elements, the 'New City Centre' is realized by the negation and the destruction of the city of which it was supposed to be the centre. From this point on, the doubling of social reality will correspond to a doubling of the city.

Insularity as ultimate poetics of habitation

As a reaction to an increasingly oppressive and absurd rhetoric of Official Discourse, a large part of the inhabitants of the city used as a last resort, in an effort to resist and to protect their proper identity, an existential strategy that could be termed 'insular existence'. This insular existence was, in most instances, realized either by an individual effort to procure a cultural education that differs from official culture and ideology, or by the foundation of clandestine groups that practiced unofficial culture.

It also seems that the same spirit of resistance and exigency for self-expression brought about a specific *vernacular architecture*. This type of architecture,[19] insular itself and quite distinctive for totalitarianism, is characterized first of all by a relation to nature that is elemental,[20] poetical and mythological. The elemental presence of nature, never minaturized nor rhetoricized, is reduced to a restricted typology. The elements include: vegetation (vine), the aerial (the windmills), flight (the bird), the sky-horizon (the look into the distance) and mineral matter (industrial waste).

Another instance of insular vernacular architecture seems to have developed because of the closures and increasing isolation of living quarters. Although the community still retained an open attitude, this was no longer a social, communal openness as before, but a symbolic one expressing a hope for escape from a hostile immanence. The specific relation between housing and public space, a relation progressively formed by the natural elements themselves, constitutes itself in an attitude of *urban camouflage*. If the vernacular architecture of democratic societies is characterized by an originality pushed to the limits of eccentricity, the vernacular architecture typical for a totalitarian society calls for an *enfolding*, a camouflage of habitation with natural elements or with materials totally devoid of colour (often industrial waste or waste from construction sites).

At the same time that the city's inhabitants became isolated and withdrew into a 'elemental nature', Political Discourse reverted to the use of a monstrous 'elemental mechanism'. During the grand propaganda spectacles, tens of thousands of human beings were orchestrated in perfectly synchronous movements, sitting side by side on the benches of a stadium, embodying, and offering their bodies to, immense *tableaux vivants* of pointillistic accuracy.

During these grotesque anthropo-mechanical shows, which became increasingly more excessive and absurd, representatives of Official Discourse took part as the only spectators of a transformation of society's individuals into an anonymous mass that reproduced and mirrored the fragments and images taken from the self-same Discourse. These huge 'bachelor machines' became the norm of 'dialogue' between the political and the social and stand as emblems of the progressive erasure of the human subject.

To further exacerbate matters, the regime still increased its already overbearing monopolisation of the mass media while at the same time denying individuals access to modern technologies of expression and communication. Permission was needed from the political (secret) police for all such activities. It even became increasingly more difficult to own a typewriter, for specialist shops no longer stocked them; they had to be acquired second-hand, if at all. In other words, the authorities denied the individual access to that which Walter Benjamin defined as the very condition of modernity. This access, of course, remained a privilege of the representatives of Authority.

It is clear from above examples that the human model promoted by Authority was that of the individual as automaton. Conversely, the habitant of the vernacular expresses another model of existence, that of the autonomous individual, who, in the political context of the time, stands for a form of a resistance to totalitarianism.

All the mechanisms considered in this paper are based on the quasi-causal capacities of signs. These determinist-semiotic capacities produce measurable effects and are fundamental to a good number of disciplines and cultural effects: for example, psychoanalysis, therapies that make use of the placebo effect, public commercials, and the impact of virtual images. The social aspects studied appear to define themselves by generalization and a frequently excessive exploitation of the deterministic potential of signs. This can only be seen as an attempt, in the face of impossibility, to conceal an ideological derivative and to manipulate reality on a large scale through signs and language.

The totalitarianism installed by Ceausescu can easily be seen, and this is probably true of all other forms of totalitarianism, as, to paraphrase a well-known title of Roland Barthes, 'a dictatorship of false signs'. It was this dictatorship that conferred on Official Architecture the status of a centrally placed false sign.

Notes

1 For example, circumstances made it nearly impossible to possess, or gain access to, a typewriter or a copying machine.

2 Hannah Arendt, drawing on lived experience, denounced the situation produced by this 'incorporation' and passing into 'oblivion' as 'banality of evil'. Hannah Arendt, *Eichmann in Jerusalem: A Report on the Banality of Evil*, 1963; French translation, Paris: Gallimard, 1966.

3 A recent instance of the dysfunctionality described in this study, had direct consequences for the present paper: in August 1995, a copy of the English translation, posted from Romania to France, was irreparably lost 'without a trace'. This is a clear indication of the persistence of aforementioned mechanisms in post-communist Romania. Of course these mechanisms can be observed, usually in an innocuous form, in all types of societies (even in the most democratic ones).

4 For example, it was strictly prohibited to film or photograph any aspects of either the demolition or construction work. This constitutes an interdiction of another view/the view of the other, the exclusion of an objective viewpoint (to keep from view that which could be memorized and transmitted). Furthermore, the regard of the other would effectively break the spell of the spectacle.

5 The sacredness is proffered and displayed by the vast enclosure around the building that makes it inaccessible (in the very middle of the city, the distance from the enclosure to the building varies from 150–550 metres and the terrain is quasi-pyramidal in form). The People's House became a Forbidden City – Bucharest receiving resounding echoes from Beijing.

6 The official guided tour of the People's House will not fail to remind visitors of the extraordinary dimensions, the record volumetric enormity, the huge amount of marble used, etc.

7 This condition of altered ontology of the city dweller and the city calls to mind, the situation of the inhabitants of cities or countries under siege or in a state of war.

8 According to Denis Hollier's classification of architectural genres, starting from but reversing the axiological criteria in Hegel's *Aesthetics*, it is possible to catalogue Official Architecture, which signifies itself, in the class of 'independent architecture'. Pointing out the lack of exteriority in this kind of architecture, Hollier states that 'symbolic architecture can only be self-referential, can only describe itself, can only say that which it is.' Denis Hollier, *La prise de la Concorde, Essais sur Georges Bataille*, Paris: Gallimard, 1974, p. 24.

9 See Jean-Claude Coquet's analysis of the diverse modalities of the institution of a semiotic subject. Coquet further states that the meta-subject manifests itself through, 'the power to transform the other….This function alone, being transitive, non-reflexive, recurrent, suffices to define [the meta-subject].' Jean-Claude Coquet, *Le discours et son sujet*, Vol. 1, *Essai de grammaire modale*, Klincksieck, 1984, p. 71.

10 In this respect, it is worthy to note the strange and ambiguous text (unsigned) on the 'tourist' brochure sold at the entrance to the People's House. The following quotations, signed by international 'personalities', are cited in the brochure: 'let us forget the one who is said to have commissioned the work and revere the one who built it' (Jean-Paul Carteron, President of Forum Crans Montana); 'this enormous palace, a palace of a megalomaniac, but at the same time, a masterpiece of Romanian architecture' (Catherine Lalumiere, Secretary-General of the European Council).

It should be noted that the building (now renamed 'Palace of Parliament') houses the Parliament of Romania and the Centre for International Conferences; that it is one of the most frequently visited buildings in Bucharest, frequently praised by foreign visitors.

11 Paul Ricoeur has noted the indissoluble complicity between totalitarianism and fiction, 'the concept of the totalitarian system is based on fictional invention upheld

by propaganda and terror.' Ricoeur underlines that totalitarianism reaches absurdity at the point where fictional coherence encounters rigour of organization, and concludes by quoting Hannah Arendt (from *The Totalitarian System*) on the specificity of totalitarianism: 'totalitarian organization requires the members of the society to act 'in strict accordance to the rules of a fictive world'. See Paul Ricoeur, 'Preface' to Hannah Arendt's *Condition de l'homme moderne*, Paris: Calman-Lévy, 1961, p. VII.

12 Street markets and shops would suddenly brim over with merchandise usually hard to get or unavailable.

13 See Gilles Deleuze/Félix Guattari, *Kafka, Pour une littérature mineure*, Paris: Minuit, 1975, p. 134; English translation: *Kafka, Toward a Minor Litterature*, Minneapolis: University of Minnesota Press, Minneapolis, 1986, pp. 74–5.

14 Sylviane Agacinski points out a similar phenomenon of 'monumentalization' of political discourse in Nazi Germany: 'totalitarianism in its national-socialist form...likened the political to art and the tyrant to the architect in a number of its ideological discourses.' S. Agacinski, *Volume, Philosophies et politiques de l'architecture*, Galilée, Paris, 1992, p. 12.

As early as 1929, Georges Bataille noted a perverse tendency at the core of the architectural–political relationship, stating, in a paradoxical voice, that 'in the morphological process, people do not represent but an intermediary stage between the apes and the grand edifice....If one challenges architecture, where monumental constructions are the veritable masters throughout the world, hoarding the servile multitudes under their shadows, imposing admiration and astonishment, order and constraint, one is at the same time, in a manner of speaking, challenging man.' See Georges Bataille, 'Architecture', in *Documents 2*, May, 1929, reprinted in OCI, p. 172.

15 'Panoptical space' was invented by Jeremy Bentham at the end of the eighteenth century for use in the 'penitentiary system'. The panopticon is based on two different spatial unities: a central space (the watchtower) from which it is possible to observe without being observed and a peripheral space (the individual prison cells) totally exposed to the supervision of the (invisible) central space and where the prisoner is seen but cannot see. His discovery of the use of panoptical spaces and various other surveillance techniques led Michel Foucault to an extensive analysis of the different penal systems in society. See Michel Foucault, *Surveiller et punir: Naissance de la prison*, Paris: Gallimard, 1975; English translation, *Discipline and Punish: The Birth of the Prison*, Penguin, 1977. See also M. Foucault, 'L' Oeil du pouvoir', in Jeremy Bentham, *Le Panoptique*, Paris: Belfond, 1977.

16 With the term 'phoboptical', I wish to indicate 'fear of seeing' and, especially, 'fear of seeing the other'.

17 There is a splendid semantic correspondence between the etymological sense of the word 'epoch', a word derived from the word *ephokhé*, in ancient Greek, which signifies 'stopping, interruption, suspension' and 'halt'. A. Bailly, *Dictionnaire grec-français*, Paris: Hachette, 1950, p. 792.

18 Space as abstract, *a priori*, homogenous and infinite; place as concrete, caused, heterogeneous and discontinuous.

19 Etymology provides a remarkably apt definition for our purposes: vernacular is derived from *verna*, which figuratively signifies 'indigenous; born in the country' but literally means, 'slave by birth, born in the master's house'. F. Gaffiot, *Dictionnaire abrége Latin-Français*, Paris; Hachette, 1936, p. 693.

20 The concept 'elemental' is here used in the sense introduced by Emmanuel Lévinas in *Totalité et infini, Essai sur l'extériorité*, Boston: Kluwer Academic, 1961.

16 The People's House, or the voluptuous violence of an architectural paradox

Doina Petrescu

Right in the historical and geographical center of Bucharest, an impressive building strikes the eye by its particular style. It is The Palace of the Romanian Parliament, a 'giant' built during the 'golden age' of the dictatorial regime and born in the mind of a man for whom the notion of 'reasonable size' did not exist.

The Guinness Book of World Records lists the building in second place according to its 330,000 m² surface, that is after the Pentagon, and third place according to its 2,550,000 m³ volume. Still, there is a 'first place' that no other building in the whole world could compete for, namely that of *the most disputed one*, as no other construction has, until now, been the target of such a great number of epithets, varying from 'genius' to 'monstrous'.

Extract from official tourist guide to the Palace of the Romanian Parliament [emphasis added]

In 1990 one of the first issues of *Architext*, the Romanian journal of architecture, included an article on the 'People's House', which revealed – somewhat surprisingly – how favourably this most terrifying and controversial of buildings was viewed by much of the population, despite the contempt in which it was held within architectural circles. Construction work had long since been suspended and the People's House was effectively in a state of half-ruins, half-unfinished construction. At that time, it was being debated whether to complete the edifice or tear it down. The former option has since been chosen, and the building has now been invested with its new function as the 'Palace' of the Parliament. The building continues to receive both criticism and admiration.

Leafing through the official tourist guide to the Palace of the Romanian Parliament, whose editors take pride in presenting it as the 'most disputed building' (presumably in the world), one is struck by a continuing dilemma: is the People's House a 'wonder' or a 'monster'? I intend to interrogate the paradoxical ambiguity that lies at the heart of this dilemma, on which the specialists and non-specialists seem so divided. At the same time, I want to preserve this ambiguity and offer it as a form of interpretation which connects the paradigm of the 'monster' with that of the 'wonder'.[1] I will try to link the one with the other, *teras* and *thauma*, as I attempt to trace the ridge that separates the two slopes, a ridge that we could name the terato-thaumato-logical paradox. My interpretation, then, will try to argue that it is the same technique, the same mechanism, that causes this perplexing response in front of both wonders and monsters.

The voluptuous violence of the paradox

The People's House appears to have been constructed according to the logic of the 'wonder'. It is clearly the result of a tyrant's mad ambition to create a contemporary 'wonder', such as tyrants have constructed throughout history. There are plenty of indications for this, such as the aspiration for an unprecedented grandeur ('the largest civic construction in Europe'), and comparisons to other 'wondrous' constructions ('three times as large as the Louvre').

'To astonish' seems to be the principal function of a wonder. And whether confronted with wonders or monsters one asks oneself the same question: how is this possible? The wondrous edifice is 'that which poses, in one way or another, a question that can have no response. Its violence – voluptuous violence – is that of a paradox. An impossible object, inconceivable, is nevertheless constructed, real, undeniable.'[2] To provoke astonishment or stupefaction: this is the terato-thaumatical teleology, the voluptuous violence of the paradox.

For the People's House, 'stupefaction' (or indeed 'stupidity') remains an architectural goal as well as an ideological one. Born of totalitarian ideology, this 'house' makes one 'stupefied': stupid, giddy, dumbfounded, paralyzed (as inherent in its etymological roots in the Latin word, *stupeo/stupere*). As an effect of the Medusa, stupefaction is – as Freud has shown – profoundly linked to castration.[3] Thus a first monster opens our collection: the Medusa, a monster that uses its scopic powers to capture its victims. Passing on to totalitarianism, communist ideology seizes the powers of the Medusa, changing seduction into horror, metamorphosing its subjects into petrified victims. The fascination in 'monsters' shows us, as Bataille puts it, the extent to which 'mankind craves stupefaction'.[4]

The language of 'enigma'

To question without the possibility of getting an answer, this is what constitutes the 'voluptuous violence of the paradox'. Let us simply consider the violence inscribed in the scene of the Sphinx: in front of the Sphinx one is condemned either to death or to commit murder, and whether one answers or not amounts to the same thing. This a prime example of the disproportionate violence of the enigma.

The language of the Sphinx – the language of monsters – is that of the enigma. The monster knows how to give a sign, but does so in a language inaccessible to our knowledge.[5] Referring to the Egyptian pyramids (counted as one of the seven wonders of the world) Hegel remarked how 'the edifice itself is constructed like a problem'. One still speaks of the 'secret of the pyramid' and a complete science has been founded to attempt to recuperate this secret. But, perhaps there is nothing to recuperate, because, as Bernard Goetz points out:

the secret isn't lost; there has never been a possibility of formulating it as such, 'in the clear and precise language of the mind'. The astonishment that we experience is not related to faults in our knowledge. The Egyptian edifice has never had a function other than to provoke this emotion. It has never held another language than that of the silence of the enigma.[6]

The 'House' attributed so violently, so cynically, by its appellation of, and to, 'the people', is perhaps itself conceived as a problem. Indeed, perhaps this is corroborated in the following quotation from an article by Mihail Moldoveanu: 'Certain of the foundations were constructed without anyone knowing what they were in support of. The president-architect came on site each day with fresh ideas.'[7] Named and attributed to 'the people' to which it would never be accessible, the 'house' does indeed emphasize its own closure, it points out what it offers as closed. It offers its closure. Without disclosing the elements of the project, incessantly changing his mind about the function, Ceausescu perhaps had the intention of staging an 'enigma'. The enigma is (inscribed) in the construction itself and holds within itself the (insoluble) key to our 'innocent culpability'.[8]

Provocation, defiance, denial

The People's House, just like an enigma, is even, on account of its structure, a 'provocation'; a provocation addressed to the clarity of mind, reason and rationality. This Sphinx challenges us to stop and answer, even when there is no answer possible. How can one respond to a monster? How can one be responsible *vis-à-vis* a 'monster', in the space where 'the accident' makes a monument, where the 'case', *casus*, of the fall of an ideology becomes representation?

Just like the monster, the monument gives off signs of warning. (Etymologically, they share the same root; from the Latin, *moneo/monere*). By definition, they make us keep our vigil; by definition they keep us thinking. Monsters defy the order of nature. Through 'the monsters, the prodigies and the abominations…we see the work of nature, reversed, mutilated, curtailed.'[9] They defy the taxonomy, the economy of meaning, the *right* meaning.

The architecture of Ceausescu is a challenge to order, to architectural orders, to urban order(s). It defies and exceeds. It carries the disproportionate measure of *hubris* and the violence of the hybrid. The 'hybrid' is literally 'the product of a violation'. In the present case, there is a violation of reason by a totalising *hybris* of an ideology, a violation of the city by a strategic implantation, a violation done to architecture itself by disregard for its rules. Still more violent is the fact that this architecture perpetuates by itself the trace of its violation: marked in stone is 'the desire' of architecture but so is the violence which leads to its satisfaction.

This desire of architecture, Ceausescu's 'architecturophilia', is first and foremost an 'architecturomania': the mania of architecture, architecture as mania, as madness, the delirious become architecture. It is well known that Ceausescu himself worked on models of the 'People's House', directly inscribing it with his own symptoms. Its architecture is a 'symptomatic figuration', but also a symptomatic protection. It is Representation – the main function of the language of that which I call Theatre of Power – as a defence against an intolerable representation. Let us keep in mind Romanian reality of the 1980s, the economic crisis, the national debt, the threat of famine, and not least the isolation of Romania in the international community.

Psychosis – as Freud tells us in 'The Neuro-Psychoses of Defense' – 'disavows reality and tries to replace it'. The present case concerns the denial of an oppressive reality and the replacement of it by a 'wonder'. Principally, hallucinatory psychosis manifests itself by:

> the accentuation of the idea which was threatened by the precipitating cause of the onset of the illness. One is therefore justified in saying that the ego has fended off the incompatible idea through a flight into psychosis....The ego breaks away from the incompatible idea; but the latter is inseparably connected with a piece of reality, so that, *in so far as the ego achieves this result, it, too, has detached itself wholly or in part from reality.*[10]

For Ceausescu, the People's House is the edifice that protects and affirms his proper separation from reality: it is the monument which he built to commemorate his separation from reality. What is represented by this architecture is the incompatible, the intolerable, that which Freud called *unverträglich/ unerträglich*. Perhaps Ceausescu's People's House can help us to think that which is an architecture of the incompatible, the intolerable (as monsters do, of course). The scene of this hallucination, though, extends from the architectural sphere in to the social sphere. A whole city but also a whole country, indeed, a whole nation was captured and inscribed in his delirium.

And, as Deleuze once said, 'si vous êtes pris dans le rêve de l'autre vous êtes foutu'. This was the human condition of the individual: *être foutu*, a being entirely socialized, an ideological marionette, or worse, 'an ornamental detail' in the great living compositions, the huge *tableaux vivants* existing under the dictator's rule. Let us recall the paranoid jubilation of the festive spectacles. Let us recall the terrifying images of the masses waving their coloured scarves to write his name with their bodies, to transform into a living calligraphy his signature.

The architecturomania of Ceausescu has to do with the desire for immortality, the obsession to preserve forever the memory of his name.[11] Indeed, the one and only purpose of a 'wonder' is to be a monument and to preserve the memory of its founder. 'From a pragmatical point of view, that which defines the wonder, that which makes the wonder, is that an edifice be known throughout the whole of the *Oekoumene*. This is why the wonder may seem to be the ideal vehicle for assuring the immortality of a proper name'.[12]

This is how, as regards immortality, this heaving monster in stone gathers speed and becomes a good vehicle. The immortality of a name remains, albeit in a negative form. Even effaced the name persists as 'effaced', 'crossed out'. That which was in the beginning the 'People's House', and then the 'Palace of the Parliament', is commonly called 'Ceausescu's Palace'. And perhaps this is an indication of a diabolical calculation at work whereby the immortality of his name is assured by any and all means. His signature remains *sous rature*, buried in the foundations. The act of burying one's name is already to count on death.

Ceausescu calculated and counted on immortality for the price of his proper death. Perhaps the People's House was from the outset meant to be a 'crypt',[13] and as such it is a projection into the future of an endless mourning, a project of 'saving his death', saving the immortality of Ceausescu's death: a mortgage and *un mort-gage* left for the future by an ideological neurosis. And *le gage engage*...

In restating the psychoanalytical notion of the 'crypt', one could say that that which remains *sauf* – without, excepted, saved – in the People's House is 'the monument of a catastrophe and the permanent possibility of his return'.[14] The monumental function of the People's House is to keep the place of the disaster *sauf*.[15]

Let us note that the construction of a 'crypt' constitutes a phallo-thanatic symbol. For, to build up, to erect, is to show off power, potency. The erection of the monument puts on show the erection of Ceausescu himself, 'the small one' becoming 'a great one'.

It still remains to interrogate the role of the edification of the People's House in the light of the events of 1989 which led to his death. After the storming of the Bastille, the devastation of the Louvre or that of Versailles, it is known that 'revolutions attack monuments'. In this sense, in his article 'Architecture', Georges Bataille affirms that, 'the great monuments are raised up like dykes, pitting the logic of majesty and authority against all the shady elements. It is in the form of cathedrals and palaces that Church and State speak and impose silence on the multitudes.'[16] And it is well known, in psychoanalysis, that all erections entail symbolic castration. 'No erection without castration', as Derrida once said, tongue in cheek.

The 'crypt' belongs to the vocabulary of the symptomatical projection–protection in the face of anguish. The ideological phallocentrism of Ceausescu leads to 'the anguish of castration'. The trial of architecture is equal to a trial of virility, a very real one, in the face of the imminence of the cut. But still, with his passion for architecture, Ceausescu knew how to maintain his libidinal investment, there in the obstinate force of his architecture. He knew how to maintain pleasure, in the face of 'the death of pleasure'. Like all tyrants, Ceausescu conceived of using the force of architecture to perpetuate his virile power. Architecture continued his dictatorship, because, as Ceausescu well knew, architecture has by itself a dictatorial power: 'The storming of the Bastille is symbolic of this state of things: it is difficult to explain this impulse of the masses other than by the animosity the people hold against monuments which are their true masters.'[17] It is precisely the figure of the masses, the people, which one finds cryptogrammed in this 'house'; like an object of anguish, like a threat of castration. Naming the People's House, Ceausescu signed the monument dedicated to the object of his anguish, excluding himself, saving himself.

Power of interruption and overthrow

In Panovsky's 'Meaning in the Visual Arts', the sphinx is seen as 'an anomaly easily explained by the fact that the organism in question is not a homogenous one but a heterogeneous one.'[18] To be sure, the anomaly of the People's House remains associated with a certain heterogeneity. The 'monstrous body', as Greg Lynn has noted, when produced by 'differential combinations' is, 'at the same time a whole and a collection of associated parts.'[19] The heterogeneity of the People's House is a consequence of a depository of a set of phantasms, residues, clichés and remains which make up a body, a mass, a unity, while guarding at the same time a rupture with all forms of totality. This is massification, a conglomeration, but also a system of opposites and contradictory tensions that infuses it with the power of residue and resistance – resistance as 'disaster', in Blanchot's terms.

Neither a style nor an addition of styles, the People's House is rather a style in the non-style, as non-style, a non-architecture in architecture; it is architecture maintained in rupture with itself. Achronical and anachronical, ataxical, atopical – like monsters – it resists time, classification and localisation. Unlike all its references, the People's House conserves, in the manner of monsters, its unique character in its own disaster.

Monsters introduce dissemblance in resemblance. They do not resemble their progenitors or parents but are issue of disarticulation, of the 'explosion of the secret alliances'. They do not reproduce. They do not participate in perpetuation, continuity, progress. Being a radical interruption in a genealogical curve, they are on a death line. They are reserves, remains.

The 'wonder' interrupts the continuity of the context wherein it is inscribed. It has the power of disruption, the power of overthrow. Discussing the Cheops pyramid, Goetz notes:

> The edifice seems to overthrow the law of nature and those of the space it occupies. It disrupts the harmony of the landscape and that of the site. It does not try, like the Parthenon, for example, to ponder its own weight and presence in relation to the place and surroundings that preceded it. On the contrary, it poses itself like an infraction. Quite contrary to 'contextual' architecture, which respects the 'already-there', the wonder imposes itself like a radical novelty which will in time profoundly derange the habitudes of perception.[20]

Negation and revolution

The logic of the wonder leads to a negation of the context and entails imposition as infraction, as a radical novelty. In the case of the People's House the infraction is performative. It could be maintained that the demolition, the erasure of a part of the city in order to annul all adherence to an urban context, was in this same logic. It is indeed the role of the wondrous edifice to 'overthrow the communal places of bodies and space' because 'voluptuous and royal is the work that commits this violation by suspending the working of the earth over the heads of the spectators.'[21] The overturning of an urban site summit (in this case, the hill of Arsenal in Bucharest) and the erasure of symbolical places (like a churches or historical monuments), in front of the citizens, transforms them into impotent spectators of the destruction of their proper grounds, and this is a consequence of a scenario that corresponds to the staging of 'the wonder'. Indeed, 'the wonder' should place itself, pose itself like a negation of that which is not itself, therein lies its force of attraction, as if the universe there found its point of deflagration, as if the habitudes of perception, comportment and aesthetical rules which reigned in its place and in all the places, before its edification, suddenly become inoperative.[22]

'The wonder', without exception, results from negative aesthetics, morality and politics. As Goetz points out, 'the negation, be it provisional and local, within ordinary constraints of existence, this power of suspension inherent in a certain treatment of space and in a certain type of architecture, will not be without the raising of the problems which are all at once, aesthetic, political and moral.'[23] This is the power of suspension, of overthrow, but also of revolution. It is a common trait of 'monsters' and 'wonders' to preserve a dialectically viable form. In the dialectic of forms there are monsters that have the power of reversion. Bataille begins his article 'The Deviations of Nature' by quoting a phrase from Pierre Boaistuau's *Prodigious Histories*:

> Among all the things that can be contemplated under the concavity of the heavens, *there is nothing that awakens the human spirit more powerfully*, that delights the senses, that brings more awe, that provokes in the creators an admiration or horror, greater than do the monsters, the prodigies, and the abominations by which we see the works of nature *reversed*, mutilated, curtailed.[24]

Monsters reverse the order of nature, but in a way, they also awaken the spirit.

It is important to examine dialectically this architecture, be it wondrous or monstrous, for it contains and anticipates the reversion, the revolution, and at the same time it also, perhaps, brings forth something else: a glimpse of hope. The wondrous/monstrous (architecture) conditions the passage, the change. (Let us not forget that, frequently, we find monsters in the role of gatekeeper.) It marks the crisis and the imminence of change. The People's House is like a 'critical point' from which something can change.

Translation by Geir Svansson and Sanda Macaet

Notes

1   Here I use the term 'wonder' as it is employed in an architectural sense, to refer to exceptional, individual buildings, as in the 'Seven Wonders of the World'.

2 Benoît Goetz, 'L'Edifice Paradoxal', in *Mesure pour mesure, Architecture et Philosophie*, Cahiers du CCI, Paris: Editions du Centre Pompidou, 1987, p. 127.

3 I shall return to this subject later.

4 Georges Bataille, 'Les écarts de la nature' (1930) in *Oeuvres Completes*, vol. 1, Paris: Gallimard, p. 228.

5 Monsters have always been considered a bad omen, a sign of divine will, an effect of a language which does not belong to us but which addresses us talking in another language than ours. Monsters 'talk' to us and make us speak a 'foreign language'.

6 Goetz, 'L'Edifice Paradoxal', p. 126.

7 Mihail Moldoveanu, 'Le ventre du Bucharest' in *Monuments historiques* 169, 1990, Paris, p. 113.

8 Using the term 'our', I myself may be committing a violation. In spite of all explication, there still remains the enigma of the specialists, the politicians, in short, a whole nation that has accepted, consented, consigned this enterprise, be it by their 'response' or by their 'silence'.

9 Bataille, 'Les écarts de la nature', p. 228.

10 Sigmund Freud, 'The Neuro-Psychoses of Defence', *Die Abwehrneuropsychosen, GWI*, in *The Standard Edition* III, trans. J. Strachey, London: Pelican, 1985, p. 59. Emphasis added.

11 Namely, the myth of the Ceausescu-epoch as 'the golden age', the summit of history, etc.

12 Goetz, 'L'Edifice Paradoxal', p. 124.

13 I recall here the psychoanalytical notion of 'crypt' introduced by Maria Torok and Nicolas Abraham in *Le verbier de l'Homme aux loups*, restored in philosophy by Jacques Derrida in 'Fors', his preface to Torok and Abraham's book.

14 Maria Torok and Nicolas Abraham, *Le verbier de l'Homme aux loups*, Paris: Aubier-Flamarion, 1976.

15 I use the French word *sauf* as belonging to the 'crypt' lexikon, in the same sense that was introduced by Derrida in 'Fors'.

16 Bataille, 'Architecture', in Neil Leach (ed.), *Rethinking Architecture*, London: Routledge, 1997, p. 21.

17 Battaille, 'Architecture'. Translation slightly amended.

18 Erwin Panowsky, *Meaning in the Visual Arts*, Chicago: University of Chicago Press, 1955, p. 62.

19 Greg Lynn, 'Body Matters' in *The Body*, Journal of Philosophy and the Visual Arts, London: Academy Editions, 993, p. 63.

20 Goetz, L'Edifice Paradoxal', p. 125.

21 Philon quoted by Goetz, 'L'Edifice Paradoxal', p. 126.

22 Goetz, *'L'Edifice Paradoxal'*, p. 111.

23 Goetz, 'L'Edifice Paradoxal', p. 126.

24 Bataille, 'Les écarts de la nature', p. 228. Emphasis added.

17 Utopia 1988, Romania; Post-Utopia 1995, Romania

Dorin Stefan

Utopia 1988, Romania

Free meditation in front of the closed gates of the town.

I was dreaming that I had to reach the north entry of the town before the sound of the third stroke of the bell had faded in the four winds. To reach my place across on the southern side of town, I would have to make it by the first stroke of the bell, so that I could find shelter by the end of the third stroke. But somehow I became distracted, and found myself outside the walls, facing the closed gate. There, inside the citadel, in the very centre, a stone statue with its insignia was being erected. I had long since moved from the centre, and found a place by the walls. Now I was back by the wall, but on the wrong side. If I walked around the outside of the walls I could come to within a stone's throw of my place within the citadel. Standing by the wall I wondered which was in fact the 'other side' of the wall. Could it be the one in front of me as I stood there, or was it that one on the inside which I would normally face? As I looked at it now, the wall appeared to have two 'other sides'. Before I used to look towards the centre, and my view would be obstructed by the stone statue – the in-sign-ia (symbol of power). Now, as I looked into the distance, I seemed to discover 'the sun, the space and the green'. Seen from the outside the wall was transparent. I could see the square full of people again, the stone statue removed. Then the wall became a mirror reflecting the horizon.

The horizon. Yes, I remember, 'the horizon must be recaptured'. It is in this once-the-people's-square that I used to have my place. It is here that my friends and I practised architecture out of our love of the people. Now that my architecture is disliked in the square-of-the-stone-statue, and – as a consequence – I have left the citadel to practise my profession outside the walls; now that I have been excluded from the citadel, as I face the closed gates, I stand pondering my calling.

Architecture, I believe, is half spatial and half social. However – without rejecting this principle – I have started to ask myself just in what sense social and to what extent spatial, now that the-once-the-people's-square is occupied by the statue.

'Technique and conscience'

Leaving aside academic definitions of architecture and confronting the professional side of the discipline, I now find myself searching for an unsophisticated answer devoid of both rhetorical beauty and didactic purity. In these circumstances, is architecture anything but solitary transcendence?

I have been taught in the spirit of the harmonic dovetailing of the parts, in the interplay of volumes in light, in rationalism as a language of architecture, and I know of the alternative tradition of 'complexity and contradiction' and the theoretical importance of 'decomposition'. Still, all this and more faded in front of the closed gates of the citadel.

The heavy-handed insignia now dominates everything with its display of force. No meaning here – the paradoxical emptiness of the sign with no meaning. Any meaning collapses behind the empty ideological eclecticism of the official style. No persuasion. Just the brute material force of the insignia as it takes over the centre.

As a defence against the inflexible insignia of the official style, architecture must be infused with certain speculative concepts: architecture as transition, diffusion, dispersal, nonconformity, transparency, fluidity, organicism, fragmentation, a rhizomic architecture, a nomadic architecture, an architecture which always resists stratification. And from his marginal position, the philosopher will help us to 'deconstruct' the hierarchies and binary oppositions, exposing the possibilities of the signifier, and revealing the potential for the aleatory play of meaning. Against the strict objectivity of the insignia, we seek a complex, discursive approach; against the limitations of the mandate, we seek a conscious freedom of choice. The joy of the game, liberation from the model, challenging the system: these are the ways to resist the insignia.

I was dreaming of returning to the citadel, and I saw the stone statue. Through it I saw the alternative of sincere criticism as opposed to eclecticism, the sensitivity of the shift breaking the axis, the interpretation of the real as opposed to the pattern of bureaucracy, the truth of the context as opposed to the manipulation of conformity.

Reconquered horizon.

Technique and conscience.

Strategy and dissemination.

Post-Utopia 1995, Romania

Today we are free.

Yet in our free towns and our free architecture we still do not have water – let alone hot water – central heating or electric lighting at night. All we have are holes in the roads, rubbish dumped on the street and, generally speaking, an acute shortage of financial resources.

So are we really free?

But if, nonetheless, you choose to put your faith in Romania and to pursue the mysterious discourse of architecture, you have to find a way.

Strategy 1: autobiography as a therapeutic method for understanding and asserting the context

Or, to use a well-known phrase in the social and political context of contemporary Romania, I would rather talk about my grandfather than about architecture.

My grandfather represented adventure and the picturesque. He was a miner who travelled across the country pursuing productive holes in the earth. This is why he never had a home. He was permanently in love with *spritz*.

My father represented stability and comfort. He built his own house, avoiding the 'crisis of translation' of the architect, by being both conceiver, builder and user of his own building. Without realising it, he practised what Yona Friedman and Nicholas Negroponte would have called 'an architecture of participation'.

Meanwhile I, as their descendant, am an architect. I have a mission to translate the user's needs, wishes and intentions into built spaces. I abstractise. I use languages. I play a game between the spiritual and material worlds. This game cannot be played outside the context, whether general or specifically Romanian: the geography, population, religion, culture, technology, economics and so on. I was shaped under the complex of the Brancusi phenomenon: a peasant's son who emerged from the deep level of the specific context of Romania to challenge the cultural avant-garde, a Romanian who took the Western world by storm, and who wrote a page in the history of modern culture. However, in my case the deep cultural context was stultified by communist ideology, and all I was left with were western ideas. In my professional work, I therefore had to adopt a personal approach which aimed at undermining the 'official line'. This tactic took two forms: firstly, the necessity to engage with contemporary western ideas, and secondly, the urge to escape the spectre of an ideological subculture.

Strategy 2: conscience as theory

How can you pursue architecture as a cultural act, when constrained by utilitarian concerns as necessary as the air that we breathe?

Option 1: overinvest the simplest constructive gesture and redirect it towards architecture. When nothing is architecture any more, everything has to become architecture. The notion of the 'design project' is undermined. When, either through subjective reasons (the absence of culture) or through objective ones (the lack of qualified workmen) the design project is constantly being changed, interpreted, mutilated, adapted, in the absence of any protective legal framework, the project has to be replaced by 'design guidelines' which must be followed under the strict control of the architect on site. The architect no longer 'designs', but merely indicates a way to build.

Option 2: adopt an elitist position with respect to the rest of society. In responding to one's professional vocation and the calling of the site, you need to situate yourself within the world's cultural horizons, and be convinced that society depends upon your spiritual efforts.

Strategy 3: impotence as practice

What can you do when there is no technology, no quality materials, no experienced workforce, and no clear framework to the construction process or legislation to ensure quality control? One suggestion might be to transform this impotence, clumsiness and lack of know-how into something positive.

In view of the present circumstances, carefully designed details have to be replaced by welding and casting; the developer's improvisations and the client's desire to modify the building on site (in the spirit of Ceausescu, who used to move with a gesture of the hand not only walls and stairs, but entire districts of housing) have to be accepted when the building solutions seem too complicated.

You could try the following conjectural tactics:

- a non-conformist approach generated by the changing syntax of materials.
- a non-conformist language of detailing (welding, casting, prefabricated blocks).
- a flexible range of textures and materials which could accommodate the intervention of client and developer without compromising the overall impression.
- an approach towards the building as a form of stitching, as a planned sewing together.

An alternative strategy:

Try to use postmodern cultural concepts, such as the 'ephemeral', 'difference', the 'fragmentary', the 'open-ended', but approach them from the opposite direction. In other words, let the context dictate, instead of attempting to dictate the context.

Follow a strategy already pursued elsewhere. The rupture produced by communist ideology was concretised by the lack of continuity at all levels (political, social, cultural, professional and so on) to the extent that Romania today is in the same situation as Western Europe after the Second World War. It therefore has to follow a well-worn path (and I keep noticing how modern architecture is constantly being rewritten these days with Le Corbusier's rough details).

This may be a short-lived personal experience, or just an impression. But once Western materials and techology have taken over the Romanian market and have imposed their rule, we might have to resort to a third strategy of control, to guard against problems that result from profit margins, mediocrity and mass production.

18 Rediscovering Romania

Ioana Sandi

In its post-Cold War configuration, Europe appears like a schizoid whole whose parts do not relate. Whether the divide between East and West is of a purely economic nature, and whether one can speak of a cultural condition which runs deeper than strictly material terms, the question about the future identity of Europe is as intriguing as it is impenetrable.

An obvious way to understand current developments in Europe is as a live model for the workings of an ever-expanding market. Any of the current theoretical models for the development of market economy, from the theory of the accursed share to the flexible accumulation of capital, offers a vision of the future of Eastern Europe. In simple terms, one half of Europe is completely developed, saturated with infrastructures and communications networks, and literally covered in all kinds of human construction. The other half is, both physically and metaphorically, a vast expanse of wilderness. This is the Europe which has yet to be developed.

If this simple physical model fails to do justice to the cultural complexity of such a situation, it does at least provide us with a point of departure: in a decade or two, Western Europe will sense the presence of Eastern Europe in a radically new way. The 'Westernisation' of Eastern Europe is sure to happen, as nation after nation is absorbed into a culture of consumption, leaving the whole continent with a new structure. This prospect of economic growth gives us one reason at least to take Eastern Europe seriously.

In the West, Eastern Europe already is a kind of concern. How else might one explain the continuous stream of attempts to grasp its apparently elusive nature, the sheer amount of media coverage nonetheless failing to provide a coherent picture, with its anecdotal, hesitant and often contradictory coverage of images and events? One day, for example, a tourist trip to the otherwise blissfully undeveloped mountain villages of Maramures in northern Romania, is dismissed in *Time Out* magazine by a journalist who fails to appreciate the unheated rooms or the 'disgusting cocktail of Nescafe and Coca-Cola', seemingly much enjoyed by local folk. Another day, a *Building Design* correspondent struggles through a lecture by the Hungarian architect Imre Mackowecz, comprising two hours of religious incantation, only to conclude that maybe it is better after all not to live in a post-communist country. Then, a heart-breaking picture of a gypsy child on the front page of *The Independent* illustrates a story of the orphans who will die during the winter not only in Romania, but throughout Eastern Europe.

The idiosyncratic nature of this kind of reflection seems to run deeper every day. Between the wildly exotic and the ridiculous, the charitable and the accusatory, the interest shown in Eastern Europe operates as a parallel discourse to the reality of the place, a discourse which always follows at a cautious distance, and which allows one, if necessary, to ignore the problem altogether.

For the frequent traveller between the two European extremes, it does not take long before the need to understand the roots of such confusion becomes a daily intellectual exercise, as does the desire if not to dissolve the differences, then at least to hear them discussed in a more fruitful way. What both guarantees the urgency and relevance of such thoughts, but also complicates them, is the underlying certainty that whatever the contradictions, one is still operating within a recognisably European arena; that no matter how far the boundaries stretch, this is not America, Asia or Africa, but Europe.

To use a somewhat hackneyed analogy, it is as though Eastern Europe is emerging from fifty years of sleep. There is no question that this sleep has been traumatic, and has altered the structure of society in ways that are only beginning to become apparent. What is more important, perhaps, is that the rest of the world has changed in the meantime, and that what has been lost cannot be regained. So, to take the analogy a bit further, Eastern Europe is like an adult which has awaken from this sleep with the mind of a child and the tastes and values of its grandparents. For the people who exist under such distorted historical conditions, the question becomes how to deal with this built-in anachronism, yet also how to adapt to a world that has been out of reach for so long. For their Western European counterparts, the question remains equally challenging, the problems compounded by the survival in the East of values and beliefs long discredited in the West. And what makes the East of Europe so unacceptable to the politically correct West is ultimately its racism, sexism and general intolerance. The somewhat cautious approach adopted by the West towards Eastern Europe, an approach strangely at odds with its otherwise liberal values, can be seen partly as a consequence of a superiority complex.

The duty of the European mutant, then, is to work against this climate of suspicion, to speak of experiences and situations not easily accessible through the general media, with the aim of unveiling the less obvious qualities which might arise from the historical turmoil; to shed a more positive light on the differences, and to hint at what it is that the East can offer to the rest of Europe.

After 50 years of isolation, Eastern Europe is innocent and is undergoing a journey of rediscovery. In Romania, this journey is difficult, enthusiastic and intense.

Rediscovering politics

The image of a nation glued to the television screen night after night may not appear too strange; after all, the world's first televised revolution was broadcast from Bucharest. However, there is more to this phenomenon than meets the Western eye. In a paradoxical response to America's dependence on broadcast programmes, the shattered structure of Romanian civil society is gradually being stitched back together by television.

That television can acquire an active political dimension appears as a utopian dream for those in Western countries which have become so saturated with this medium. It seems preposterous to assume that we are now witnessing in Eastern Europe a resurrection of public values and political meaning just precisely when these notions are losing their currency in the rest of Europe. It is maybe even more difficult to see television as the vehicle and the site of this real political exchange. A closer look at the role of the media in a totalitarian regime will nevertheless show that this is not so unlikely.

The aim of a totalitarian regime is to fragment society into a group of unconnected individuals, so as to make them easier to control. Such atomisation is achieved over a period of time by means of deliberate measures done in the name of some professed ideal (communism, fascism and so on), measures which appear at the time violent and ruthless. This condition is maintained through a variety of oppressive means which prevent any form of individual political exchange. One of these is poverty, the condition in which survival becomes more important than politics. Another is fear and distrust, where even those who appear to be suffering may simply be acting on behalf of the secret police. Yet another is the concealment or distortion of information. The ideologically controlled mass media therefore play a crucial role in the totalitarian structure by providing no real information, yet equally offering all the information that is permitted.

Television takes on an enormous significance when it becomes the site of revolt, and – against a background in which it had provided a distorted, fiction-alised account of reality – provides genuine information. One can imagine the cathartic power of the moment when, for the first time in decades, television starts to broadcast what is actually happening, events of vital importance. In a condition of social and political crisis, the immediacy of the consequences of what is shown on the screen expands the significance of a medium which is otherwise sterile and abstract.

It is in this context, then, that television becomes the locus of a real debate. For the course of the country, and the life of the people, it matters greatly whether a certain political event is screened, whether a certain political figure makes a meaningful speech. Against the growing proliferation of commercial programmes and channels, those which discuss political questions remain of crucial interest to much of the population.

Rediscovering ethics

Is fundamentalism the mark of an underdeveloped society? Should the religious surge in Eastern Europe be seen as fundamentalism? Religion can be seen as one of the ways – perhaps the easiest, for being part of a tradition – of fulfilling the need for an ethical understanding of the world, for a reformulation of values and moral ideals which have been deliberately erased under a totalitarian regime.

The violence of the totalitarian regime and its sacrificial upheaval has brought Eastern Europe to a point of crisis so acute that no action can be seen to be beyond good and evil. Today everything is judged, so that the issues of right and wrong are very exposed and under continuous interrogation. The intensity of this state of affairs can be hard to grasp from the point of view of contemporary Western thought, so aware is it of cultural difference and the provisionality of truth; but things look different from the East. In Romania, the revolution provided a judgment degree zero against which good is forever separable from evil. There is an ultimate common denominator to all further deliberation: people have died for liberty. In the face of such a universal truth, Western relativism is simply not an option.

Romania is blessed – or cursed – with its recent brand of martyrs. Their sacrifice rings a strange note in turn of the century Europe. Dying for something you believe in, for your freedom and that of others, still happens, still matters. How can one understand the kinship with a stranger whose death has given you freedom? It is this kind of martyrdom – of the most real, unpretentious and banal kind – that distinguishes a cultural figure or a popular hero from a true hero who opens a way to the ethical. Probably the best approximation of the sacrifice of these often anonymous individuals is their number: something running into thousands, although the exact figure has yet to be disclosed. The realisation that these people have suffered something as tragic as death so that many others might acquire some form of liberty fades in the mists of time, or is simply forgotten in the general turmoil. Then, all of a sudden, you come across somebody who has lost a son or mother, and whose personal tragedy connects with your own life, with where you are now. Finally, all arguments gradually boil down to the point of no further reduction: human sacrifice.

For the Western eye, this raises the question of how to reconcile this renewed potential for ethical life with the flagrantly 'unethical' racism, sexism, xenophobia and corruption which seem to have swept the whole of Eastern Europe, and which have proved so unappealing to potential foreign investors. The two issues belong, though, to different categories. If the values seem conservative and old-fashioned, or at time even repulsive to those in the tolerant Western world, they are mostly the result of decades of isolation and ideologically induced hatred of difference. What is perhaps more important is that the seeds of change are there, opened by the very possibility of asking ethical questions, of holding a meaningful debate about what is good.

Rediscovering economics

Watching capitalism at work in its most anecdotal form can provide great entertainment. In Romania, just as in Russia or the rest of Eastern Europe, people seem poised to reenact and even surpass the Hollywood gangster stories, which were the closest one came to an image of America under the previous regime. Because there is so little, wealth is created with real passion and those who are successful are regarded with great interest and admiration; but equally with hostility.

The process is interesting in two ways. Firstly, it is fascinating to watch how industrialisation rises and falls as if in a fast-forward repeat of the twentieth century in the West; how the massive heavy industry is recognised as redundant and abandoned, without a fraction of the struggle that surrounded the same phenomenon in the West; how small businesses take off by themselves – provided they have the chance – as does international large-scale collaboration and transaction.

Secondly, it is perhaps even more fascinating to witness the passionate lifestyles spawned by these new economic circumstances, the lifestyles of those who are at last free to live as they always wanted, or thought they wanted, so obviously indebted are they to Western cultural models. Hence extreme exhibitionism and conspicuous consumption determine consumerist priorities, to the extent that a smart Western car, a good sound system and a proper satellite dish come before a good place to live. Every other film is the latest American mainsteam movie, possibly showing months before its release in London or Paris, while McDonald's is the favourite hang-out. Street vendors hawk pirate pop albums the very day that they are launched internationally. A world of contradictions and contrasts is born.

Rediscovering architecture

Like most of Eastern Europe, Romania has half a century of culture with which to catch up. This does not mean that there had been no cultural production under communism. On the contrary, a specific and very powerful kind of cultural response had been generated against the oppressive regime: the act of cultural resistance. Apart from the dissident act, all production had been forced to develop survival strategies of disengagement, which inevitably threw any cultural move on to an abstract plane. The return of leading Eastern European intellectuals to the roots of Western philosophy, and the impressive scholarship which emerged, are good examples.

Devising a way of thinking that copes with the current transformations in Eastern European countries seems to be an altogether different task. The decades of dissident writing and 'abstract' philosophy carry little relevance to the present culture and its need for articulation. When interesting and meaningful articulation does occur, as in the writings of H.R. Patapievici, it is at first treated with great suspicion and hostility before it eventually wins considerable popularity.

In architecture, things are probably more difficult to predict than in any other aspect of culture. For decades, not only has any chance of architectural development been blocked by lack of money and state control, but a completely new image (more than a typology) of the built environment has been created; the one we recognise when we speak about socialist architecture. Whether or not there is any value in this kind of construction is a difficult question. What is clear is that there is a very limited degree flexibility within existing structures, as in the case of the extensive low-quality mass housing projects, or the 'ideological' buildings, both of which appear to resist alternative patterns of use or habitation.

New architecture will therefore not happen on barren ground, but on a strangely perverted built landscape, which includes the typical socialist tower blocks (now part of the familiar environment for many people) and the grotesque institutional structures. Contemporary architects, who have mostly been trained according to totalitarian guidelines, respond to the question of how to build by rummaging through the toolbox of twentieth-century architecture, in a rerun of the 1980s in the West. However, the question of style is perhaps not that important against the scale of construction which will undoubtedly take place in Eastern Europe.

Despite the emerging typologies or physiognomies of buildings, there are two factors which make the journey of architectural rediscovery in Eastern Europe so interesting. Firstly, there is the status of architecture as a cultural act. Architecture remains important. For instance, a bank will still insist on the use of expensive materials to signal a place of wealth and financial security, and a hotel will still aspire to an early twentieth-century ideal of glamour to provide the setting for a whole range of business from government transactions to more dubious local deals. Sculptural shapes and new volumes are still in demand as landmarks in an otherwise barren built environment.

That such an old-fashioned attitude to architecture should be back in vogue may be seen as part of the pervasive anachronism of Eastern Europe. It is strange, after all, to expect a bank to express itself in built terms when wealth no longer relates to a place of storage but to fluctuating impulses of digitalised information and, on a daily basis, to anonymous, omnipresent personal cards and cash dispensing machines in walls. It is hard to imagine the value of such an attitude when the very future of architecture in the West seems to have been displaced into a mix of infrastructures, transactions and planning.

Secondly, in Eastern Europe there are simply no rules for architecture. There is no established way of building, no coherent construction industry and, most of all, no recognisable criteria by which to judge what might be a good place in which to work, rest or play. After decades in which architects were practically reduced to being automata for the state, they are now working in what emerges as one of the most liberating professional climates in the world.

Eastern Europe at the end of the twentieth century is a barren, dangerous, exotic, unknown and very intense part of the world. All the more reason, perhaps, for the West to take it seriously.

V
Tombs and monuments

19 Berlin 1961–89

The bridal chamber

Neil Leach

Figure 19.1 Bride with binoculars, looking at her parents in East Berlin

What are we to make of the wall that divided Europe? How might we begin to theorise such a wall from an architectural perspective? It is against the rich background of the wall in history that the full sociological implications of the particular wall that divided East from West are set in relief. For we have inherited an understanding of the wall as an architectural element which has been accorded a social status beyond its purely physical properties. Indeed, for some it has had a pivotal role as the very generator of society. While Vitruvius had claimed that it was fire which brought humankind together, Alberti argued that it was the roof and the wall which first gave rise to society, by drawing men together and providing them with 'a safe and welcome refuge':[1]

> Some have said that it was fire and water which were initially responsible for bringing men together into communities, but we, considering how useful, even indispensable, a roof and walls are for men, are convinced that it was they that drew and kept men together.[2]

This principle extended beyond the simple enclosure of the house to include the wall of the city itself. Throughout antiquity, the wall served not only to protect the city but also to unite the citizens, to the point where the citizens invested their very identity in the wall. The city wall came to symbolise the unity and protection of the citizens to the extent that the wall was the city, and the city was the wall. Even when there was no wall – as was the case with Sparta – the very absence of the wall fulfilled this role, for the Spartans were so confident in their military prowess, that they prided themselves in not needing any defensive walls.[3]

City walls, as Alberti comments, 'were therefore considered particularly sacred, because they served both to unite and to protect the citizens.'[4] The sacred nature of these walls was reflected in the clear ritual adopted by the Romans in laying them out.[5] The ploughshare, which was always associated with life and fertility, would be used to cut a furrow in the soil so as to demarcate the line of the walls. Where the plough was to cross a gate it would be lifted and carried over that space. By lifting the plough in this way, the gates would not form part of the wall. The dead could therefore be carried through the gates in order to be buried outside, without polluting the sacred furrow of the wall. Such rituals served to reinforce the symbolic content of the wall.

Against this tradition of the wall as the very originator of society and domesticity, how might we view a wall that had the opposite effect, a wall that denied society, that tore Europe apart? What are we to make of a wall that divided families, a wall that kept brother from brother, sister from sister, husband from wife, bride from mother, a wall that was anything but 'a safe and welcome refuge'? What are we to make of a wall that was also known as the 'iron curtain', a wall whose very name evoked an inflexible, unrelenting, terminable sense of death? How are we to understand this wall, the wall that divided East from West, a wall that we shall refer to henceforth as 'the Wall'.

The full horror of the Wall is brought out by the elaborate and gruesome

Figure 19.2 Two women meeting, Harzer Straße, Berlin, August 1961

machinery which was devised to make it as efficient as possible. Contemporary efforts to improve the technical efficiency of the domestic wall – the thermal, structural and acoustic properties of the wall – have a sinister parallel in the attempts to render this 'other' wall likewise as efficient as possible, its purpose being to prevent the transmission not of cold or noise, but of human beings. Of significance here was the strip which was regularly ploughed afresh so as to reveal the traces of those attempting to escape. The plough was used here to demarcate not the sacred and inviolate territory of the wall across which polluted corpses could not pass, but precisely the opposite, an open expanse on which the escaper could be shot. Like the fields in the myth of the Golden Fleece sown with dragon's teeth, these fields brought forth soldiers, whose remit here was to shoot to kill. The plough was used to till the fields not of life but of death, strips of land which were referred to as the 'death-strip'.[6]

Around Berlin the Wall took on a distinctly architectural dimension. In early versions the architecture of the Wall was clearly a domestic architecture. The

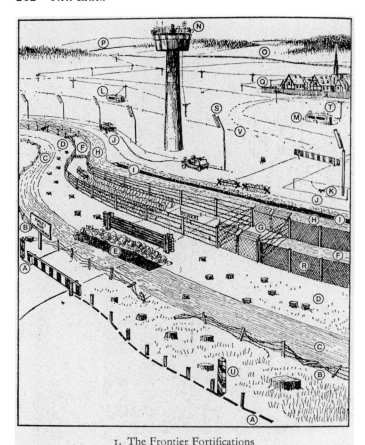

1. The Frontier Fortifications

KEY

A. Actual Border line
B. Old barbed wire
C. Original 10-km ploughed strip, now overgrown
D. Clear-felled area
E. Vehicle trap
F. Mined strip flanked by barbed wire or metal fences
G. Way through double fence
H. Second ploughed strip
I. Barrier trench
J. Track for heavy vehicles and foot-path
K. Guard dog on sliding lead
L. Concrete bunker

M. Earth bunker
N. Watchtower with searchlights, phones, infra-red aids and possibly radar
O. Barrier cordoning off hinterland
P. Barrier of 5 km forbidden zone, with police control
Q. Wall round village
R. Tall stamped metal fence
S. Floodlighting
T. Field telephone
U. Border marking stones and striped obelisk
V. Trip wires

Figure 19.3 Diagram of the defences of the Wall

original Wall was built using standard materials of domestic construction: mortar, concrete blocks and bricks. Whatever was ready to hand was used. Materials included fence posts and precast concrete beams intended for domestic floor construction. The very materials which had been used – in Alberti's definition –

Figure 19.4 The body of Peter Fechter being carried away by GDR border guards, Berlin, 17 August 1962

to bring society together were being used to tear society apart. Domestic materials – bricks and concrete blocks – were being used against themselves, against the logic of the domestic. Indeed, as the Wall was being constructed, the doors and windows in the houses immediately to the east of the Wall were bricked up, the very innocence of the materials highlighting the macabre and sinister nature of the task.

Figure 19.5 Bricked-up facade, Bernauer Straße, Berlin, 16 October 1961

The image of the bricked up facade evokes the memory of the ancient Greek myth of Antigone, in which Creon, the ruler of Thebes, ordered Antigone to be walled up alive in a cave for acting against the state.[7] Creon ordered this despite the fact that Antigone had been betrothed to his own son, Haemon. Instead of joining Haemon in the bridal chamber, Antigone was condemned to the cave. The cave therefore became her 'bridal bower':

ANTIGONE: So to my grave
            My bridal-bower, my everlasting prison,
            I go, to join those many of my kinsmen
            Who dwell in the mansion of Persephone...[8]

The 'crime' of Antigone had been to disobey manmade law. It was a case of the classic Greek dilemma between manmade and natural law, between *nomos* and *physis*. Antigone's two brothers, Polynices and Eteocles, had both been killed in battle, Polynices attempting to overthrow the city of Thebes and Eteocles struggling to defend it. Creon had decreed that in retribution the corpse of Polynices was to remain on the battlefield to be devoured by vultures, whereas Eteocles was to be accorded a full state funeral. Antigone, however, defied Creon and buried Polynices, setting into motion the tragedy that was to consume them both. Just as Antigone effectively became a martyr for obeying the natural law, so too Creon came to suffer for committing the ultimate *hubris* of overstepping the mark and overruling that law. For his actions led eventually to the death not only of Antigone, but also of Haemon.

The myth of Antigone has parallels in the Romanian legend of the walled-up bride, where the mason, Master Manole, was obliged to build his wife into the wall of a monastery under construction in order to prevent it from collapsing.[9]

Figure 19.6 Bricked-up doorway, Harzer Straße, Berlin, 1962

According to the legend, Master Manole was the leader of a group of masons who undertook to build 'a high monastery, unequalled on earth' at Arges for the Black Prince. Each night the work of the previous day collapsed, until Manole was instructed in a dream to wall in the first wife or sister of the workmen to appear at dawn. This proved to be Manole's own wife, and Manole was obliged to build her into the wall. Her sacrifice ensured that the walls did not collapse and that the monastery could be completed. With Manole the sacrifice was a sacrifice in the name of art. With Antigone it was a sacrifice against the name of art, if by art we understand the natural. In the case of Antigone the unnatural, artificial law prevailed. Antigone represents the other walled-up bride, the bride who was sacrificed against the natural law.

The walling up of sections of East Berlin constituted the triumph of the unnatural over the natural, the state over the family. Antigone therefore becomes the emblematic motif of the Berlin condition: the family torn apart and denied by the state. Just as Antigone had been walled up in her own bridal chamber of death, the houses around the Wall were themselves bricked up. The domestic, furthermore, was violated by an architectural language that was itself domestic. The house, the family home, was entombed with the very bricks with which it was built. Finally, once the house had been walled up, suffocated, denied the very houseness of the house, it was erased so completely that only the bare traces remained, a ghost of a house left to haunt those in the West. If, as Walter Benjamin has said, to live is to leave traces, here have been the traces of life.[10] If, by extension, to remove the traces is somehow to extinguish the very evidence of life, these houses – these lives – were themselves extinguished.

It is in this context that the full import of the Wall becomes apparent. The Wall violated the domestic. The Wall denied the family. The Wall denied society. The building of the Wall, the emptying of the buildings around the Wall, the bricking up of the windows and doors, and the demolition and ultimate erasure of those buildings constituted an architecture of denial. Yet the Wall was not only an architecture of denial, it was also a denial of architecture. The Wall became a form of anti-architecture, a grotesque denial of the very social value of the art of building. All that architecture had stood for over the ages was now being subverted, challenged and denied by the logic and the violence of the Wall.

Figure 19.7 Building under demolition, Lohmühlenplatz, Berlin, March 1966

Notes

1 Vitruvius, *Ten Books on Architecture*, Morris Hickey Morgan (trans.), New York: Dover Editions, 1960, p. 38.
2 L.B. Alberti, *On the Art of Building in Ten Books*, Joseph Rykwert, Neil Leach and Robert Tavernor (trans.), Cambridge, MA: MIT Press, 1988, p. 3.
3 Referred to by Alberti, p. 102.
4 Alberti, p. 190.
5 On this see, for example, the account by Plutarch of Romulus founding Rome, in *Plutarch's Lives*, Bernadotte Perrin (trans.), London: William Heinemann, 1967, vol. 1, pp. 119–21.
6 Significantly, when the ancients wished to destroy a city – to erase its memory – they would plough it over.
7 Antigone, the daughter of Oedipus, was of royal blood, and could therefore not be put to death, although to be walled up alive in a cave was tantamount to being put to death.
8 Sophocles, 'Antigone' in *The Theban Plays*, E.P. Watling (trans.), Harmondsworth: Penguin, 1947, p. 150.

9 For the complete ballad see Mircea Eliade, *Zalmoxis: The Vanishing God*, Willard Trask (trans.), Chicago: University of Chicago Press, 1972, pp. 164–70.
10 Walter Benjamin, 'Paris, Capital of the Nineteenth Century' in *Reflections*, Edmund Jephcott (trans.), New York: Schocken Books, 1978, p. 155.

20 Reflections on disgraced monuments

Laura Mulvey

When Mark Lewis and I embarked on the project that was eventually to become the documentary film *Disgraced Monuments*, we did not intend it to be only about the disgrace of public monuments in the former Soviet Union. During the winter of 1989, indeed, Mark had been first impressed by this symptom of the collapse of communism when he saw, on the Canadian television news, a gigantic Lenin being removed from the centre of Bucharest. The removal was rendered particularly ritualistic by the presence of young priest who, representing the return of religion while exorcising the spirit of communism, held up a crucifix to the twelve-ton bronze statue as it swayed on a crane.

Figure 20.1 Mark Lewis, 'On the Monuments of the Republic, 2'

The early treatments of *Disgraced Monuments* looked quite generally at the symbolic roles played by statues caught up in political and historical upheavals. As Mark points out in his article 'What Is To Be Done?':

> Clearly the impulse to attack and destroy public works is part of the general attack on the continued presence of signs of the *ancien régime*. It is confirmation also that in moments of 'madness', publics will treat these monuments almost as if they were the actual leaders themselves....For instance in a report from 1871 on the destruction of the Vendôme column, the London Illustrated News gave this account of what happened after the column was felled: '[The crowd] treated the statue [of Napoleon] as the emperor himself, spitting on his face, while members of the National Guard hit his nose with rifles.'[1]

After the defeat of the Commune, the Vendôme column (itself on the site previously occupied by a statue of Louis IV) was restored, signalling the return of the *status quo ante*. In *October*, Eisenstein evokes such a reversal cinematically and symbolically: the beginning of the revolution is marked by a mass attack on the statue of the Czar which is thrown in pieces on the ground; then, as the February revolution fails, the film is literally reversed and the statue thus magically restored, complete, to its throne.

Moments when public monuments attract excessive attention contrast with the normal course of events when they attract very little:

> The most striking feature of monuments is that you do not notice them. There is nothing in the world as invisible as monuments. Like a drop of water on an oil skin, attention runs down without stopping for a moment....We cannot say that we do not notice them; we should say that they de-notice us. They withdraw from our senses.
>
> Robert Musil[2]

However, once they have attracted the attention of the crowd, the monuments' meaning can become unstable, shifting significance between the before and the after of their disgrace. On the one hand, their disgrace and removal may encapsulate, as image and emblem, the triumphal overthrow of an *ancien regime* for which they had presented a public face, often at odds with the private perceptions of the people. On the other, their ultimate fate raises questions about continuity and discontinuity, memory and forgetting, in history; about how, that is, a culture understands itself across the sharp political break of revolution.

In the aftermath of the French Revolution of 1789, the crowd attacked the royal tombs at the cathedral of St Denis. In response, the Abbe Gregoire took an important intellectual step. He argued that, after the Revolution, within the context of a new conception of the state and its collectivity, the monuments of the past no longer belonged to Church and King, but to the citizens as their national, cultural heritage. Once the monuments ceased to represent existing, oppressive, structures of power, they could acquire the cultural value that is bestowed by time and history. To destroy them, he said, would amount to 'vandalism'.

The monuments of modern dictatorships present perhaps more political difficulties and also have less clear aesthetic significance. It may seem only right to wipe out the triumphalist remnants of a fascist regime, especially when a people suddenly finds itself able to impose a collective, symbolic vengence on these objects and especially when their aesthetic value reflects their political significance. But it is here that the issue of memory, and repression within history, might need to be considered. The monuments erected by a hated regime may also, after its fall, perform an emblematic function in reverse. Samir al Khalil, for instance, discusses the future of Saddam Husain's Victory Arch, (erected in Baghdad in 1989 to celebrate the end of the Iran–Iraq War). Arguing that the monument should be allowed to stand, he says :

> What will future generations of Iraqis see in this monument: a symbol of the demonic machinations of one man which they will once again [as once the crowd destroyed statues of King Hussein and General Maude] try to tear down on the day of his overthrow, or an unforgettable testament to their country's years of shame?[3]

Originally, we had hoped that the documentary could include a variety of historical instances and political debates, but as it happened, *Disgraced Monuments* had to focus exclusively on events in the Soviet Union. When, in August 1991, the old guard's coup failed, anti-communism erupted into the streets and the statue of Dzerzhinsky was removed to scenes of carnivalesque celebration. Seen on television screens across the world, this moment created an infinitely repeated and generally recognised emblem for the collapse of Soviet communism. The more general questions we had been researching then provided a backdrop for a reflection on this moment of iconoclasm and its significance for people's understanding of seventy years of communist rule.

Change and continuity

> Every turning point in our society has begun its new history with a struggle with old monuments. This was a struggle with the past which was realised, primarily, as a struggle with monuments. So removing the statue of Dzerzhinsky [founder of the secret police that later became the KGB] in August 1991, has become a symbolic act. On the one hand, it signified a stage in the development of the contemporary social situation, but, on the other hand, it was also a repetition of the events of 1917.
>
> Natalya Davidova, art critic interviewed in *Disgraced Monuments*[4]

Tension between continuity and change is evident in Lenin's own trajectory from image maker to image, from active inaugurator of a new order of monumental art in the years immediately after the Revolution, to passive icon, celebrated as a 'cult' after his death in 1924. Lenin, standing aside from the debates about art and politics that were absorbing intellectuals and artists in the post-revolutionary period, wanted to use monumental art as a means of 'enlightening' a mainly illiterate people. Under the decree 'Concerning the Monuments of the Republic' (1918) plaques were erected celebrating revolutionary figures, such as Marx, Spartacus, Robert Owen and Danton, writers, such as Tolstoi and Dostoievsky, and composers, such as Chopin and Scriabin. At the same time, under the same decree, 'Monuments Erected in Honour of the Tsars and their Servants' were removed. Lenin seems to have been inspired both by the utopianism of writers such as Campanella and Thomas More (translated by radical publishers in the earlier years of the century and republished by the Petrograd Soviet in 1918) and also by his own, as an Enlightenment intellectual, revulsion at popular religious superstition. Thus, some churches were closed and statues of saints removed in order to mark a sharp break with traditional beliefs.

It was, perhaps, these traditional beliefs, starved of objects to venerate, that re-emerged after Lenin's death and fed the cult of the dead leader. The embalming of his body, for instance, followed in the tradition of the Orthodox saints, whose bodies failed to decompose after death; and his portrait began to stand in for the religious icons he had hoped to eclipse through education and reason. Walter Benjamin, in Moscow in 1926, notes the continued presence of religion and 'the traditional adoration of images' and, at the same time:

> The cult of Lenin's image is taken to incredible lengths here. There is a store on the Kusnetzky most that specialises in Lenin, and he comes in every size, pose and material.[5]

It was in the aftermath of the cult of Lenin that Stalin could launch his own cult of personality. The vacuum that followed Stalin's death and disgrace in the 1950s was in turn filled by a return to the cult of Lenin. The studios of the official artists that we visited in 1991 were filled with maquettes of Lenin statues dating from the 1950s and 1960s. The poses had become fixed and stereotyped: Lenin with one arm outstretched, with both arms outstretched, standing still, walking forward, sometimes holding a cap, sometimes wearing a cap and so on. One favourite anecdote was of a statue which had got muddled and appeared with Lenin both holding and wearing a cap. Above all, over and over again, people connected the latest wave of iconoclasm with Lenin's own first removal of Tsarist statues and religious icons. As Nikita Voronov said of 1991, 'So you could say that Lenin's decree ordering the removal of monuments lives on and is victorious.'[6] The problem of the monuments returns to the problem of history. If seventy years of communist rule had been marked by these waves of iconoclasm, many of the people we interviewed in 1991 said that an ability to live with monuments to the heroes of communism would now mark an ability to live with the past, however hostile to that past they might be personally.

I think we must analyse [the Stalinist era], or at the very least, recognise the links of our generation to the 'zone of silence' generation and our links to that culture. It's easier to struggle with monuments than with concrete reality. We can pull down monuments and raise new ones. And that's the only reality the people have encountered since August 1991.

Andrei Rodionov, *Disgraced Monuments*[7]

Changing meanings

The formal nature of a monument affects its ability to survive. A few years before the Revolution, an obelisk was erected outside the Kremlin walls to celebrate three hundred years of the Romanov dynasty. In 1918 it was transformed into the Obelisk to Revolutionary Thinkers and the names of the tsars were replaced with names such as Marx, Engels, Winstanley, Campanella, More, Fourier, Proudhon, Saint-Simon and so on. It was the abstract, symbolic, nature of the obelisk that allowed it to be recycled in this way. On the other hand, the later monuments that belonged to the cult of personality were significant through recognisable resemblance. In semiotic terms, they are iconic signs and always have the threat of disgrace hanging over them. However, the meanings of even these monuments can be unstable. As Mark Lewis points out:

> Like the fetish, the public work serves two ends, the one ultimately under-mining the other. The monument covers up the crimes against the public in so far as it is able to temporarily 'smother' the possibility of remembering specific histories in terms of the violence that engendered them; instead, it commemorates a history or event in terms of a pernicious heroism or nationalism. At the same time, the monument exists as a perpetual marker, a reminder of those very crimes. It waves a red flag, so to speak, on the site of its repressions. And when the symbolic order is thrown into crisis, the public monument's semantic charge shifts and the work becomes less heroic in form but rather begins to take on the characteristics of a scar.[8]

Once disgraced, the passing of time can shift the monument's meaning further, out of the political into emotional or cultural resonance. Many people have noted that fallen statues can acquire a certain kind of pathos. This seemed to be particularly so of the vast Soviet monuments, lying incongruously and ignominiously on the ground. They lose their dignity as children play on them, and, like Gulliver in Lilliput, their very scale underlines their helplessness. In time, they can also acquire a curiosity value and find a demand abroad. Or, like the Stalin statue abandoned in the countryside, slowly sinking into the ground, covered with moss and ivy, they take on something of the romance of ruins and the mysteriousness of Ozymandias.

In Moscow we noticed a third kind of monument, whose meaning was simply due to its actual existence in place and time. In response to Gorbachev's decision to open up the hitherto selective and repressed history of the Soviet

Union, a demand gradually developed for a monument which would acknowledge and commemorate the victims of Stalin's repression. In the absence of any agreement about what this monument should be, a large stone was taken from the Solvetsky Gulag and placed facing the Lubyanka, the KGB headquarters. The Gulag stone is neither symbolic nor iconic; it has an indexical relationship to commemoration, setting up a literal, physical, link with the history it represents. Its position was all the more pointed as the empty plinth, on which the Dzerzhinsky statue had once stood, still occupied the centre of the square. Without representing anything in itself, the stone became invested with a collective memory which had not previously found expression in the public space of the city:

> This monument is a document of the times, like all other monuments in Moscow. For the very first time we determined our own attitude to the past, as opposed to the way it had been done previously, when a monument represented the official version of our memory.
>
>   Natalya Davidova, *Disgraced Monuments*[9]

Repetitions

In addition to the particular monuments, set in the public spaces of the city, made out of valuable material such as granite or bronze, the communist iconography was supplemented by vast numbers of small statues or busts cast mechanically and circulated on a massive scale. In one foundry we discovered a series of large cupboards, each of which was filled with rows of brown paper packages, each neatly tied with string. Only one would have the paper torn away, to reveal the features of either Marx, Engels or Lenin. Thus, from a practical point of view, identifying the occupant of the cupboard but also presenting a surreal and telling image of mass production and repetition. At another foundry we were told:

> Our factory was founded in 1949 for the main purpose of casting bronze statues of our leaders. At first we cast statues of Stalin. Then, after his death, we began to cast statues of Lenin. We made small busts of Vladimir Ilyich Lenin. These were presented as awards to the winning competitors on workers' holidays....These busts comprised 90% of our output. Since perestroika, our production lines have changed. We have stopped making the small busts. Now we make things for the general public, whatever people will buy.
>
>   Head of the Artistic Department, Skulptorny Combinat[10]

Although the objects cast had changed to reproductions of churches and tourist memorabilia, there was a sense that the free market economy would not sustain this kind of mass production.

The mass repetition of the leaders' images that characterised Soviet output

Figure 20.2 Mark Lewis, 'The Studio', 1993

was, after the collapse of communism, replaced by another kind of repetition, a return of the past. The cultural, political and economic vacuum that enveloped the Soviet Union at this point seemed to only allow a move backwards, to the imagery and iconography of the pre-Revolutionary era. In a historical and collective return of the repressed, gradually, the tsars were returning into public space. A statue of Alexander II was returned to its old place in the Kremlin, replacing a statue of Lenin. But most particularly, we noticed that sculptors were working on images of Peter the Great. Peter and Stalin have both been seen to be 'modernisers' of their country, most particularly, in their different reorganisations of agricultural labour, the reform of serfdom and collectivisation of farming, respectively. In this context, the return to Peter the Great seemed to represent a complex form of nostalgia and one that ran the risk of doubling for Stalin. In front of a recently installed statue of Peter in St Petersburg, a little girl laid a bunch of flowers, just as children had laid flowers at the feet of statues in the unveiling ceremonies of the communist era.

The visible return to Peter, and the possible ghostly condensation of Stalin within his image, suggested another kind of return that was both a haunting from the past and an anxiety for the future. Naum Kleiman, Eisenstein scholar and Director of the Eisenstein Museum, told us about Eisenstein's interest in the huge equestrian statue of Peter the Great (made by the French sculptor Etienne Falconnet in 1782). He had sketched a story-board for a film of

Pushkin's poem, 'The Bronze Horseman', written in 1833. In the poem, the statue uncannily comes to life, and pursues the unfortunate hero, Yevgeny, through the streets of St Petersburg until he loses his sanity. Eisenstein's return to the Pushkin poem suggested a series of returns and hauntings, incorporating both the presence of Stalin and the future resurrection of Peter himself in the post-Communist era. The poem, and Eisenstein's interest in it, evoked the theme of repetition in Russian history as well as the uncertainty of the future of the Russian people in the absence of public political and cultural debate along the lines that almost everyone we interviewed suggested and desired.

We filmed the most of the material for *Disgraced Monuments* in Moscow and Leningrad in 1991; Mark shot supplementary material in 1992. The issues about the relationship between culture, history, mythologies and politics, represented particularly pointedly in the debates about public monuments in the public space of the cities, that we discussed with the people we interviewed seem to have dropped even further from sight as economic crisis has dominated the former Soviet Union. We were very fortunate to have had the opportunity, as foreigners, to witness the clarity and complexity with which people addressed the issues at that time, between the failure of the August coup and the final collapse of communism four months later.

Figure 20.3 Mark Lewis, 'The Dialectic'

Notes

1 Mark Lewis 'What is to be done?' in A. Kroker and M. Kroker (eds) *Ideology and Power in the Age of Ruins*, New York: St Martin's Press, 1991, p. 3.
2 As quoted in Lewis "What is to be done?', p. 3.
3 Samir al-Khalil, *The Monument: Art, Vulgarity and Responsibility in Iraq*, London: Andre Deutsch, 1991, pp. 133–4.
4 'Disgraced Monuments: the script', as published in *PIX 2*, London: British Film Institute, 1997, p. 108.
5 Walter Benjamin, 'Moscow Diary', *October*.
6 'Disgraced Monuments: the script', p. 104.
7 ibid., p. 106.
8 Lewis, 'What is to be done?', p. 5.
9 'Disgraced Monuments: the script', p. 109.
10 ibid., pp. 106–7.

21 Attacks on the castle

Hélène Cixous

I was in Prague two weeks ago, it was the first time, and the only thing I absolutely wanted to see was Kafka's tomb. But to-see-Kafka's-tomb does not simply mean to see Kafka's tomb. I was at last in Prague and I wanted at last to see the hand, the trace, the footprint, that is to say the natural and naked fleshy face of the author of the Letter, that is to say the eyelids of god. It is now thirty-five years that I have fought for this day, a long combat and obscure like all combats. One never knows in the heat of the struggle who one is everything being mixed up, desire, fear, hostility of love, one fights, desire is a battle between oneself against oneself, an imagination of obstacles to stop oneself from going off to lose the war.

But finally I was there, too bad. The long-awaited day was inevitable. I wanted to see Kafka's tomb. Knowing perfectly well (having verified it so many times) that you cannot see what you want to see, I went to the cemetery to see what I could not see. It's the law. All is law. It's because of desire. The law makes its nest in the peel of desire. Go on: you will not enter. If you did not desire to go, there would be a chance that the door would open. I went to Israelica street. And then the cemetery was closed. So we went around the cemetery which is immense. I had no hope. Every now and again there were portals of forged iron, the car drove by the portals, heavily chained. All were closed. At one particular moment, the car stopped near a large rusted portal with chained iron bars. I pressed myself against the portal, because it was written you will press yourself against the rusted portal of the promised land, I had forgotten. And there before me was Kafka's tomb, and I was before him.

It is a clean tomb, modern, the stone is a raised stone, those who have seen it before me say it is black, but this one is white, my one, the one I saw standing facing me standing facing it was thin white upright, *my size*. It was turned toward me and on its brow the words Dr Franz Kafka looked at me.

I have already seen this tomb look at me with eyes metamorphosed into letters of a name. It was in the cemetery of Algiers, I looked at my father look at me with his eyes that said his name gravely to me, as do children and dead people: Dr. Georges Cixous.

So standing face to face my hands on the rusted bars I knew that I always looked for the same face solemnly simplified to childhood.

The tomb and I were separated by the high locked portal, and it was good. Desire and fear answered together was unhoped-for. I clutched the bars.

There are three cities I would like to go to and I will never make it. Though I can do everything to try to get there, in reality I do not make it, I mean it's impossible for me to find myself there in the flesh in the streets in the squares in the roads in the walls bridges towers cathedrals façades courtyards quays rivers and oceans, they are still well guarded. These are the cities I have the most meditated on, lay siege to frequented and run through in dreams in stories in guides I have studied them in dictionaries I have lived in them if not in this life then in another life.

Promised Pragues. You dream of going. You cannot go. What would happen if you went?

How can one not go to Athens even while going there? Freud asked himself for decades until the September day when he decided to go to Corfu from Trieste where he was staying with his brother. 'Corfu?!' a friend said to him. 'In the middle of summer? Insanity! You would be better off going to Athens for 3 days.' And indeed the Lloyd's steamer left that afternoon, but the two brothers were not at all sure. Therefore they were quite surprised when in spite of everything that was opposed to Athens they found themselves there, they were standing on the Acropolis in reality, but Freud only half believed it: it all existed as the two brothers had learned in school. From the schoolbook to the landscape the consequence was quite good. It was too beautiful to be true. But Freud never would have been able to find himself in Athens either totally or half-way if he had not decided to go to Corfu.

And where should I go, to what city other than Prague so as to arrive in Prague only by guile or by chance without having wanted it?

I went to Vienna. Walking down the Berggasse at a sharp slope to ring at Dr Freud's door, I felt Prague breathing a short distance away. There we were on the road that separates-unites Vienna and Prague. The car went neither to the right nor to the left. We passed a few kilometers from Trnava where Michael Klein my grandfather was born. I have never been there. But Trnava exists in the Atlas. At the time the border floated in the wind and you were one day Czech one day Austrian and every day Bohemian. An inhabitant of Turnau of Trnava. One day Dr Franz Kafka of Prague came to stay at Turnau, at the hotel where my grandfather Michael Klein had come to deliver fresh produce from the farm yesterday. I lived all of this. It is like the day Dr Freud had just left the Berggasse to go to Gmund when Dr Kafka passed in front of Dr Freud's house his head lowered, because it was a dream of a missed encounter.

I did not go to Turnau where I will never go, but my life passed close by. Fields of poppies and of blue flax spread between us the blue and red sheet of separation.

For centuries my desire has been haunted by a being called sometimes die

Altneusynagoge sometimes Staronova Synagoga and that I call the Oldyoung Synagogue. And always I roam outside the Old Jewish Cemetery, Alt Jüdischen Friedhof, absolute desire without commentary blind confident. What do I want? I will see. I am expected. I am expecting it. I am waiting for myself there.

In dreams I have often gone there. The cemetery there is immense and sweet like an ocean. Squirrels dance around pine trees, merry reincarnations of the dead. I search. I want to see the tomb that is my cradle. I want to see my cradle, the cradle of my tombs, the tomb of my childhood, the source of my dreams and of my worries.

Everyone has gone to the Old Jewish Cemetery except me. My children my friends my loves everyone has gone without me before me for me beyond me to lean over my cradles. My mother too, except me.

Nevertheless I was waiting for the possibility. I cannot go lightly to see the tomb of my cradles. I was waiting for the person who would accompany me, the being who would be necessary enough delicate enough to break with me the bread of awaiting. The messiah of the Oldyoung synagogue. But if he did not come, ever?

But on the other hand, we cannot never have gone to our tomb-cradle; it is an obligation. We must go to the sources before the hour of death. It's that all human destinies are launched from a tomb. We do not always know it, but in the end we return to port.

One day I thought everything started from there, enough backing away since in the end I will go let's go there now so I went there as a lone woman as a silent woman as a widow, as a person and on the exterior of all dream.

No sooner inside – there I was pushed back like an attack. How to take it? I look everywhere for the door, the entrance, the defect. Passing by the Charles Bridge and its squads of statues planted like impassive saints coming off on the side of Mala Strana, by the alley of the Saxons, then by Velkoprevorske Square by Prokopka alley up to Malostravske Namesti at a brisk pace passing in front of the Schönborn palace then going up by Bretislavova until the Nerudova and there you go back down the slope until Mala Strana without ever managing to penetrate.

The next day, second try: on the quays up to the National Theatre, then coming back up to Starometske, passing by Miners' road, it was fleeing just in front of me. Ten times I asked directions in German, they stared at me as a false ghost, no one spoke the tongue of my parents any more. Effacement effacement thy name is City.

Thirdly by Celetna road passing in front of the house at the Golden Angel up to Ovocny square, the fruit market, from there up to the Tyl Theatre the flowered balconies of which had thrown themselves out of the interior stage of the Opera by the window on that day – because the play takes place at this very moment on the Old City Square. It was Sunday. Then, on the square, instead of the black and plump monument to Jan Hus, there is no monument, no square everything is conjured away, neither can you see the Starometsky Orlo, the clock on which yesterday the sun and the moon still turned, nor the palaces, nor the houses, the centre of the universe is covered this Sunday with a flood of feet in sneakers. It was the marathon that had attacked the city introducing the virus of the Sneaker. The City had fallen? Sneaker, Praguean horse, so with your Synecdoche you have vanquished the impregnable city!? Around the tank to Jan Hus topped with hundreds of sneakers the air was fluorescent blue. Venus of the whole country, the victorious sneakers rolled thousands of cans with the effigy of Coca-cola under the chaos of their hooves. Suddenly exhausted, the macabre carnival collapsed, loosing its masks. A universal tee-shirt enveloped the remains of the disemboweled City. From the shroud emerged only the two untamable horns of the Tyn church.

But the next day the Castle began again.

There has never been a more pricked-up city.

A City? An army. There is none more combative more erect, more provocative. A City? A heroine, called Prague. At dawn barely is one rising, she is already up, her lances standing, her helmets pricked. From the heights of her hills she apostrophes you: Try to take me! She stamps her foot, she envelops herself in her stone coat. Wherever one is, raising one's head, she is there – brandished phallic modest, omnipresent and inaccessible. There is none more impregnable. Certain cities remain intact, the crowds believe they trample them – the regiments of tourists banderilla it with foreign flags, course through the roads, occupy the arcades, no attack will ever force the City to surrender.

Over the centuries suitors had presented themselves, had conquered it, tamed it they thought; they hurried to build their palaces, during the construction anxiety aged them, knowing that the walls would outlive them made their flesh sweat. But one after another, they constructed, it was the City that wanted it. It was fate to build until you're done in; then there was a gust of wind, the lords fell successively: into ashes and into bloods and the palaces were there, calm under the snow.

No, this is not a City.

A reserve of centuries of alleys of tombs.

Centuries: alleys: tombs: it is all interchangeable.

I do not know why, why Prague, Prague, why so many centuries flow in your alleys? Full of powder of generations, flasks of constructions.

Stratigraphy of the layers of the Praguean bark. Columns of dates, piles of styles.

10th century–1050, *c.*1050–*c.*1260, *c.*1260–1310, 1310–1419, *c.*1450–1526, 1538–1580, *c.*1580–1620, 1611–1690, 1690–1745, 1745–1780, 1780–1830, 1895–1914, 1918–1939: spreading Gothic high Baroque neo-Renaissance, neo-Baroque Functionalism and Constructivism Late Renaissance (Mannerism) pre-Romanesque architecture (Prague Castle, Vysehrad, Brevnov) primitive Gothic Rococo (late Baroque) Art Nouveau (Secession) high Renaissance Romanesque architecture Romantic Historicism: neo-Romanesque style, neo-Gothic primitive Baroque late Gothic (flamboyant, of Vladislav)

Everything started with the Castle, Vysehrad in 1050 Otto architecture, and the Castle gave to the site the tables of the law: and you shall build on the Red Sea, and you shall build hotels and churches on the dark lake of blood. All will end with the Castle. But this is a fable: and that is the Castle of Babble with sleeping inhabitants. A single dead person keeps watch still, like a candle lit in a match box at 22 Alchemists Road.

Everywhere cranes rise in an assault of the sky. No this is not yet a city, it's an idea, it's a fury of interminable inconstruction. Nothing but Pelions and Ossases. The idea is at the end to build the city one day on the summit of the heap.

I was in Prague for the first time and Prague was not there. She had just left, or else it was he, the spirit of the City, the doctor K, the inhabitant of our 'Right this minute' house. We have heard about it this Odradek, this bobbin that is not a bobbin, that is not only a bobbin, and that stands on two small sticks as on two legs. One could think that it was useful once and that it is broken, but that is a mistake. It is something that was described by Dr Franz Kafka standing on two small stick legs, it has all the appearance of the thing that has lost its meaning, but one cannot speak without being mistaken, because Odradek is extremely mobile, while I speak, he runs off and he is no longer here. One can only look for him.

So where is he? Is he in the dictionary, in a museum? No, 'he is now in the attic, now in the stairwell, now in the halls and now in the entranceway.' He gets around a lot. He has no lodgings, he is in all the parts of the house that do not lodge, that are not counted, places where one only passes through or else disappears.

Or else was it I who was not there? When we are alive we do not know we are ghosts.

What are we in the promised cities? The contemporary dead of our descendants, the future returning ghosts. It is Sunday today I pass in front of the 'Right this moment' house that K. left just now sixty years ago to go to his office. He went out the door and he took off. A person who is not yet born will pass by here in forty years, and will wind the cut string onto our bobbin.

Time is a square wheel. Running fast enough in the alleys I could perhaps catch him who passed through here even before I was born before I was born.

For this it suffices that the centuries be well guarded inside the Castle.

Imaginary memories, imaginary life: I have already lived here we lived on the fourth floor, by the window of the living room you could see the corner of the City Hall. No more imaginary a life than my other ancient lives. The country of the past belongs to the same continent as the imagined country. They meet and mingle their fields, their squares, their sweet salt waters. At the back of the picture the streets of Oran intersect the streets of Prague.

We dream of going to Prague. We do not know how to go. We fear. We go. Once inside we do not find it. We wander for a long time in the Castle. If there had not been the minuscule door 22 Zlata Ulicke, the minuscule door in Gold Street, to cast the anchor for a minute, we would never even have landed at all.

Where is the Synagogue? Where is the door?

Happily, we never get there. It was too late. It had just closed. We would not have succeeded in entering.

Blessed be the closed doors and the rusted portals. You wanted to enter?

Happily we failed.

Where is the Oldyoung Jewish cemetery enchanted with squirrels? – Here, here, between the dark severe walls, just in front of your nose. Above our humiliated heads powerful volleys of crows scream their brusque abrupt menaces. It is a harsh miracle, these crows: they caw like lions inside a minuscule square of sky just vertical to the minuscule hanky-full of dead people. The old Jewish cemetery raises its invisible well filled with tombs up to the feet of the sky, you do not see the end of it, the crows scream up there: it's here, it's here. I had never seen cemetery so high and so small, like a roll of dead people that climbs and descends from the bottom of the earth up to the bottom of the sky. Make room, thunder the crows, let the dead climb past!

I had not been told that the cemetery was so small. I had not been told that the thousand year city leaves only the end of its nose of tombs and a few worn teeth visible at the surface of the century. The tombs bury the tombs. Twelve layers of tombs.

I had not been told of the doll houses, the doll Synagogue, the doll people.

Everything dwarfed. Everything sacred.

Your Prague is not in Prague, as you can well see. Promised Prague is in the sky under the earth.

I clutched the bars in my rusted hands. In front of me svelte distracted white the tomb looked at me with its bright eyes of words. How alive and young you are, I thought. While all the other ghosts in the palaces, behind the sgraffitoed walls, all the ghosts are dead. 'You have not changed, I said.'

Translated by Eric Prenowitz

Index

Note: Page numbers in **bold** type refer to **figures**; page numbers followed by 'n' refer to notes.